VISUAL FACTFINDER

HISTORY TIMELINES

First published by Bardfield Press in 2005
Copyright © Miles Kelly Publishing 2005

Bardfield Press is an imprint of
Miles Kelly Publishing Ltd,
Bardfield Centre, Great Bardfield, Essex, CM7 4SL

Some of this material also appears in *1000 Facts on History Timelines*

2 4 6 8 10 9 7 5 3

Editorial Director: Belinda Gallagher

Copy Editor: Jeremy Smith

Editorial Assistants: Amanda Askew, Hannah Todd

Picture Researchers: Liberty Newton, Laura Faulder, Jennifer Hunt

Production Manager: Elizabeth Brunwin

Designed and packaged by Q2A Creative

Scanning and reprographics: Anthony Cambray, Mike Coupe, Ian Paulyn

British Library Cataloguing-in-Publication Data
A catalogue record for this book is available from the British Library

ISBN 1-84236-540-1

Printed in China

www.mileskelly.net
info@mileskelly.net

VISUAL FACTFINDER

HISTORY TIMELINES

Consultant: Rupert Matthews

BARDFIELD
PRESS

Contents

4

Age of Revolution

Modern World

HISTORY TIMELINES

How did the Black Death get its name?

Who was the last wife of Henry VIII?

When were East and West Germany reunified?

The answers to these and many other questions can be found in this amazing book of almost 2500 facts. Beginning with the formation of the Earth, a timeline spans the history of the world right up to the present day, including the development of early civilizations, world wars and explorations and inventions that have changed our planet. A list of key dates provides a quick and easy way to access information.

4600–1.6 million years ago

c.4600 million years ago Dust and gas floating in space came together to form the Earth. Our planet's early atmosphere contained little oxygen. One large continent, Gondwanaland, and other smaller continents made up the landmasses.

c.3500 million years ago The first life forms on Earth – single-celled bacteria and blue-green algae – appeared.

c.600 million years ago Gradual increase in oxygen and formation of the protective ozone layer led to the evolution of multi-cellular organisms.

c.500 million years ago A variety of creatures such as shelled invertebrates, marine plants and fish appeared. Within the next 100 million years, land plants and animals began to flourish. The northern landmasses came together to form Laurasia.

c.360–290 million years ago Tropical forests flourished and reptiles began to appear. Laurasia and Gondwanaland merged together to form a single landmass, Pangaea.

c.245–146 million years ago Laurasia and Gondwanaland split. Reptiles, particularly dinosaurs, dominated this period. Conifers, ferns and redwoods were common by the end of this period, leading to a rise in herbivorous dinosaurs.

◀ *The coelacanth appeared about 350 million years ago. It was thought to have become extinct some 60 million years ago, but was found again in 1938.*

159–144 million years ago
Archaeopteryx, which had common physical features with both birds and dinosaurs, flourished during this period.

***c.*146–65 million years ago** Modern continents began to form. Flowering plants, marsupials and other mammals appeared. By the end of this period, dinosaurs became extinct, perhaps due to climatic changes.

***c.*65–2 million years ago** Mammals dominated the Earth. An increase in grasslands coincided with the appearance of grazing animals such as horses and giraffes. *Australopithecus*, the first hominid, and *Homo habilis*, the first human, appeared.

***c.*1.6 million years ago** Glaciers covered most parts of the northern and southern continents, causing large-scale deaths and migration towards the Equator. The glaciers advanced and retreated several times over the next period.

▼ *Compared to the skulls of modern humans, Neanderthals had prominent brow ridges, a low, sloping forehead, a chinless and heavy jaw and large front teeth.*

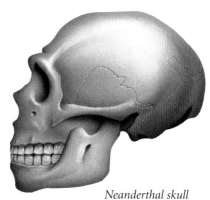

Neanderthal skull

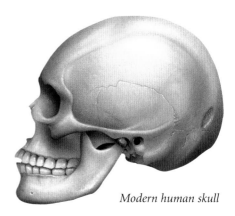

Modern human skull

15

2 million years ago–9000BC

c. **2 million years ago** *Homo habilis* made tools for hunting; and, later, *Homo erectus* used fire to cook. Serrated axes made of pebbles and flint were used as tools.

c.**200,000 years ago** *Homo sapiens* appeared at the beginning of this period. They developed stone and wood tools such as knives, axes, spears and arrowheads. They migrated from Africa into Asia and Europe.

c.**90,000 years ago** Fully modern humans evolved in Africa. They then spread out to the rest of the world. Other forms of human gradually died out.

c.**50,000BC** The burial of dead bodies became an important ritual.

c.**35,000BC** Tools with handles were devised. For example, stone spearheads attached to wooden handles appeared during this time. Groups of hominids began to form settlements.

c.**30,000–15,000BC** The bow and arrow were invented. Towards the end of this period humans crossed over to America on land bridges created by glaciation.

c.**15,000BC** In Dordogne, France, the famed Lascaux cave paintings were made. The paintings and engravings depicted animals, humans and mythological creatures.

c.**11,000–10,000BC** Wheat was cultivated in northern Mesopotamia, the area between the rivers Tigris and Euphrates, in West Asia. The availability of water and development of irrigation techniques led to the decline of hunter-gatherer societies and an increase in settled agricultural communities that reared domestic animals. Dogs were among the first animals to be domesticated.

c.**9000BC** Jericho, one of the earliest settlements and farming communities, was established on the western bank of the Jordan River.

*c.***9000–3000**BC In the Pachmarhi Hills, central India, Stone Age people made rock paintings of scenes from daily life.

These paintings depicted a variety of animals, birds, insects, male and female forms and plant life.

▼ *A stone-age hunter. These early people made a variety of chipped stone tools for many different purposes.*

8000–7000BC

*c.*8000BC Mesopotamians began using clay tokens of different shapes to keep accounts of land, food and livestock.

*c.*8000–6000BC The people of Jericho made textiles from linen, which they dyed and decorated with shells and beads. Statues were made by moulding clay and plaster on reed frames.

*c.*7500–6500BC In Turkey, towns had a central square with buildings arranged around it. The bases of buildings were made of stone, while their upper layers were usually made of mud. The Anatolians of Turkey used copper as a decorative and precious metal.

*c.*7400–6700BC The people of Mexico began forming agricultural communities and grew vegetables such as pumpkins and gourds.

*c.*7000BC In Greece early Stone Age settlements had formed. The people in these settlements cultivated food crops and sailed the Aegean Sea.

*c.*7000BC Humans reached South America. Initially they formed small groups and hunted for food.

*c.*7000–6000BC Mesopotamians began making pottery utensils

*c.*7000–5000BC In China, small agricultural settlements developed. People cultivated rice and made simple pots and baskets.

▶ *An ancient Chinese village. Animals such as pigs, dogs and cattle were domesticated in China around 5000BC.*

...FASCINATING FACT...
The world's oldest bakery was discovered at the pyramid workers' village at Giza. It was tall, cylindrical and had a conical top. The firebox was at the bottom and there were shelves inside for cooking the dough.

7000–4500BC

*c.***7000–4500BC** The earliest permanent Egyptian settlements were established. These had huts and granaries. Stone and bone tools and ceramic utensils were used.

*c.***6000BC** A primitive agricultural settlement that grew wheat developed at Mehgarh, west of the Indus Valley. This area later became a part of the Harappan or Indus Valley civilization.

*c.***6000BC** Catal Hüyük in Anatolia was a developed agricultural settlement where inhabitants also reared domestic animals.

*c.***6000BC** The aboriginal people of northern Australia made rock paintings of fish and crocodiles and other animal life.

*c.***6000–4500BC** People in the Iberian Peninsula cultivated crops and domesticated animals, but they were mostly nomadic.

*c.***5000BC** In Greece, the early simple hut dwellings developed into more permanent buildings and by 3400BC fortifications were made around some settlements.

*c.***5000BC** Agricultural people arrived in southern Italy by boat. They formed settlements in which they built houses, cultivated wheat, reared sheep and cows and made pottery.

*c.***5000–4000BC** In China, there were several settled cultures with distinct artistic styles. People built wooden houses. They could weave and make weapons, utensils and decorative objects with wood and stone. Lacquer work was used for decoration.

*c.***4500BC** Settled farming began in Spain. Villages were formed and huts and pens were made with branches.

*c.***4500BC** The practice of burying the dead became more widespread. In Catalonia, Spain, the dead were buried in graves that had chambers to hold several bodies. At the same time, huge stone tombs were built in Portugal.

▼ *Early farmers used tools such as sickles to harvest crops. Farming became a major occupation as humans gave up their nomadic lifestyle and formed settlements.*

4000–3600 BC

*c.***4000**BC Egyptians discovered weaving and dyeing, and began making clothes.

*c.***4000**BC People from Turkey migrated to Sumer, south of Mesopotamia. They farmed, traded and developed a number of crafts. These Sumerians later invented cuneiform writing, the ox-drawn plough and wheel.

*c.***4000–3000**BC In Uruk, one of the biggest centres of the Mesopotamian culture, pottery began to be mass-produced.

*c.***3650–3300**BC Egyptian society was divided into distinct social classes. This was most evident in the different types and sizes of graves.

*c.***3650–3300**BC Faience, a blue-green ceramic glazing characteristic of early Egyptian art, was developed.

*c.***3600**BC A primitive form of writing was developed in Mesopotamia.

▼ *The invention of the wheel was one of the most important landmarks of human civilization. By 3200BC the Sumerians had built four-wheeled carts like the one shown here.*

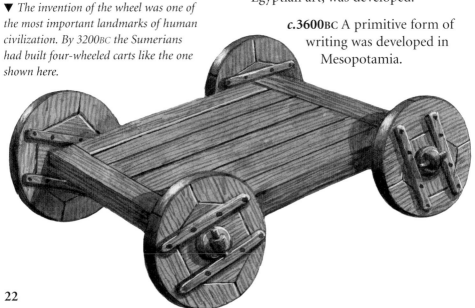

*c.***3500**BC Independent city-states gained power in various parts of Mesopotamia. Palaces and temples were decorated with stone carvings and mosaics made of coloured stone.

*c.***3500**BC The Chinese studied cracks on heated ox bones and turtle shells to tell the future. Jade was used widely in making figurines and jewellery.

*c.***3500**BC In the Indus Valley, ceramics, copper artefacts, carved seals and stone beads were made during this time. Pottery was decorated with abstract patterns.

*c.***3200**BC Settlements around the Aegean Sea flourished. The people of these areas cultivated olives, grapes and cereals. Metalwork was widespread.

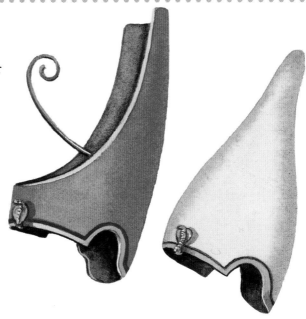

▲ *The crown of Lower Egypt was red and had a low front and tall back. The one for Upper Egypt was white and cone-shaped.*

*c.***3100**BC Menes, also known as Narmer, a king from Upper Egypt, unified Lower and Upper Egypt to form one kingdom. He made Memphis, near modern-day Cairo, his capital. Menes is considered to be the first Egyptian pharaoh.

3100–2800BC

▲ *The builders of Stonehenge transported some massive blocks of stone all the way from the Preseli mountains of southwest Wales, a distance of over 215 km.*

c.3100BC In Britain, the first stage of building Stonehenge began.

c.3100–2700BC Hierakonpolis, in Egypt, was an important city during the rule of the first and second dynasties.

c.3000BC The Minoan civilization emerged in Crete. It was one of the earliest great civilizations of the world.

c.3000BC Maize was grown in an area that is now Belize in Central America, and cotton was woven to make clothes.

*c.*3000BC In Italy spinning and weaving began, as did the manufacture and trade of metal objects. Since tin (which is required to make bronze) was not available in Italy, most people continued to use stone, wood and bone tools.

*c.*3000–2350BC Mesopotamian trade with Persia, present-day Iran, resulted in the former acquiring gold and silver objects decorated with precious and semi-precious stones.

*c.*3000–2000BC Marble quarries in Naxos and Paros in the Cycladic Islands produced a lot of stone. The local sculptors made abstract sculptures for burial purposes.

*c.*2950–2575BC The Egyptian calendar was invented. It was the first known calendar and had 365 days in a year, divided into 12 months of 30 days. The extra five or six days were added at the end of the year and were not part of any month. However, the months were not named until the 6th century BC. The calendar continued to be used by astronomers in the Middle Ages.

*c.*2800BC In the Indus Valley a complex written language had developed by this time.

... FASCINATING FACT ...

The Minoan civilization derives its name from its founder Minos. According to legend, Minos was the son of Greek gods Zeus and Europa. He became king with the help of Poseidon, the Greek sea god, and colonized the Aegean islands after defeating the sea pirates in that area.

2698–2472BC

2698BC The Chinese calendar was introduced.

*c.*2640BC Silk was manufactured in China. In the beginning it served as a writing surface.

*c.*2630BC In Egypt, the Old Kingdom pharaoh Djoser built the first pyramid, the Step Pyramid, at Saqqrāh in Memphis. Djoser's chief minister Imhotep was its architect.

*c.*2575–2551BC Pharaoh Snefru built the Bent Pyramid at Dashur, Egypt. The special technique employed in building the Bent Pyramid was used in the construction of another giant pyramid for Snefru, the North Pyramid.

*c.*2575–2150BC The process of preserving dead bodies – mummification – became highly scientific and ritualistic in Egypt.

*c.*2551–2528BC Khufu, Snefru's son, built the Great Pyramid at Giza, Egypt. It is the largest pyramid and was considered in ancient times to be one of the Seven Wonders of the World.

▲ *The Great Pyramid at Giza, Egypt, is a major tourist attraction.*

*c.*2500BC Khafre, Khufu's son, built the Great Sphinx at Giza. The face of the Sphinx is believed to resemble Khafre.

*c.*2500–1700BC Mohenjo-Daro and Harappa, major cities of the Indus Valley civilization, flourished. They had well-planned streets, large two-storey homes and a developed plumbing and sanitary system.

*c.*2500BC The Chinese discovered acupuncture, a method of medical treatment involving insertion of small needles into the skin of the patient.

*c.*2490–2472BC Menkaure, Khafre's successor, built the third and smallest pyramid at Giza. All the pyramids at Giza had mortuary temples attached to them and were surrounded by smaller pyramids for royal relatives.

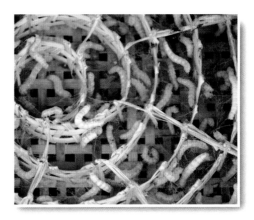

▶ *Natural silk is produced from silkworm cocoons. Silk was first produced in China.*

...FASCINATING FACT...
The Indus Valley civilization was probably the first to have an advanced plumbing system. The Indus people had two-storey brick houses with a central courtyard, living rooms and bathrooms. Each house had its own well, and clay pipes below the houses carried waste to sewers that ran beneath the streets.

2400–2000BC

*c.***2400**BC The Egyptians discovered papyrus, an early form of writing material. The stem of the papyrus reed was cut into strips, dried and flattened.

*c.***2334–2279**BC Sargon, one of the earliest conquerors in world history, ruled Mesopotamia. He founded the Akkad dynasty and brought parts of Syria, Turkey and western Iran under his control. Sargon was the first leader to organize a formal military force.

*c.***2300–2000**BC The Mesopotamians established contact with the people of the Indus Valley, leading to trade between the two civilizations.

2218BC Gutians, a tribe from the hills east of the Tigris River, ended the Akkadian rule in Mesopotamia.

*c.***2200–500**BC Ziggurats were built by the Sumerians in various parts of Mesopotamia. These mud brick temples were large and rectangular or square in shape, with step-like platforms placed one above the other.

▶ *The Egyptians recorded important events using hieroglyphic writing.*

The platforms were landscaped with trees and shrubs.

*c.***2200**BC Egypt was weakened by crop failure and social upheavals, which led to the decline of the Old Kingdom, followed by a period of disorder, when Egypt split into several parts.

*c.***2040**BC The pharaoh Nebhepetre-Mentuhotep united Egypt and founded the XIth dynasty. He made Thebes his capital and his reign marked the beginning of the Middle Kingdom, which lasted until 1640BC.

*c.***2000**BC The Indus Valley civilization declined. According to some historians the cause was a change in the course of the Indus River, which caused the fertile land to dry up. Other theories suggest that the civilization declined because floods destroyed the crops or because overgrazing by animals made the land infertile.

***c.*2000**BC** The Mesoamerican Olmec civilization developed. The civilization flourished in the lowland gulf coast of southern Mexico. The Olmecs made advances in commerce and the arts.

***c.*2000**BC** Metal began to be widely used in Egypt and Mesopotamia. Household objects such as knives, bells, weapons and even jewellery were crafted out of metal.

29

2000–1800BC

*c.*2000BC The development of astronomy in Egypt meant that people could try to predict the annual Nile floods.

*c.*2000BC Babylon, one of the most famous ancient cities, was established on the banks of the Euphrates river. Bronze was used widely to make tools, weapons and utensils.

*c.*2000BC In North America, the Bering Strait and the Arctic, hunter-gatherer communities in North America developed more efficient stone tools.

*c.*2000BC The Sumerian epic *Gilgamesh*, the first literary work of this kind, was written. It is the story of a mythological Sumerian hero, written on 12 clay tablets in cuneiform script.

*c.*2000BC The aboriginal people of Australia painted human and animal figures in an 'X-ray' style, showing the bones and internal organs.

*c.*2000–1600BC Sumerian rule collapsed and the Amorites from Arabia conquered Mesopotamia. The new rulers preserved the native culture but introduced their own language.

*c.*2000–1000BC In Italy, there was a gradual migration of people who came from the north by land and from the east by sea. They formed settlements in various parts of the country and probably spoke an early form of Italic language.

...FASCINATING FACT...

Ancient Greeks, especially the women, liked chewing gum.
They chewed mastic gum, the resin obtained from the bark of the mastic tree, a shrub-like tree native to Greece and Turkey. It cleaned their teeth and prevented bad breath.

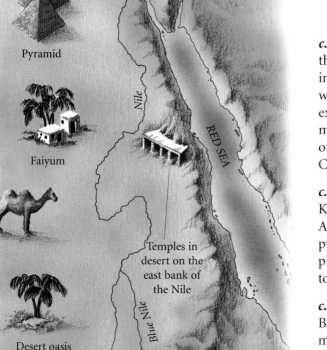

Pyramid

Faiyum

Desert oasis

Nile delta

Nile

RED SEA

Temples in desert on the east bank of the Nile

Blue Nile

White Nile

*c.***1900–1350**BC In China, the city of Erlitou gained importance. This city was well-known for its exquisite bronze work. It may have been the capital of the Xia dynasty, the first Chinese royalty.

*c.***1817**BC Egyptian Middle Kingdom pharaoh Amenemhet III built his pyramid at Hawara. It was probably the last pyramid to be built.

*c.***1800**BC Ancient Babylonians devised basic mathematical calculations, such as multiplication, division and square roots.

◄ *Despite regular floods, the Nile was the lifeline of ancient Egypt.*

31

1800–1550BC

c.1800BC The Mesoamericans had given up hunting and settled down to village life. Pottery making was widespread.

c.1792–1750BC Hammurabi ruled during this period. He was one of the most famous and revolutionary Babylonian kings. He laid down the first known code of laws regarding acceptable social behaviour, duties of citizens and crime and punishment.

c.1766BC The Shang dynasty came to power in northeast and north central China. Remarkable bronze vessels were produced during this period for storing wine and food.

c.1700–1000BC In southeast Spain the Argaric people moved their homes to hill tops and changed the shapes of their dwellings from circular to rectangular. Collective burial gave way to individual graves below houses.

▼ *An Egyptian charioteer driving into battle against the Hyksos. The word* Hyksos *is derived from the Egyptian phrase* Heka-khasut, *which means 'rulers of foreign lands'.*

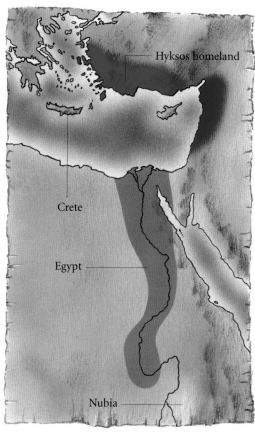

Hyksos homeland

Crete

Egypt

Nubia

▲ *Hyksos ruled over Egypt until they were defeated by the Pharaoh Ahmose I.*

*c.*1650BC Mycenae, in Greece, became an important centre.

*c.*1630–1531BC Hyksos, people of mixed Semitic-Asian origin, conquered and ruled Egypt.

*c.*1600BC The Minoan civilization reached its peak on Crete. The Minoans built great palaces decorated with colourful and delicate paintings, and made elaborate earthenware.

*c.*1600BC Aryans, nomadic warriors, invaded north India and drove the Dravidians, the original inhabitants, further south.

*c.*1580BC The highly developed and refined Minoan culture of Crete began to have an important influence on the Mycenaean civilization that was developing in Greece.

*c.*1550BC Pharaoh Ahmose I defeated the Hyksos and took over Egypt and Nubia, which was to the south of Egypt. During his reign the country prospered.

33

1504–1400BC

c.1504–1492BC Tuthmosis I was the first pharaoh to make his tomb deep within the cliffs of the Valley of Kings at Thebes. Thereafter, all royal tombs were built underground to save them from grave robbers. Only a mortuary temple (in which offerings were made to their spirits after their death) was made in the valley, on the banks of the Nile.

c.1500BC The kingdom of Kush was established to the south of Egypt.

c.1500BC The Mayans of Central America began using latex from rubber trees to make rubber. They used the rubber to make balls for a ball game. They also made crude pottery utensils.

▼ *A Minoan vase.*

▲ *A Minoan mask. The Minoan civilization was named after King Minos who, according to Greek mythology, kept a half-bull, half-human monster called the Minotaur in his palace.*

*c.*1500BC Egyptians invented the first portable clock, a sundial. It had five graded markings and a stem that cast a shadow when placed facing east-west in the morning and placed in the opposite direction at noon.

*c.*1500BC People migrated to the Micronesian and Polynesian islands and formed settlements.

*c.*1500–1100BC The Mayans developed terraced farming to grow corn in northeastern Mexico.

*c.*1472–1458BC Queen Hatshepsut ruled Egypt. A powerful ruler, she often wore a beard and dressed like a man.

*c.*1450BC The Myceneans from Greece invaded Crete and destroyed many villages on the island.

*c.*1420BC The Mycenaeans invaded Crete for the second time after an earthquake had weakened the Minoan civilization, which then declined.

*c.*1400BC In the Soconusco region, along the Pacific coast of Guatemala, the dead were buried ceremonially and ceramic figurines, stone bowls and jewellery were placed in their graves.

▼ *Treasure buried in the pyramids made them the target of grave robbers. The interior design of pyramids became increasingly complicated to confuse grave robbers.*

*c.***1391–1353BC** The Egyptian New Kingdom pharaoh Amenhotep III built the famous Luxor temple on the eastern bank of the Nile. It was dedicated to Amun-Ra, the king of the gods.

*c.***1353–1336BC** Pharaoh Amenhotep IV, also called Akhenaton, made Amarna the capital and religious centre of Egypt. He forced his subjects to give up old religious traditions and instead to worship the Sun god Aton.

*c.***1353–1336BC** Nefertiti, Akhenaton's wife, ruled the kingdom with her husband.

*c.***1350BC** The first public building in Mesoamerica, a mud and timber structure on an earth platform, was built at the important settlement of San José Mogote in the Valley of Oaxaca.

*c.***1350BC** The famed Lion Gate was made at the entrance to the fortress at Mycenae, Greece. Within the fortress was a palace, a shrine, a granary and houses for people who served in the palace.

◄ *Akhenaton means 'the one who is beneficial to Aton'. The pharaoh built the city of Akhetaton as the centre for the worship of Aton, sun god in ancient Egyptian religion.*

▲ *The Temple of Abu Simbel, built by Rameses the Great, was carved into a sandstone cliff.*

*c.*1336–1327BC Tutankhamun, the boy-king, ruled Egypt from Memphis. He ascended the throne at the age of nine and returned the country to its old religious traditions. His tomb in the Valley of Kings, one of the best preserved, was excavated in AD1922.

*c.*1319–1292BC Horemheb ruled Egypt. He was the commander of the Egyption army in northern Egypt before he ascended the throne.

*c.*1279–1213BC Rameses II or Rameses the Great was pharaoh of Egypt. He built the remarkable temple of Abu Simbel in Aswan.

*c.*1258BC Rameses II signed the oldest known peace treaty in the history of mankind. The treaty was between Egypt and the invading forces of the Hittites from Turkey.

*c.*1250–1200BC The Hebrews left Egypt to settle in Palestine. They wandered in the Sinai Desert for several years, and then set about conquering Palestine.

1250–1100BC

*c.***1250**BC The city of Troy in western Turkey was sacked by an army of Mycenean Greeks.

*c.***1225**BC The Assyrians captured southern Mesopotamia and Babylon. The Assyrian state was organized for war and quickly became the centre of a large empire.

*c.***1200**BC The Olmecs used volcanic stone to make large sculptures. The workshop where these were made is called the 'Red Palace', a large wood and mud structure with red floors and walls.

*c.***1200**BC The people of southern Palestine fell ill with a mysterious illness. This may have been the first outbreak of plague.

*c.***1200**BC The Mayan settlement of Chau Hiix, in Belize, was established.

*c.***1200–1000**BC Small settlements developed in the West Bank area of Palestine.

*c.***1200–300**BC At Chavin de Huantar in the Peruvian Andes, an urban culture flourished during this period.

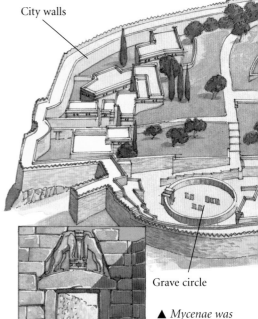

City walls

Grave circle

The Lion Gate

▲ *Mycenae was one of the major centres of Greek civilization in the second millennium* BC .

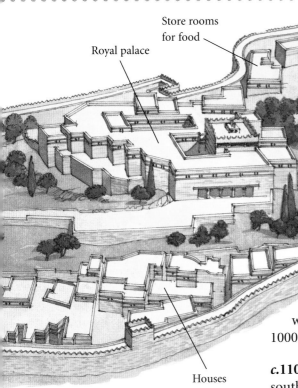

Store rooms for food

Royal palace

Houses

*c.***1100**BC The Indo-Aryans began using iron tools. They began practising Vedic religion, based on the book known today as the *Rig Veda*, the earliest of the four *Vedas*. It was probably compiled between 1000 and 2000BC.

*c.***1187–1156**BC Rameses III ruled Egypt. The world's first recorded labour dispute occurred during his reign, due to a delay in sending monthly rations to temple builders at Thebes.

*c.***1100**BC Phoenicians migrated to southern Iberia and formed settlements. They gradually gained control of the native communities in this area.

*c.***1100**BC The Dorian Greeks invaded Mycenae and the city was destroyed in a blazing fire. With this the Mycenean civilization came to an end.

1069–1000BC

*c.*1069BC Egypt was in turmoil due to internal warfare and an empty royal treasury.

*c.*1045BC The Zhou dynasty replaced the Shang dynasty in China. The Zhou dynasty can divided into two periods: the Western Zhou (*c.*1045–771BC) and the Eastern Zhou (*c.*770–256BC). During the Western Zhou period the capital was near Xi'an in the west, which shifted east to Luoyang during the Eastern Zhou period.

*c.*1045–479BC The *Wu Ching*, or the Five Classics of Chinese literature, were written. The five books are *I Ching* (Book of Changes), *Shu jing* (Book of History), *Shi jing* (Book of Songs), *Li ji* (Book of Rites) and *Chun qiu* (Spring and Autumn Annals).

*c.*1004BC David, King of Israel, captured Jerusalem from the Jebusites and made it his capital. David united Israel and during his reign Jerusalem became an important political and religious centre.

*c.*1000–750BC This period was known as the Greek Dark Age. The Greek economy collapsed and the population declined due to constant warfare. The Greek settlements reduced in size and trade, and agriculture suffered.

*c.*1000–800BC Horse riding developed on the Eurasian steppes.

*c.*1000–450BC Small city-states developed in the southern part of Arabia. Saba was one of the oldest and most powerful among these and was a force to reckon with until AD1.

*c.*1000–300BC The Central American settlements of El Mirador and Nakbe were established.

*c.*1000BC In Tabasco, Mexico, a great Olmec ceremonial centre was built. It was used until about 600BC.

*c.*1000BC Etruscans, who were probably from Asia Minor, migrated to Italy. Over the next 200–300 years they colonized a large area of central Italy. They built large stone forts and introduced the potter's wheel to Italy.

▲ *The ancient Maya people built great pyramid temples. They were built with limestone blocks and decorated with reliefs and inscriptions.*

1000–900BC

*c.*1000BC Iron became a popular metal in Europe and western Asia as people gained experience in heating, melting and forging techniques. The book of *Genesis* in the Bible mentions that Tubal-Cain, a descendant of Adam, was an expert ironsmith.

*c.*1000BC In south India the dead were buried in terracotta sarcophagi. Graves contained ceramic utensils and iron tools.

*c.*965BC Solomon succeeded David as the king of Israel and was famous for his wisdom and wealth. He reorganized the country into 12 administrative districts and initiated a vast building process that included the construction of the Temple of Jerusalem.

*c.*950BC In Mesoamerica, the Olmec settlement of San Lorenzo declined and La Venta gained importance. La Venta was originally built on an island in the Tonalá River. Today, it is part of a large swamp. Many of the ancient artefacts found here were moved to an archaeological museum.

*c.*928BC The kingdom of Israel was split into two parts. Israel was in the north with Samaria as its capital and Judah was to the south with its capital in Jerusalem.

*c.*900BC In Chalcatzingo, in the central Mexican highlands, a series of broad terraces were cut out of rock and carvings of ritual scenes were made.

*c.*900BC Trade flourished between the various Mesoamerican settlements, resulting in cultural exchanges. The largest and best known Olmec sites were situated along rivers.

*c.*900BC Anuradhapura was established in Sri Lanka. It was later the capital of the island country from about 300BC to around AD1100.

*c.*900–840BC The Assyrians conquered Syria and Turkey.

*c.*900–750BC Villanovan settlements flourished near Bologna, Italy. These were populated by Etruscans and later grew into cities.

▼ *The old city of Jerusalem, founded about 4000BC, is surrounded by massive stone walls.*

▲ *Little is known about Homer, who is regarded as the author of the epics* Iliad *and* Odyssey. *It has even been said that Homer was blind.*

*c.*850–480BC The Greeks developed the first true alphabet from an earlier system used by the Phoenicians.

*c.*800BC Greece revived after a period of decline known as the Dark Ages. The Greeks learned a new technique to smelt iron ore through contact with Eastern traders. The technological innovation helped them produce better tools and weapons at a lower cost.

*c.*800BC In the southwest of North America, large villages with dome roofed pit houses emerged.

*c.*800BC Merchants from the coasts of Phoenicia founded the city of Carthage in North Africa near modern Tunis.

*c.*800BC Sixteen *mahajanapadas* or 'great states' were formed in North India. The northeastern kingdom of Magadha eventually dominated over these warring states.

*c.*800BC In Mesoamerica, the Olmecs constructed a large earthen pyramid at La Venta. This was probably a religious structure.

*c.***800–700**BC In Greece, the poet Homer is believed to have composed his famous epics *Iliad* and *Odyssey*. The *Iliad* describes the legendary conflict between the Greeks and the city of Troy. The *Odyssey* narrates the story of the Greek hero Odysseus after the Trojan War.

*c.***800–500**BC In India, the Sanskrit texts *Brahmanas* and *Upanishads* as well as the *Sama*, *Yajur* and *Atharva vedas* were composed. These texts contained hymns relating to religion, rituals and philosophy, and formed the foundation of Hinduism.

776BC The first Olympic Games were organized. The festival was thereafter held once every four years and had participants from all over the Aegean.

*c.***775**BC A solar eclipse was documented by Chinese astronomers, making this the first recorded astronomical event.

▼ *The Trojan Horse is part of the legend of the Trojan War fought between the Greeks and the people of Troy. It is told that the Greeks hid themselves inside the huge, hollow wooden horse thought to be a gift. When the Trojans brought the horse into their city, the Greeks attacked and defeated the people of Troy.*

45

▼ *The Egyptians continued to use hieroglyphs for writing on monuments long after improved writing systems were used for everyday purposes.*

*c.*753BC According to legend, Rome was founded by the bandit chief Romulus. According to legend, Romulus and his twin brother Remus were raised by a she-wolf who found them left for dead in a river. A woodpecker also brought them food. The woodpecker, like the wolf, was considered sacred to Mars, the Roman god of war.

c.750BC Chalcidians, from the western part of the Greek mainland, colonized parts of Italy. Several settlements emerged in Italy, each having their own culture and language.

*c.*730–710BC In Greece, Messenia was invaded by Sparta. The invaders conquered Messenia and took the residents as slaves.

*c.*712–332BC Egypt was invaded and ruled by the Nubians from the south, the Assyrians from northern Mesopotamia and the Persians.

*c.*700BC In Central America, the Mayans developed a written language. The script used pictures and symbols.

*c.*700BC In India, society was divided into different classes by the caste system. The *brahmins* (priestly class) were the highest caste, followed by the *kshatriyas* (warrior class). Then came the *vaishyas* (traders), followed by the *shudras* (lowest class).

*c.*700BC In Greece, most domestic buildings were made of mud bricks and had thatched or tiled roofs.

*c.*700BC The Greek poet Hesiod was born. *Theogony* and *Works and Days* are two of the epics written by him.

*c.*683BC In many Greek city-states, monarchies gave way to republics where maintaining law and order was the responsibility of archons (magistrates).

*c.*650BC This is considered to be the beginning of the Archaic period in Greek art. This period was characterized by attention to human anatomy and depiction of scenes from literature and mythology.

650–600BC

*c.***650**BC In Greece, timber was replaced by stone in public buildings. Different types of columns developed and sculptural decoration on the exteriors of buildings became popular.

*c.***630**BC Greek poet Sappho was born on the island of Lesbos. She composed several lyrical poems about personal emotions such as love, friendship and enmity. The style in which she wrote was simple, direct and very descriptive.

*c.***630–561**BC Nebuchadnezzar II reigned over Babylon. He attacked Judah and captured Jerusalem. Various building projects were undertaken in Babylon during his reign, including the construction of the Hanging Gardens of Babylon, considered in ancient times to be one of the Seven Wonders of the World.

*c.***621**BC Draco, a lawmaker in Athens, set down a strict and almost tyrannical code of laws that was named after him. Surviving records of the laws he wrote, together with later accounts by Aristotle and

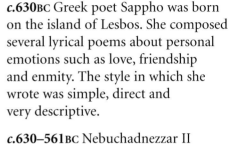

◀ *Nebuchadnezzar II is regarded as the greatest ruler of the Chaldean empire of Babylon.*

Plutarch, show that in Athens the death penalty was given to anyone who committed even the smallest crime. The laws of Draco specified that the criminal must be punished by the state.

*c.*616–579BC Lucius Tarquinius Priscus was king of Rome. He is said to have created the marketplace later known as the Roman Forum.

*c.*600BC The religion of Zoroastrianism was founded by the prophet Zoroaster, also known as Zarathustra, in central Asia.

*c.*600BC Thespis, the Greek poet, originated the actor's role in a drama. He is considered to be the inventor of tragedy.

*c.*600BC In Tartessus, southern Spain, the Greeks from northern Ionia established a trading station, trading with the Phoenicians, Carthaginians and people from Brittany.

*c.*600BC The technique of making cast iron was developed in China. This helped the Chinese make stronger pots, tools and weapons.

*c.*600BC The Mayans developed the practice of agriculture and irrigation. They made canals to bring water to their cities in Central America. These ancient tribes mainly cultivated corn, beans and squash. The farmers used a special method to clear the jungles and also terrace the slopes of the mountains to grow crops on.

...FASCINATING FACT...
Women in ancient China considered it inappropriate to be examined by doctors. Doctors made house calls and made their diagnosis after studying an ivory figurine on which patients marked the body parts that were troubling them.

▲ *This is a statue of Lord Buddha, the founder of Buddhism. The word 'buddha' means 'the enlightened one'.*

*c.*600BC In southern Mexico, masonry buildings were made at San José Mogote in Oaxaca. The corridor floor was inlaid with a carved panel.

*c.*600BC The Egyptians invented the first astronomical tool, the *merkhet*. It could measure time by studying the positions of the stars. It was also used by builders to mark the most suitable position for buildings.

*c.*600–300BC In India, several important books such as the *Arthsashtra*, *Natyashastra* and *Manusmriti* were written, laying the foundations of disciplines such as administration and warfare, dance, the visual arts and architecture.

*c.*594–574BC Solon, a well-known poet, became the leader of Athens. He abolished most of Draco's harsh laws and drew up a code that was more humane. Solon also revived the Athenian economy, minted Athenian coins and introduced weights and measures.

*c.*563–483BC Buddha lived during this period, in India. He is founder of the religion Buddhism.

*c.*560BC Renowned Greek mathematician and philosopher Pythagoras was born on the island of Ionia. He is credited with formulating several important mathematical theories, the most well known among them being the Pythagorean theorem.

*c.*551–479BC Chinese philosopher Confucius lived during this period.

*c.*545BC The Achaemenid Empire of Persia took control of several city-states in Central Asia. The religion of Zoroastrianism spread from these cities throughout the empire.

*c.*543BC In Magadha, northern India, Bimbisara established the Saisunaga dynasty.

*c.*540–520BC The Persians conquered the Greek city-states in Asia Minor and captured Egypt.

▼ *A statue of Buddha at the Golden Pavilion, Japan.*

509–490 BC

509BC King Tarquin the Proud was expelled from Rome, which then became a republic. Rome began a series of wars to conquer the Etruscans. The Etruscan civilization was one of the most prominent civilizations in modern-day Italy before the rise of Rome. Their territory was northwest of the Tiber River, now in modern Tuscany and parts of Umbria.

508BC The nobleman Cleisthenes reformed the government of Athens so that it had a democratic government. All citizens participated in the government and elections were held for the first time. Women and slaves still had few rights.

c.500BC In Mexico, the city and religious centre of Monte Albán was established on a hill above the Valley of Oaxaca. Villages in the valley, such as San José Mogote, began to decline.

c.500BC In present-day Nigeria, settlements were formed and people began to make iron tools.

c.500BC In India, Mahavira founded the Jainism religion.

c.500BC In India, Buddism and Jainism gained popularity as people rebelled against the rigidity of Vedic traditions.

499–494BC The Ionian settlements in Greece and those in Asia Minor revolted against their Persian rulers. The Persians were successful in crushing the Ionian revolt.

c.496–406BC Greek playwright Sophocles lived during this period. He was the author of tragedies such as *Oedipus the King* and *Antigone*.

492–449BC Greece and Persia were engaged in a series of battles, which are collectively referred to as the Greco-Persian Wars.

c.490–430BC Greek sculptor Phidias lived during this period. He was the chief sculptor of the Parthenon and created the statue of Zeus for the Temple of Zeus at Olympia.

▲ *The Parthenon in Athens was built by the Greek architects Ictinus and Callicrates.*

*c.*490BC Athens defeated invading Persians in the Battle of Marathon. It was a historic win as the Athenian army was much smaller and less well equipped than the Persians.

*c.*484–430BC Greek historian Herodotus lived during this period. He wrote a valuable account of the Greco-Persian wars.

*c.*484–406BC Greek playwright Euripides lived during this period. He was the last great tragic dramatist of ancient Greece. His plays include *Medea*, *Hippolytus* and *The Trojan Women*.

*c.*480BC The Greeks fought the Persians in the Battle of Salamis, part of the Greco-Persian Wars. The small Greek naval fleet managed to defeat and destroy a large Persian fleet comprising 800 galleys. This was the first battle at sea recorded in history.

*c.*478BC Athens became the most powerful state in Greece. It formed and led the Delian League, an association of Greek states that contributed monetary and military resources to fight foreign invasions. The members met annually at the island of Delos and their treasury was kept in the Temple of Apollo.

◀ *Most of what we know of Socrates comes from the writings of his students Plato and Xenophon.*

▶ *Legend has it that Pheidippides (or Phidippides) ran a distance of 40 km from Marathon to Athens to convey news of the Greek victory in the Battle of Marathon.*

c.475–221BC The Zhou dynasty broke up into several small warring states.

c.470–399BC Greek philosopher Socrates lived during this period.

c.462BC Military leader Pericles became the head of the state of Athens. His leadership coincided with Athens'

'Golden Era'. One of Pericles' achievements was the building of the acropolis (ancient Greek citadel) in Athens.

c.461BC Sparta gave up its membership of the Delian League due to differences with Athens. It formed the Peloponnesian League, which included most states in Peloponnese, all of which had strong armies, and Corinth, an old rival of Athens, which had a strong navy.

. . . FASCINATING FACT . . .
In ancient Greece only young men from aristocratic families were educated. At the age of 18 they had to spend two years in a gymnasium, where they were prepared, physically and mentally, to enter adulthood. To study subjects such as philosophy, mathematics and logic, students had to attend Plato's Academy or Aristotle's Lyceum.

451–400BC

*c.*451–450BC *The Twelve Tables of Roman Law* were the first set of laws laid down by the Roman Republic.

*c.*450–388BC Greek playwright Aristophanes lived during this period. He wrote 40 plays including *Wasps* and *Clouds*, and is regarded as the greatest comic dramatist of ancient Greece.

449BC Pericles began to build the Acropolis and the Parthenon temple dedicated to the goddess Athena. It is one of the most important buildings of the Greek civilization, and represents the Greek style of architecture and sculpture at its best.

*c.*445BC After leading the Greek cities to defeat Persia, Athens tried to enforce its own rule on other Greek states.

431–421BC The Peloponnesian War began when Athens broke a treaty with Sparta. All Greek cities took sides. After ten years of fighting, the two sides agreed to a truce.

430BC Plague struck Athens and about one thousand people died. The Athenian leader Pericles was one of them. Without Pericles, Athens was unable to defeat Sparta. In 421BC the Athenian general Nicias agreed to a truce.

*c.*428–348BC The Greek philosopher and teacher Plato lived during this period. He was a student and close friend of Greek philosopher Socrates.

415–405BC After a period of six years, known as the Peace of Nicias, Athens renewed the war with Sparta. Losses at war and political chaos at home eventually contributed to their defeat. The Peloponnesian War weakened the Greek cities and ruined their economy.

*c.*400BC *Tao-te Ching,* or *Classic of the Way of Power,* was written by Lao-tzu. The Taoism religion was based on this.

*c.*400BC Celtic-speaking Gauls from continental Europe occupied northern Italy.

▶ *The Parthenon in Athens has suffered considerable damage over the centuries, but its basic structure remains intact.*

▲ *Aristotle studied a wide range of subjects, including logic, philosophy, politics, physics, psychology and zoology.*

*c.*400BC In southern Mexico, the Zapotecs used a 365-day solar calendar as well as a 260-day ritual calendar. Interestingly, unlike many of the tribes that inhabited Middle America at the time, they had no traditions or legends that recorded their migration or origin. The Zapotecs are said to have believed that they were born directly from rocks, trees and jaguars.

*c.*400BC In Mesoamerica, the Olmec city of La Venta lost its importance following the destruction of many of its sculptures and structures.

384–322BC Greek philosopher and scientist Aristotle lived during this period. His theories and teachings had a far-reaching effect on the western world. Aristotle was a student of the Greek philosopher Plato. He believed that the answers to anything can be found in logic and all his teachings are based on this belief.

337BC Philip II of Macedonia defeated Athens. He formed the League of Corinth, of which all states except Sparta were members.

336BC Philip II was assassinated and his son Alexander became king of Macedonia.

*c.*335BC Aristotle founded the Lyceum in Athens. The Lyceum was a school that specialized in teaching biology and history.

333BC Alexander the Great invaded the Persian Empire leading a joint Greek-Macedonian army. He conquered Egypt and became pharaoh. Alexander founded the historical city of Alexandria and made it his capital.

331BC Alexander the Great defeated the Persians in the Battle of Gaugamela. This defeat brought about the fall of the Persian Empire. Alexandria became the largest city in the Mediterranean basin. It had two royal libraries, one in a temple of Zeus and the other in a museum. The libraries were said to contain around 700,000 scrolls.

330BC The Greek culture came to western Asia with Alexander's conquest of these areas. This influenced the architecture and town planning of areas where Macedonian and Greek soldiers settled. The settlers also popularized the Greek language.

▲ *A great general, Alexander was only 20 years old when he became king. He is famous for overthrowing the Persian Empire.*

59

327–300BC

327–326BC Alexander the Great invaded Taxila in northwestern India and defeated King Porus.

c.326BC The Circus Maximus was constructed. This hippodrome, or stadium, was the largest in Rome, and chariot races were held in it.

323BC Alexander died in Babylon after conquering Egypt, Bactria and the Indus Valley and spreading Greek culture in the east.

c.312BC The Romans built the first aqueduct, the *Aqua Appia*, to bring water to Rome. An aqueduct was a channel built to convey water, chiefly for providing a densely populated region with a supply of fresh water.

c.310–230BC Greek astronomer Aristarchus lived during this period. He discovered that the Earth revolves around the Sun. Other conclusions that he is credited with are that the Sun is larger than the Earth and that the Earth rotates upon its axis, causing day and night. He is also believed to be the first who suggested the Earth's axis is inclined, and that it is this that causes the change of seasons.

c.306BC Epicurus, the Greek philosopher and teacher, founded a school called *Ho Kepas* (the garden) in Athens. His was the first institution to admit women.

c.304BC Chandragupta Maurya, King of Magadha, expanded his empire by obtaining the Indus Valley from Seleucus, one of Alexander's successors. He made Patna his capital and founded the Maurya dynasty.

301BC The generals of the Macedonian army fought the Battle of Ipsus among themselves to gain control of Alexander's empire. After a stalemate, they divided the empire between themselves.

c.300BC Shaft tombs were built in Jalisco and Colima in western Mexico. The tombs, with a number of ceramic vessels and figures, were hidden deep below, at the bottom of the shafts.

*c.*300BC Cuicuilco, in Mexico, became an important centre. It had a circular pyramid and several large public buildings.

▼ *The ancient Romans built 11 aqueducts to supply water to the capital. The longest of these could bring water to Rome from a distance of as much as 92 km.*

...FASCINATING FACT...
Ptolemy II, King of Egypt, founded the Library of Alexandria at the beginning of the 3rd century BC. He asked every country in the world to send copies of their books, making it the largest collection of its time.

300–250BC

*c.***300**BC The city of Teotihuacán was established. One of the greatest Mesoamerican cities, it was situated near springs that provided water for irrigation. Obsidian, used for making tools and weapons, was also found here in large quantities.

*c.***300**BC Indian traders brought Buddhism to the Greco-Bactrian kingdom of Southwest Asia.

◀ *It took 12 years to build the Colossus of Rhodes. The statue was toppled by an earthquake in about 226*BC. *In* AD654, *invading Arab forces broke up the statue and sold off the bronze.*

*c.***294–284**BC A giant bronze statue of the Sun god Helios was erected at Rhodes, Greece. The Colossus of Rhodes was 32 m high and was considered to be one of the Seven Wonders of the World. Arabian invaders destroyed it in AD653. According to legend, the statue stood astride the harbour and ships passed between its legs. In reality, however, it is believed that the statue stood on a peninsula overlooking the harbour.

*c.***290**BC In India, Mauryan king Bindusara expanded his kingdom southwards to include the Deccan Plateau. In south India, the Chola dynasty dominated.

*c.***290–212**BC Greek mathematician and inventor Archimedes lived during this period. He discovered the law of buoyancy, which is also known as the Archimedes principle.

264–241BC The Romans defeated the Carthaginians in the First Punic War and captured Sicily. The war broke out because of conflict between the Sicilian cities of Messina and Syracuse. One faction called on Carthage for help and another faction called on Rome for assistance.

*c.*260BC Asoka succeeded his father Bindusara. One of India's most famous rulers, Asoka converted to Buddhism after the Battle of Kalinga. He played an important role in spreading Buddhism and the message of non-violence throughout the country.

*c.*251BC Asoka's son Mahendra helped spread Buddhism in Sri Lanka.

*c.*250BC In India, the stupas (domed Buddhist shrines) and large rocks were engraved with Buddhist texts and royal announcements in Prakrit, Greek, Aramaic and the Brahmi script, the first Indian script.

▼ *Teotihuacán was one of the largest cities of its time. The ruins of the city contains great palaces, plazas and temples. The Pyramid of the Sun is one of the largest structures built in the ancient Americas.*

232–150BC

*c.*232BC In India, Emperor Asoka died and the Mauryan Empire began to crumble.

221BC Antiochus III, also known as Antiochus the Great, became king of the Syrian Empire.

221–207BC The Qin dynasty unified all the warring states and ruled China. King Shih Huang-ti, who declared himself the first emperor of China, built the Great Wall of China.

218–201BC The Second Punic War between Rome and Carthage began when Rome broke the treaty of 241BC. The Carthaginian general Hannibal led an army to Italy, where he defeated the Roman Army in 216BC.Rome refused to surrender and defeated Carthage in 202BC. Rome became the most powerful state in the Mediterranean.

206BC In China, Liu Bang founded the Han dynasty. The Han dynasty can be divided into two periods, the Western Han dynasty (when the capital was to the west at Chang'an) and the Eastern Han dynasty (when the capital was to the east at Luoyang). Chang'an was one of the largest cities of the time.

*c.*200BC In the southwest of North America, famine led to the decline of village cultures.

189BC The Romans defeated Antiochus III of Syria at Magnesia.

*c.*180BC The last Mauryan king was killed by his commander-in-chief, Pushyamitra Sunga, who established the Sunga dynasty. The Satavahanas came to power in southern and central India.

*c.*160BC Greco-Bactrian forces, from the area around modern-day Afghanistan, invaded northwestern India. They ruled the area until the Scythians from central Asia invaded in 80BC.

*c.*150BC In Greece, *Venus de Milo*, the famous statue of the goddess of love and beauty, was carved. The statue is now at the Louvre Museum in Paris.

▲ *Carthaginian general Hannibal led an army of 20,000 infantry and 6000 cavalry in the Second Punic War. Hannibal's army crossed the Alps successfully during the expedition.*

65

150-70BC

c.150BC The eruption of the Xitle volcano in Mexico resulted in the mass migration and resettlement of people in the northern part of the Basin of Mexico.

149–146BC The Third Punic War between Rome and Carthage resulted in the destruction of Carthage and led to Roman control over the western Mediterranean.

146BC The Romans invaded Greece and by 30BC the entire area of Greece was a part of the Roman Empire.

138–78BC Nobleman Sulla won the first civil war in Rome and became dictator of the Roman Republic.

106–43BC Cicero lived during this period. He was a great Roman orator, lawyer, scholar and writer, who was in favour of Rome continuing as a democratic republic.

c.100BC In China, the practice of providing terracotta armies around graves gave way to large stone

▶ *Gladiators were men who fought in amphitheatres to entertain ancient Romans.*

sculptures on top of the tomb and on either side of the path leading to the grave. This practice continued for several centuries.

100–44BC Julius Caesar lived during this period. He was a Roman general who rose to become dictator of the Roman Empire between 46 and 44BC.

90BC Those people in Italy who were ruled by Rome gained the right to be Roman citizens, giving them important civil rights such as the right to vote.

c.73–71BC Gladiators of Rome revolted against the Republic in the Gladiatorial War. Spartacus, a gladiator from Thrace, was leader of the revolt.

c.70–8BC In Rome, Virgil and Horace composed some of the greatest literary classics. Horace was famous for his lyric poetry and satire in Latin and Virgil's best known composition is the epic *Aeneid*, which recounts legends of early Rome.

63BC–AD1

▲ *A statue of Julius Caesar, dictator of Rome.*

63BC The Romans defeated the Jews and occupied Palestine.

53BC The Parthians of Iran defeated the Romans in northern Mesopotamia.

51BC The beautiful Cleopatra VII was made queen of Egypt by Julius Caesar. When Cleopatra VII ascended the Egyptian throne, she was only 17 years old.

44BC Brutus, Cassius and other aristocrats in the Senate murdered Julius Caesar in an attempt to restore democracy.

*c.***37–4BC** King Herod was appointed to the throne of Judea by the Romans. He built several public buildings in Judaea.

31BC After a series of civil wars, Octavian, the nephew of Julius Caesar, defeated his final enemies at the Battle of Actium. Among the defeated were Roman general Mark Antony and Queen Cleopatra of Egypt. Octavian then made himself pharaoh of Egypt.

27BC Octavian assumed the title Augustus and became the first emperor of Rome. The Roman Empire included large parts of Europe and Asia, northern Africa and the Mediterranean islands.

*c.***4BC** Jesus Christ was born in the village of Bethlehem, in Judea, during the rule of King Herod.

*c.***AD1** Teotihuacán, in central Mexico, grew into a large city due to the migration of people from surrounding areas. It had a population of about 40,000.

▶ *Cleopatra, Queen of Egypt, persuaded Roman general Mark Antony to join her in war against Rome.*

AD1-30

◀ *Saint John the Baptist was imprisoned and later executed by King Herod Antipas.*

*c.*AD1 In North America, the Cherokee tribe lived in the southern Appalachians. They settled in the region of modern-day Virginia, West Virginia, northwestern South Carolina, northern Georgia and northern Alabama.

*c.*AD1 In China, grave goods became more elaborate and included clothes, jewellery and models of soldiers and attendants.

*c.*AD1–125 In the southwest of North America, the cave-dwelling Anasazi formed flourishing agricultural settlements.

*c.*AD1–100 The Friesians, a Teutonic tribe of German-speaking Europeans, settled in the area of the modern-day Netherlands.

*c.*AD1–10 Greek inventor Hero of Alexandria made an *aeolipile*, the first steam engine. Unfortunately it was not put to actual use. His writings on mechanics include the study of mechanical problems of daily life and the construction of several kinds of engines.

AD14 Tiberius succeeded Augustus Caesar as the Roman emperor. His reign was marked by revolts in Germany, Gaul and other parts of Europe. He ruled the state efficiently and carried out some reforms.

*c.*AD25 Luoyang, in China, was the capital of the Eastern Han dynasty. With a population of 500,000 people, it was the most populated city of its time.

*c.*AD30 John the Baptist was imprisoned by King Herod Antipas of Judea. Herod Antipas later beheaded John the Baptist when his step-daughter demanded John's head as a reward for dancing in front of the king's guests.

*c.*AD30 Jesus Christ was crucified on the hill of Golgotha in Jerusalem. His teachings later formed the basis of the Christian religion.

*c.*AD30–64 Saint Peter was appointed the first leader of the Christian Church. He is recognized as the leader of the 12 apostles. Saint Peter's Basilica in Rome is said to be built on the site of his grave. Roman Catholics regard him as the gatekeeper of heaven

▲ *The teachings and deeds of Jesus Christ are recorded in The New Testament and form the basic principles of Christianity.*

AD33–60

c.AD33–100 Christianity spread to the Roman provinces around the Adriatic Sea.

AD37 Gaius Caesar, better known as Caligula, became the third Roman emperor.

AD41 Claudius succeeded Gaius as the emperor of Rome.

AD43 The Romans conquered southern Britain and built a bridge across the Thames at a site that is now London.

c.AD45 The discovery of a shorter sea route to India by the Greeks led to the development of Calicut, on the western coast in south India, into an important trading post.

AD46 Greek biographer Plutarch was born in Chaeronea, Greece. His essays, biographies and historical writings inspired many Europeans centuries later. Plutarch has about 227 works to his credit.

c.AD50 The Mayan city and pilgrimage centre of Teotihuacán, in Mexico, was developed on a grid pattern, which was later copied in several other cities.

c.AD52 Christianity came to India when St Thomas, an apostle of Jesus Christ, arrived in modern-day Madras.

▶ *Queen Boudicca of the Iceni led a rebellion against the Romans.*

· · · FASCINATING FACT · · ·

The ancestor of the apples that we eat today is the wild apple that grows on the mountains of Kazakhstan. Ancient Greek and Roman traders who passed through the Silk Road brought the fruit to the western world. Apple trees are grown using the grafting method, which was developed by the Chinese in 2000BC.

AD**54–68** Roman emperor Nero ruled during this period. He was very cruel and ill-treated his subjects. He even had his own mother, Agrippina the Younger, murdered.

AD**60** Queen Boudicca of Iceni (modern Norfolk, England) revolted against the Roman occupation of her territories. She burned London and killed 70,000 Romans before being defeated.

AD64–100

AD64 Large areas of Rome were destroyed by a huge fire. Nero rebuilt the city with Greek-style buildings.

AD69 Vespasian founded the Flavian Dynasty in Rome and ended the civil wars that followed Nero's reign. He built the Colosseum in Rome.

AD70 The Israelites rose in revolt against Roman rule by fighting the Jewish War, but were defeated in battle. The Romans burned the Temple of Jerusalem.

▼ *The ancient Romans used paving stones to lay the surface of the road. The stones were cut so they fitted together closely.*

▶ *Trajan erected a 40-metre-tall carved marble column in Rome.*

AD79 The Roman towns of Pompeii and Herculaneum, as well as several smaller settlements, were buried when the volcano Mount Vesuvius erupted.

AD96 Nerva Caesar Augustus ascended the Roman throne. His reign was one of peace and prosperity.

AD98 Trajan became the emperor of Rome. He expanded the eastern boundaries of the empire and built several public buildings, roads and aqueducts.

***c*.AD100** Paper made from wood pulp was invented in China. Its use slowly spread across Asia and into Europe.

***c*.AD100** The Mesoamerican Olmec civilization began to decline.

***c*.AD100** Settled farming communities flourished in the southwest of North America and communities with elaborate burial traditions existed in Ohio and Illinois.

AD100-135

c.AD100–200 In India, the Kushan dynasty replaced the Scythian dynasty.

c.AD100–200 In India, Kushan ruler Kanishka encouraged Buddhism. During this period, Buddhism spread to most parts of central Asia and China. Development of trade routes resulted in trade with Rome and Southeast Asian countries.

c.AD100–300 In Japan, farming villages grew in size. Various clans were formed, which constantly fought among themselves.

c.AD100–400 In a period of intense literary activity in India, several early Tamil classics were written in the region of present-day Tamil Nadu. Three *sangams* (literary academies) in Madurai were responsible for the development of this Sangam literature.

c.AD100–700 The Moche and Nasca Indians formed agricultural settlements in the area that is modern-day Peru. They cultivated corn, peanuts, beans and pumpkin.

▶ *Shopping for jewellery in Roman Britain. During the Roman occupation, several towns were established in Britain and Roman culture spread across the country.*

c.AD100–1000 The Champa kings ruled Vietnam and developed Hoi An into an important port and trade centre.

AD117–138 Roman emperor Hadrian took control of the empire and reformed the government of the provinces. He rebuilt the Pantheon in Rome and began the construction of a large wall, known as Hadrian's Wall, in northern Britain. It was supposed to protect Rome from the northern barbarians.

c.AD125 North Africa and Italy were struck by an epidemic disease that killed large numbers of people. It may have been a form of measles.

AD135 The Romans forced the Jews to leave the city of Jerusalem. The Romans later renamed the city and called it Aelia Capitolina.

AD138–200

AD138–161 Roman emperor Antoninus Pius ruled during this period.

AD161–180 Marcus Aurelius ruled during this period. He was a noted philosopher, and defeated several invasions during his rule.

AD161 Roman silk merchants sent by Emperor Marcus Aurelius arrived in the court of Han emperor Huan-ti. They were the first Roman delegates to reach Han China.

c.AD165 Smallpox stuck Rome and claimed the lives of about one-quarter of the population. The epidemic also caused severe food shortages.

AD177–192 Roman emperor Commodus ruled during this period. His reign marked the beginning of the Roman Empire's downfall. To display his physical strength, Commodus even performed as a gladiator. He also renamed Rome *Colonia Commodiana*, which means 'colony of Commodus'. Romans rose in revolt against his cruel and irresponsible rule.

▶ *Many Roman emperors built triumphal arches to commemorate their victories in battle.*

AD193–211 Septimius Severus established the Severan dynasty of emperors in Rome. After the end of this period the Roman Empire underwent 50 years of civil wars and revolts.

AD196 The city of Byzantium, in Turkey, was attacked and destroyed by Roman emperor Septimus Severus.

AD198–217 Roman emperor Caracalla ruled during this period. He popularized the concept of public baths called *thermae*. During his reign, Roman citizenship was extended to all free inhabitants of the empire.

c.AD200 The Bantu people, descendents of the Neolithic Nok people from west Africa, migrated into central and southern Africa.

c.AD200–500 Nalanda and Valabhi, important universities and centres of Mahayana Buddhism, were established in India.

...FASCINATING FACT...

Nerva, Trajan, Hadrian, Antoninus Pius and Marcus Aurelius were
the 'five good emperors'. Their reigns, which lasted from 96–180, were a
period of peace and prosperity in the Roman Empire. The period from
the reign of Augustus to that of Marcus Aurelius is popularly known as
Pax Romana, or Roman Peace.

AD224–313

c.AD224–641 The Iranian Sassanid dynasty ruled over Persia.

c.AD248 Vietnamese patriot Trieu Au led a revolt against the Chinese. The revolt was unsuccessful and she committed suicide.

c.AD250 In Central America, temples near the Pyramid of the Moon at the Mayan city of Teotihuacán were decorated with wall paintings. Houses were built as groups of single-storied apartments.

c.AD250 The reign of Emperor Sujin marked the start of documented Japanese history.

c.AD253 An epidemic of plague struck the Roman Empire and lasted for 15 years.

AD284–305 Roman emperor Diocletian ruled during this period. He brought peace and order after a succession of ineffective and cruel rulers. In 305 he abdicated and spent the final eight years of his life as a gardener.

▶ *Roman emperor Constantine addresses his troops after they had made him emperor.*

c.AD300 Armenia became the first Christian state when its king, Tiridates III, made Christianity the official religion.

c.AD300 In Japan, the Yamato clan suppressed its rivals and took control of most of Honshu Island and the northern part of Kyushu.

AD306 Constantine the Great was made emperor by the Roman troops in Britain. At first he ruled over only Britain and Gaul. He was the first Roman emperor to convert to Christianity and is widely held to be the 'first Christian emperor'.

c.AD313 In Korea, the domination of the Chinese Han dynasty ended and the three Korean kingdoms of Koguryô in the north, Paekche in the southwest and Silla in the southeast, were established. A small group of city-states called the Kaya Federation ruled the areas between Paekche and Silla.

AD317-400

c.AD317–420 Following a long period of warfare in China, the Eastern Jin dynasty brought peace and cultural development to part of the country. During their reign calligraphy, figure painting and poetry flowered.

c.AD320 The Gupta dynasty came to power in India under the leadership of Chandragupta, a lover of art and literature. For the next century, most of the country was united under the Gupta Empire. The Guptas controlled the land from the eastern hills of Afghanistan to Assam. The rule of the Gupta Empire is called the 'golden age of Indian civilization'.

AD324 Constantine defeated Licinius, the ruler of the Eastern Roman Empire, and became the sole emperor of Rome.

AD326 Roman emperor Constantine rebuilt the ruined city of Byzantium and made it his capital. He later named the city Constantinople.

AD330 The world's largest hippodrome, a stadium used for horse and chariot racing, was constructed in Constantinople.

AD364 After the war with the Romans, the Persians took over Armenia and most Roman areas in Persia.

c.AD372 The Huns, who had migrated from Central Asia to Europe, drove out the Ostrogoths and Visigoths from the Ukraine. The Goths fled into Roman territory, where they were a constant source of trouble to the Romans.

AD391 The Library of Alexandria, Egypt, built by Greek king Ptolemy II, was destroyed in a fire.

AD393 The Roman emperor Theodosius I banned the Olympic Games because of corruption and links to paganism.

c.AD400 The White Huns from Central Asia invaded Afghanistan. They destroyed the Buddhist culture and ruined most of the country.

▲ *Roman legion heading to battle. A Roman legion (army unit) comprised 5000 to 6000 men.*

AD400–475

c.AD400 Ancient Indian poet and playwright Kalidasa composed several literary classics in Sanskrit. His most famous work is the Sanskrit drama *The Recognition of Shakuntala*.

AD406 The Germanic tribes of Vandals, Alans and Sciri crossed the Rhine. This event marks the collapse of Roman power.

AD410 The Visigoths, led by Alaric, attacked and looted Rome. This was the first time Rome had been captured by a foreign army in 800 years.

AD410 The Huns forced the Roman Empire to pay them tribute. The Huns introduced stirrups in the west, which gave them an advantage in battle.

AD429 The Vandals invaded North Africa and conquered Carthage. The city became the Vandal capital, from where they controlled all of North Africa. The Vandals later annexed Corsica, Sardinia and Sicily. Their pirate ships controlled a large part of the Mediterranean region.

c.AD430 The British missionary St Patrick arrived in Ireland to spread Christianity. He is the patron saint of Ireland. According to legend, he rid Ireland of snakes and explained the notion of the Holy Trinity by using the shamrock leaf. Shamrock was later made the national plant of Ireland.

AD434–453 Attila was the leader of the Huns. During his leadership the Huns were successful in battles against the Visigoths, Ostragoths and the Alans.

AD451 Attila the Hun was defeated by the Romans in the battle of Chalons.

AD455 Rome was attacked and sacked by the Vandals.

AD475–476 The teenager Romulus Augustulus lead the western Roman Empire based at Ravenna. He was considered to be the last Roman emperor. The great Roman Empire came to an end when the Germanic ruler Odoacer deposed Romulus. Thereafter, the western Roman Empire was divided under barbaric rule.

▲ *The present-day St Patrick's Cathedral stands on the site of a well where St Patrick is said to have baptized converts to Christianity. The cathedral replaced the old wooden church in the 12th century.*

▲ *The Anglo-Saxons were inhabitants of Germany who migrated to England in the 5th century and settled there.*

*c.*AD476 Indian mathematician Aryabhatta devised roots and powers of numbers.

AD493 Theodoric, King of the Ostrogoths, became the ruler of Italy.

*c.*AD496 The Shaolin Temple was built at the foot of Mount Songshan in Henan, China. It was the birthplace of the martial art Shaolin boxing, which later developed into kung fu.

*c.*AD499 The Angles and the Saxons conquered what was left of Roman Britain. They established numerous small kingdoms that would later become England.

. . . FASCINATING FACT . . .

According to legend, tea was discovered in ancient China by Emperor Shen Nung. It is said that when one of the king's servants was boiling drinking water during an outing, some leaves from a wild tea plant fell into the water. The emperor found the liquid refreshing and soon tea consumption spread throughout China. Later, Portuguese and Dutch traders brought the beverage to Europe.

*c.*AD500 The city of Teotihuacán, in Mexico, covered an area of 8 square miles and was inhibited by nearly 150,000 people.

*c.*AD500 In Egypt, Nubians adopted Christianity and gave up the worship of ancient Egyptian gods.

*c.*AD500 In India, Bodhidharma founded Zen Buddhism.

*c.*AD500 The Vakataka dynasty of central India began work on the Ajanta cave paintings. These delicate paintings are among the earliest in India and depict scenes from the *Jataka* tales, which are traditional stories of previous lives of the Buddha.

*c.*AD500 In the valleys of west central Jalisco, Mexico, the Mayan tradition of circular ceremonial and administrative structures developed. They also made vast circles, which may have been used as ball courts, surrounded by several short pyramids.

▶ *The ruined ancient city of Chichén Itzá is said to have been built by Maya peoples. It was established in about the 6th century.*

AD508 Frankish king, and most important king of the Merovingian dynasty, Clovis conquered most of France and Belgium, and converted all his subjects to western Catholic Christianity. Paris was made the Merovingian capital.

AD510–610

c.**AD510** Huns from southeastern Europe defeated the Guptas of India and conquered the regions of Punjab, Gujarat and Malwa.

AD527 Justinian I ascended the Byzantine or Eastern Roman throne. During his reign a large part of Constantinople was ruined by fire. Justinian rebuilt the city, including several religious buildings, such as the famous Hagia Sophia church.

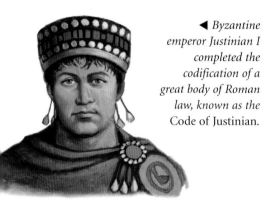

◀ *Byzantine emperor Justinian I completed the codification of a great body of Roman law, known as the* Code of Justinian.

c.**AD528** Weakened by continuous invasions, the Gupta Empire in India collapsed.

AD533–565 Justinian I brought Italy, North Africa and parts of Spain under Byzantine or Eastern Roman rule.

c.**AD541** Plague struck Europe and raged through the continent, claiming the lives of vast numbers of people.

c.**AD550** David converted the residents of Wales to Christianity. In 1120, he was canonized and became known as the patron saint of Wales.

c.**AD550–1189** The Chalukyas of Karnataka, India, ruled over parts of south and central India. They built some of the most beautifully carved temples in India.

c.**AD593** According to tradition, Queen Suiko, of the Yamato dynasty, became Japan's first queen. During her reign Buddhism spread all over Japan.

c.**AD600** Cantona, east of central Mexico, became the most important Mayan centre after the decline of Teotihuacán.

AD610 Prophet Mohammed began to preach the religion of Islam at Mecca in Arabia.

▲ *St David, the patron saint of Wales.*

AD618-633

AD618 In China, Li Yuan established the T'ang dynasty. He united the whole of China and unified the various small kingdoms.

AD622 Opposition from Mecca's leaders forced Prophet Mohammed to flee to Medina. The event is called the *Hegira* and is considered the beginning of the Islamic era.

AD629 Dagobert I, the most powerful Merovingian ruler, united the entire Frankish land under his rule. He signed a treaty with the Byzantine emperor and campaigned against the Slavs in the east. Dagobert I shifted his capital from Austrasia to Paris. He was a patron of arts and the great abbey of Saint-Denis was built during his rule.

AD629–645 Buddhist monk and scholar Hsüan-tsang visited India and Southeast Asia. He translated several Buddhist texts and helped spread the religion in China.

AD630 Prophet Mohammed returned to Mecca with the Islamic holy book, the *Koran*. He established the *sharia*, the Islamic code of laws.

...FASCINATING FACT...

According to an Arabian legend, King Shahryar married and killed a girl everyday until it was the turn of a young woman called Scheherazade. Scheherazade narrated stories to the king every night and left them incomplete until morning. The king's curiosity prevented him from killing her. These stories have been collected in the book, *The Thousand and One Nights*. The stories of Ali Baba, Aladdin and Sindbad are from this undated collection of folktales.

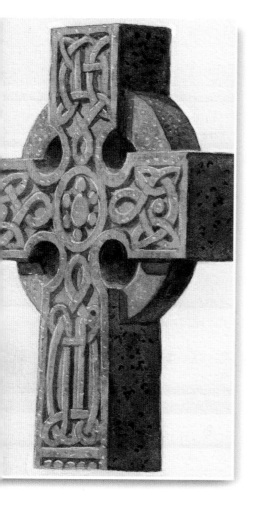

◀ *The Celtic cross is a traditional Christian symbol. It has a circle enclosing the point where the lines of the cross meet.*

AD632 After the death of Prophet Mohammed, Abu Bakr became the first caliph (leader of the Islamic peoples). Abu Bakr was Muhammad's father-in-law as well as his trusted companion and adviser.

AD632 Hassan and Hussein, grandsons of Mohammed, founded the Fatimid Caliphate, which ruled Egypt and North Africa.

AD632 English king Penda of Mercia killed King Edwin of Northumbria and took control of northern Britain.

*c.***AD632** Queen Sondok became the ruler of the Korean kingdom of Silla.

AD633–640 Muslim forces conquered Persia and attacked the Byzantine Empire. In Alexandria, Antioch and Jerusalem, Christian churches were turned into Muslim mosques as the lands fell to the Arab conquerors.

91

AD634—700

AD634 Caliph Omar succeeded Abu Bakr. He completed the conquest of Syria, Persia and Egypt in what was one of the earliest 'holy wars'.

AD636 The Arabs defeated the Byzantines at the Battle of Yarmuk. They captured Jerusalem and destroyed the wooden cross on which Jesus Christ had been crucified.

c.AD641 Buddhist king Harshavardana, ruler of Kannauj in north India, established the first diplomatic relations between India and China. He brought Uttar Pradesh and parts of Rajasthan and Punjab under his rule. Chinese pilgrim Xuanzand visited India during his rule.

c.AD650 The Mayan city of Teotihuacán was destroyed, perhaps by Toltec invaders. Its temples and buildings were burned and statues were broken.

c.AD650—888 In south India, the Pallavas founded the city of Mamallapuram, where they erected beautiful stone temples.

c.AD651 Traders and travellers from Arabia introduced Islam to China.

AD661 Supporters of Ali, Muhammad's son-in-law, formed the Islamic sect called Shi'ites.

AD 691 The Dome of the Rock was built in Jerusalem. The site on which the mosque was constructed is sacred to both Muslims and Jews.

c.AD700 In China, the T'ang capital Chang'an became the largest and richest city in the world. It spread over almost 30 square miles and was surrounded by a wall with 12 gates.

c.AD700 The Toltec city of Tula Chico was founded in Hidalgo, Mexico. The city had a population tens of thousands. The city's art and architecture resembled that of the later Aztec Empire. One of the major structures in the city was a plaza bordered by a five-stepped pyramid.

▲ *The Dome of the Rock in Jerusalem is the oldest existing Islamic monument. It was built as a shrine for pilgrims.*

AD700–850

*c.*AD700 Porcelain ware was invented in China. Its name was derived from the word *porcellana*, which Marco Polo used to describe it.

*c.*AD706 Muslim invaders drive out the Zoroastrians from Persia, in modern-day Iran. The refugees travelled eastward and eventually settled in China and Gujarat, India. Zoroastrians who settled in India became known as Parsis. Those who continued to live in Persia were forced to pay a special tax to the Muslim authorities.

AD732 Frankish king Charles Martel defeated an Islamic invasion at the Battle of Tours in France.

AD750 The Abbasid Caliphate of Baghdad replaced the Omayyads of Damascus and gained control of the Islamic Empire for the next 350 years.

AD768 Charlemagne ascended the Frankish throne and united most of western Europe. He fought and defeated the Saxons and subdued the Avars of the Danube region.

▶ *Chinese porcelain is famous for its beauty and delicacy, and the perfection of the covering glaze. It reached a peak in the Ming era (1368–1644).*

AD794 Kyoto became the Japanese capital and Emperor Kammu managed to unite the Japanese islands under his rule. Japan entered a period of cultural and artistic development.

AD800 Charlemagne was crowned emperor of Rome by the Pope. His kingdom became known as the Holy Roman Empire.

*c.*AD800 In Mexico, cities such as Yagul, Mitla and Zaachila in the Oaxaca valley became centres of power and activity.

AD814 Louis I, also known as Louis the Pious, became the emperor of the Holy Roman Empire. He carried out important cultural and religious reforms during his rule.

*c.*AD850 Several flourishing central Mexican city-states were destroyed or abandoned, probably due to internal problems or because of invasions by the Toltecs.

AD850–906

c.AD850 The Viking prince Rurik conquered Kiev and established the Rus dynasty, from which the name Russia derives. Vikings were warriors from Scandinavia.

AD850 Louis II became the Holy Roman emperor.

AD868 The *Diamond Sutra*, a Mahayana Buddhist text, was the first book to be printed. The primitive printing method involved taking rubbings of carved wood blocks.

c.AD868–1000 The Vikings discovered and colonized Iceland, Greenland and parts of North America.

AD875 Charles the Bald became the Holy Roman emperor.

AD881 Pope John VIII crowned Charles III, the German king of Swabia, Holy Roman emperor.

c.AD895 The Magyars migrated from Siberia and settled down in modern-day Hungary and parts of Romania.

AD896 The Bavarian king Arnulf was crowned the Holy Roman emperor by Pope Formosus.

c.AD900 The Toltecs ruled the area from Costa Rica to the southwest of North America, from Tula, their capital city.

c.AD906 Annam, or central Vietnam, freed itself from Chinese rule. By about 939 all of Vietnam was free.

...FASCINATING FACT...

Unlike women in other parts of the world during the Middle Ages, Viking women played an important role in society. Vikings had to pay a bride-price to the girl's father in order to marry her. While her husband was away raiding, the Viking woman managed her home and estate. Some of them served as speakers in the court and some even went to battle!

▼ *The Vikings invaded and colonized vast areas in eastern and western Europe from 800 to 1100.*

c.AD946 The areas ruled by the Abbasid Caliphate became increasingly fragmented and under the control of local rulers.

c.AD950 In China, folded books replaced paper scrolls.

c.AD950 The Rajput Tomars established their capital at Delhi, India. Delhi rose to importance and remained the seat of power of the following dynasties in India for several hundreds of years.

AD955 German king Otto the Great defeated the Magyars in the Battle of Lechfeld. He then established the country of Austria.

AD959 Edgar, King of Wessex, became king of England. He is considered the first king of England. Edgar's reign was peaceful and he was tolerant towards local customs.

AD960 The Sung dynasty succeeded the T'ang dynasty in China. During the Sung period, education gained importance and printed books and

▶ *The Chinese have quite a few inventions to their credit. Among these are coal, fireworks, eyeglasses, ice cream, pasta and paper money.*

paper became more common. Their rule is divided into two periods – the northern Sung (960–1126) and the southern Sung (1127–1279). Tai Tsung was the first emperor of the Sung dynasty and he established Kaifeng, in northern China, as his capital.

c.AD970 China became the first country to use paper money. Its use became widespread after 1260.

c.AD983 *Taiping Yulan*, considered to be the first encyclopedia, was printed in China.

c.AD985 In India, the Chola Empire reached the height of its power under Rajaraja Chola. He built the famous Brihadeeswara temple in Tanjavur, Tamil Nadu.

AD987 Hugh Capet became the king of France and founded the Capetian dynasty that ruled France until 1328.

AD988–1048

AD**988** Vladimir I, the grand duke of Kiev, converted to Christianity and popularized the customs of the Orthodox Church in Russia.

AD**997** Mahmud of Ghazni invaded north India and conquered Punjab. He was the ruler of the Ghaznavid Empire based in Afganistan.

AD**997** Stephen I became the first king of Hungary. His rule was marked by an invasion by Conrad II of Germany and wars with Bulgaria and Poland. He based the Hungarian government and Church administration on the German model. Stephen I is considered the patron saint of Hungary.

c.AD**1000** The Cholas of south India conquered Sri Lanka.

c.AD**1006–1346** In India, the Hoysala dynasty ruled the area between Chola and Chalukya Empires. The Hoysala kings were art and literature lovers. They built several elaborately carved stone temples in Belur, Halebid and Somnathpur in Karnataka.

AD**1016–1035** Canute, Prince of Denmark, became the king of England, Denmark and Norway. He issued a new law code and was a strong supporter of the Church. His rule brought peace and prosperity to England.

AD**1031** The Omayyad Caliphate ended with the death of Caliph Hisham III.

c.AD**1044** The Mons and the Burmese established the kingdom of Pagan, or Burma, in Southeast Asia.

AD**1046** Clement II was appointed Pope by the German king Henry III, ending a disputed papal succession and demonstrating imperial power over the papacy. He crowned Henry III the Holy Roman emperor. During the later years of his rule, Henry's control over Hungary and southern Italy weakened.

AD**1048–1131** The famous Persian poet, mathematician and astronomer Omar Khayyám lived during this period. His most popular literary work is the *Rubaiyat*. *Rubaiyat* was later translated into English by Edward Fitzgerald.

▲ *The Vikings, who began to raid England in the late 8th century, began to issue coins of their own, like the coin above, once they settled in the country.*

1050–1070

*c.*1050–1101 Confucianism gained popularity in China. It comprised the teachings of the 5th century philosopher Confucius.

*c.*1050 The port city of Mombasa was founded in eastern Africa.

*c.*1053 Norman warrior Robert Guiscard defeated the army of Pope Leo IX at Civitate. He later supported the papacy and ruled over the southern part of Italy.

1054 A dispute between Pope Leo IX and Michael Cerularius, the leader of the Greek Orthodox Church, led to the permanent separation of the Eastern (Orthodox) and Western (Roman) churches.

1055 Toghril Beg established the Seljuq dynasty after defeating the Shiites in Baghdad.

1056 The Byzantine Macedonian dynasty ended with the death of Empress Theodora. The Comnenus dynasty took control of the empire.

1058 Malcolm Canmore became the king of Scotland.

1066 William I (also known as William the Conqueror), duke of Normandy, defeated Harold II of England in the Battle of Hastings and seized power as the king of England.

... FASCINATING FACT ...
It is believed that sugar cane was originally grown in New Guinea.
Thousands of years ago it was planted in Southeast Asia and India.
In 500BC Indians discovered that by boiling the juice of the sugar cane,
sugar crystals could be made. The Arabs brought sugar cane to Spain
and the crusaders brought sugar to Europe.

*c.*1069 England's king, William the Conqueror, suppressed an English uprising in the northern parts of the country. He later invaded Scotland and Wales. William also carried out a survey of England, which was recorded in the *Domesday Book*. He divided his land among his sons, giving England to William II. His second son Robert II was given Normandy and Maine.

▲ *William the Conqueror's victory in the Battle of Hastings in 1066 marked the beginning of Norman rule in England.*

1070 The Italian merchants of Amalfi founded the order of the Knights of St John (also called the Knights Hospitallers) at Jerusalem, to take care of the St John hospital. In 1834, the headquarters was moved to Rome.

*c.*1070 The Tilantongo Kingdom, a small Mixtec city-state in Oaxaca, Central America, expanded its rule over a large area.

1086 Spanish king Alfonso VI captured Toledo, the Islamic centre of science. However, his success led to the invasion by the North African Almoravid Muslims, who then defeated him at Zallaqah.

◀ *A medieval knight wearing the cross of a crusader.*

1087 William the Conqueror, King of England, died in Rouen, France.

1088 Chinese inventor Su Sung constructed a water-powered mechanical clock.

1095 Pope Urban II urged all Christians to join a crusade to fight a war against Muslims.

1096 The First Crusade was fought to protect the Byzantine Empire from the Seljuk Turks. Nearly 300,000 European Christians fought in the campaign. The First Crusade succeeded in establishing

a western military state in and around Jerusalem, which lasted almost two centuries.

*c.*1096–1306 Jews were killed or driven out of Rhineland, England and France.

1097 The Battle of Niceae, part of the First Crusade, ended with the Christian army defeating the Muslims.

1099 Godfrey of Bouillon, a leader of the First Crusade, captured Jerusalem and assumed the title 'Defender of the Holy Sepulchre'. He made peace with the nearby Muslim cities and resisted an Egyptian invasion.

1120 The Order of the Poor Knights of Christ and the Temple of Solomon (Knights Templar) was founded to protect defenceless Christian pilgrims from attacks by Muslims. In the beginning the group comprised only eight or nine French knights who were given quarters near the site of the former temple of Jerusalem, which gave them their name. They flourished during the following two centuries and spread in other countries, becoming a wealthy and powerful brotherhood of armed Christian warriors.

▼ *The Crusaders succeeded in capturing Jerusalem in the First Crusade.*

105

1120 Windmills, which were invented in Persia, were used throughout Europe.

***c.*1136** Suger, Abbot of Saint-Denis, France, constructed the church of Saint-Denis in a new architectural style. This was the beginning of the Gothic style of architecture.

1145 Pope Eugene III asked the French Cistercian priest Bernard of Clairvaux to call upon all Christians to begin the Second Crusade. This was in response to the Muslim capture of Edessa.

1147 Louis VII of France and Conrad III of Germany led a vast army in the Second Crusade. The Crusade failed and the Crusaders suffered several casualties. However, the English troops succeeded in freeing Lisbon from the Moors.

◀ *Stained glass windows are an important feature of Gothic architecture. They recorded significant events and people, such as Dermot MacMurrough, who ruled Ireland during this era.*

▶ *Windmills were commonly used in England from the 12th century until the early part of the 19th century.*

*c.*1150 In Cambodia, the Khmer king Suryavarman II constructed the Angkor Wat temple complex, the world's largest religious structure.

*c.*1150 China became a major maritime state under the Sung dynasty.

1152 Frederick I, or Frederick Barbarossa, became the king of Germany. He was also crowned emperor of the Holy Roman Empire.

1152 Henry II became the king of England. He extended his empire in northern England and western France. He strengthened the royal administration and reformed the court system. Henry II's reign was marked by internal disputes among the family.

1154 Nicholas Breakspear was elected as Pope Adrian IV. He is the only Englishman ever to hold papal office. He had earlier served in France and Italy.

1164 Henry II of England issued the Constitutions of Clarendon, laws that restricted the power of the church and gave more power to the king. Thomas Becket, Archbishop of Canterbury, disagreed with the king and was forced to flee to France.

107

1165–1175

1165 William I, also known as William the Lion, became king of Scotland.

1167 Frederick Barbarossa, Holy Roman emperor, installed antipope Paschal III on the papal throne, but Paschal was not accepted in Rome.

1170 Henry II of England forced Roger, Archbishop of York, to accept royal power over the church and its administration.

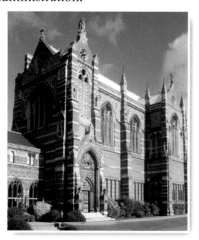

▲ *The University of Oxford at Oxfordshire, England is one of the most renowned British universities*

*c.***1170** The University of Oxford was founded in Britain after English students were barred from the University of Paris.

1170 Thomas Becket returned to Canterbury and was murdered by King Henry's knights in Canterbury Cathedral.

*c.***1170** In Central America, Chichimec nomads raided the Toltec capital at Tula, Mexico.

*c.***1171** Some Irish chieftains accepted Henry II as king of Ireland.

1171 Kurdish soldier Saladin overthrew the ruling Fatimid dynasty and seized the Egyptian throne.

1174 The Leaning Tower of Pisa, a bell tower, was constructed in Pisa, Italy.

*c.***1175** The Aztecs migrated towards central Mexico and probably destroyed the Toltec centre, Tula.

▶ *Canterbury Cathedral was built in many stages and dates back to the 6th century. It is one of the most splendid examples of Gothic architecture in England.*

. . .FASCINATING FACT. . .

The English scientist, Welcher of Malvern, was the first
to propose dividing the Earth's surface into degrees, minutes and seconds
with lines of latitude and longitude. He devised this system in 1120, after
studying a solar eclipse in 1092 and trying to calculate the time difference
between England and Italy.

109

1175–1187

▲ *Sultan Saladin of Egypt was revered as a great Muslim hero. He was renowned for his victory against the Christian Crusaders.*

1175 In Honen, Japan, the Japanese School of Pure Land (*Jodo*) Buddhism was founded.

*c.***1175** The legends of King Arthur and his Knights of the Round Table at Camelot were compiled and modified by Walter Map, a Welsh priest.

1176 Saladin, the sultan of Egypt, conquered Syria. He reformed the army and placed the land estates and collection of taxes into the hands of his Mamluk officers.

1177 Pope Alexander III signed the Treaty of Venice, a peace treaty between himself, the Holy Roman emperor and the Lombard League, which supported the Pope.

1184 A new Canterbury Cathedral was begun to replace the one in which Thomas Becket was killed. It was designed in the Gothic style by the Frenchman William of Sens.

*c.*1185 In Japan, the shoguns (generals) took power, reducing the emperor to a mere figurehead.They appointed feudal lords called daimsyo to rule different parts of the country with the help of warriors called samurai. The shogunate headquarters was based in Kamakura.

▶ *A Muslim soldier from Saladin's army. Known for his military acumen, the sultan had built up a strictly disciplined army.*

1185 Egyptian sultan Saladin expanded his empire by conquering Mosul (in present-day Iraq) and Mesopotamia.

1185 Minamoto Yoritomo established the Kamakura shogunate in Japan. During the Kamakura period Japan was under military rule and the shoguns dominated. Minamoto established his governors and stewards throughout Japan, thus creating a government that dominated the royal court. This enabled him to rule without overthrowing the emperor.

1187 Sultan Saladin defeated the Christian Crusaders at the Battle of Hattin and captured Jerusalem. He succeeded in uniting Egypt, Syria, northern Mesopotamia and Palestine.

1187 Henry II of England passed away and was succeeded by his son Richard the Lionheart.

1189-1197

1189 The Holy Roman emperor and German king Frederick Barbarossa set out to lead the Third Crusade. Barbarossa, however, died on his way to the Holy Land.

*c.*1190 The order of the Teutonic Knights was founded in a hospital at Acre to nurse the sick during the Third Crusade. It was militarized in 1198 and given lands in Germany. During the 13th century the base of operations of the Order shifted to eastern Europe. The Order later spread in Prussia.

1191 Henry VI became the Holy Roman emperor. He had to face revolts from Henry the Lion of Germany and Tancred in Sicily, but he was successful in establishing peace.

1191 Zen Buddhism gained popularity in Japan through the efforts of Chinese Buddhist priest Ensai.

1191 Richard the Lionheart of England conquered Cyprus and Acre, and defeated Saladin's army in the Battle of Arsuf in Palestine.

▶ *Known for his military prowess in battle, King Richard I of England (also called Richard the Lionheart) was a poet too. The king was celebrated as a hero in many legends.*

1192 Richard the Lionheart called for a truce with Saladin in Palestine. Saladin allowed the Christians to keep the coastal towns they had conquered and gave them safe passage to the Holy Sepulchre at Jerusalem.

1192 Richard the Lionheart was imprisoned by Leopold of Austria.

1193–1194 Richard the Lionheart was surrendered to Henry VI, the Holy Roman emperor, who demanded a ransom for his release. The people of England and Aquitaine paid the ransom and Richard returned home in 1194.

1195–1197 Henry VI consolidated his rule over Italy and Sicily.

1197 Henry VI died and civil war broke out in Germany due to the fight between his successors.

1199–1209

1199 Richard the Lionheart died in France. His brother John Lackland succeeded him. A war with Philip II of France cost John Normandy and most of his French possessions.

*c.*1200 In North America, the Cahokia tribe from the area that is now Illinois built a city with large earthen mounds used for religious purposes.

*c.*1200 Cuzco, in Peru, developed into an important Inca centre. It was also known as 'City of the Sun'. It was regarded as sacred to the Sun god.

*c.*1201 Venice became an important commercial centre in Europe under the rule of an elected ruler called the Doge.

1202 Pope Innocent III called for the Fourth Crusade. The Doge of Venice agreed to transport the Crusaders to the Holy Land. However, the Crusaders could not fight the Muslims as they were unable to pay the amount asked by the Venetians. The Venetians persuaded the crusaders to attack Zara and Constantinople.

1204 The Crusaders captured Constantinople.

1206 Mongol ruler Genghis Khan united the nomadic Mongol tribes of Central Asia. He attacked China and by 1215 had captured Beijing and overthrown the Sung dynasty.

...FASCINATING FACT...
The 13th-century Indian poet-saint Gyandev devised a game played with cowrie shells and dice, in which players moved up ladders (representing 'good') or were eaten by snakes (representing 'evil').
The game is still popular and is known by the name of 'snakes and ladders'.

▶ *Genghis Khan unified the nomadic tribes of Mongolia and founded a vast Mongolian Empire. The great warrior-ruler extended his empire across Asia to the Adriatic Sea.*

1206 Qutb-ud-Din Aybak established the Delhi Sultanate in India. He was a slave who rose to the postion of military commander in the army of Muhammad of Ghur. Qutb-ud-Din set up headquarters in Lahore (present-day Pakistan) and Delhi. He laid the foundation of the famous stone tower Qutb Minar in Delhi.

1209 German prince Otto IV invaded Italy and was crowned Holy Roman emperor by Pope Innocent III after agreeing not to capture Sicily.

1209 Pope Innocent III called for the Albigensian Crusade against the Cathari, a group in southern France which did not follow the Roman church.

1210-1218

1210 The Franciscan order was founded by Francis of Assisi with the approval of Pope Innocent III.

1212 The Children's Crusade was led by the shepherd boy Stephen of Cloyes, who led an army of children from France, and Nicholas, who led another army of children from Cologne, Germany.

1213 The English Parliament had its early beginnings in the Council of St Albans where the clergy, earls and barons held discussions.

*c.*1214 North German towns and German trading communities formed an association called the Hanseatic League. The League controlled most of the trading activities in northern Europe for the following two centuries.

1214 French king Philip II defeated a coalition of European powers including the Holy Roman emperor Otto IV and King John of England in the battle of Bouvines.

1214 Saint Dominic founded the Dominican Order in France.

1215 King John was forced by English barons to sign the Magna Carta, a document that limited the king's power and guaranteed the people certain basic rights. It was later changed on several occasions.

1216 Civil war broke out in England with the barons forming different groups.

1216 Henry III became king of England. He ascended the throne at the age of nine, and his supporters suppressed the rebels supported by the French. After beginning to rule in 1227, Henry angered the barons with his indifference towards tradition and by agreeing to supply funds to Pope Innocent II in exchange for the Sicilian crown.

1218 Pope Innocent III called for the Fifth Crusade. The crusade failed to gain much support and was postponed.

▼ *The Magna Carta, which means 'Great Charter', was signed between King John and the barons of England.*

1220 Frederick II became Holy Roman emperor. He angered Pope Honorius III because of his delay in departing for the Fifth Crusade.

1220–1223 Genghis Khan attacked and destroyed the city of Samarkand in Central Asia. He then sent two of his best generals in pursuit of Sultan Muhammad, the ruler of the state of Khwarizm, who had fled west. Genghis Khan's generals found the sultan on an island in the Caspian Sea and killed him. The generals defeated an army of Russians and Kipchak Turks in the Crimea before turning back to join Genghis Khan.

▼ *The procedure for the papal Inquisition allowed a person accused of heresy time to confess and clear himself.*

*c.*1220–1292 British scientist and philosopher Roger Bacon lived during this period. He was the first European to describe the process of making gunpowder and proposed motorized ships and flying machines.

*c.*1222 Pope Honorius III sent a formal delegation to Frederick II to persuade him to go on crusade, but the emperor delayed again.

*c.*1225 Qutb-ud-Din Aybak erected Qutb Minar, one of the tallest minarets in the world, in Delhi, India. A minaret is a turret connected to a mosque with a balcony used to call from at hours of Muslim prayer.

1228–1229 Frederick II set off on the Sixth Crusade. He obtained Bethlehem, Nazareth and Jerusalem from the Egyptian sultan through diplomatic negotiations and military threats.

1230 Pope Gregory IX sent an army to invade Sicily, owned by Frederick II. Frederick defeated the invasion and called a truce with the Treaty of San Germano..

▲ *The Holy Roman emperor Frederick Barbarossa led the Third Crusade.*

1231 Pope Gregory IX initiated the Catholic Inquisition to discover and punish heretics (those who opposed official Church doctrine).

*c.*1233 Coal mining began in Newcastle, England. The town soon gained a reputation for its high production of coal.

*c.*1237 Mongol warriors led by Sabutai, a son of Genghis Khan, attacked Russia and destroyed many cities.

119

1238-1250

1238 Muhammad I established the Nasrid dynasty in Granada, Spain. The dynasty ruled the area for 260 years and played an important part in the Islamic struggle against Christianity in Spain.

1240 Richard of Cornwall, brother of Henry III, King of England, set out on a crusade to the Holy Land.

1240–1241 Mongols invaded and destroyed Poland.

1241 Following a dispute with Pope Gregory IX, the Holy Roman emperor Frederick II invaded the Papal States and captured a number of clergymen. Frederick II later tried to make peace with Pope Innocent IV, but his attempt failed. His struggle with the papacy continued and he had lost much of central Italy by the time of his death.

1244 Mercenaries hired by the Egyptian pasha Khwarazmi captured Jerusalem from the Christian Crusaders.

1245 After new disputes with Frederick II, the new Pope Innocent IV declared that the emperor was excommunicated and deposed. Only a few nobles accepted that the pope had the right to depose the emperor, so the dispute dragged on.

1246 Frederick II occupied the throne of Austria and Styria when their ruler Duke Frederick II passed away.

1248–1250 Louis IX, King of France, led the Seventh Crusade to rescue Jerusalem from the Egyptians.

1250 The Egyptians defeated the Crusaders led by Louis IX in the Battle of Fariskur. Louis returned to France and reorganized his administrative system. He later made peace with England by signing the Treaty of Paris.

*c.***1250** The Toltec-Chichimec people took control of Cholula, in Mexico, and built new ceremonial structures around the Pyramid of Quetzalcóatl.

1250 Holy Roman emperor Frederick II died. The nobles could not agree who to elect as the new emperor until 1273 when Rudolf of Hapsburg was chosen. In the meantime, anarchy prevailed and the empire lost much of its power.

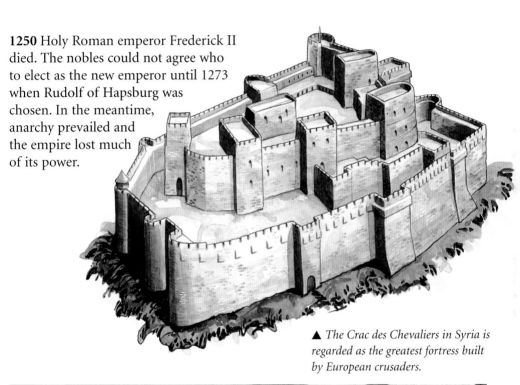

▲ *The Crac des Chevaliers in Syria is regarded as the greatest fortress built by European crusaders.*

· · · **FASCINATING FACT** · · ·
In 1266 bakers in England were asked to mark the loaves they baked so that if badly baked loaves were sold, the buyer would know who had baked it. This was the first time when a trademark was used.

121

1250–1277

c.1250 The language Urdu was born out of a combination of Persian, Arabic and Indian dialects.

1254–1324 Venetian merchant and traveller Marco Polo lived during this period. He travelled to China and spent many years in the court of Kublai Khan. He probably also served as the governor of Yangzhou during his stay in China.

1258 The Mongol army led by Hülegü Khan destroyed Baghdad, killed several of its inhabitants and brought an end to the Abbasid Caliphate here.

1258 The English House of Commons was formed. At first its membership varied greatly, as did the number of times it met.

1260–1271 Mongol king Kublai Khan gradually brought all of China under his rule. He engaged in war with countries including Burma, Java, Japan, Vietnam and Indonesia, but suffered disastrous defeats. Buddhism became the state religion during his rule.

1270 Louis IX, King of France, set out on the Eighth Crusade, but died of plague in Tunis. His army too suffered heavy losses. Louis was later made a saint by the church.

1270 Navigational charts were first recorded as being used in Europe.

1272 Edward I (also called Edward Longshanks) ascended the English throne. He instituted administrative and legal reforms, and played an important role in formulating English common law.

1273 Rudolf I was crowned Holy Roman emperor by Pope Gregory X. First German king of the Habsburg dynasty, he was recognized by the Pope only after he promised to lead a crusade and to renounce imperial rights in Rome and the papal territories.

1277–1284 Edward I of England conquered North Wales. This involved the suppression of rebellions against English rule.

▶ *Venetian traveller Marco Polo spent almost 17 years in China. His* Il milione (*'The Million'*) *is considered a classic travel book.*

1278-1300

1278 Holy Roman emperor Rudolf I attacked and defeated Ottokar II of Bohemia and captured Austria.

***c*.1285** Porcelain ware, textiles, metalwork and other decorative articles were created in government workshops and factories in China.

1286 Queen Margaret ascended the throne of Scotland. She was last in the line of Scottish rulers descended from Malcolm III.

1290 Osman I became leader of the Seljuk Turks. He established the Islamic town of Bithynia, from which grew the great Ottoman Empire.

1290 The Khalji dynasty of Muslim Turks was founded in Delhi by Jalal-ud-Din Firuz Khalji and ruled all northern India.

1292 Edward I, King of England, chose John de Balliol, King of Scotland, after being invited by Scottish nobles to decide between rival claimants following the death of Queen Margaret.

▶ *William Wallace, Scottish patriot, fought bravely against the English.*

1296 John de Baliol of Scotland formed an alliance with France, which was at war with England. Edward I defeated the Scottish army at Dunbar, imprisoned John de Balliol and took control of Scotland.

1297 Scottish patriot William Wallace defeated the English forces in the Battle of Stirling.

1297 The English army defeated William Wallace in the Battle of Falkirk. Wallace was imprisoned by the English and later executed. Robert Bruce, a descendant of Scots king David I, assumed leadership of the Scottish resistance movement. Although they had opposed William Wallace, the Scottish nobility supported Bruce.

1300 Pope Boniface VIII organized a jubilee celebration to mark the end of the century and the forgiveness of sins to Christian pilgrims.

1300–1328

c.1300 San Fernando and Chetumal were among the largest of the Mayan coastal city-states. They had crude pyramids, temples and houses.

c.1300 Various tribes migrated from the northern parts of the American southwest towards the Little Colorado River and the Rio Grande in the south.

1301 In Hungary the Árpád dynasty ended with the death of Andrew III. Civil war broke out and the country was in chaos for seven years.

1306 Jews in France were made to leave the country. In England, nearly 100,000 Jews were tortured and expelled.

1314 Scottish forces led by Robert Bruce defeated Edward II in the Battle of Bannockburn.

1320 In India, Muhammad bin Tughluq founded the Tughluq dynasty. The dynasty was weakened under the rule of Feroz Tughluq, who moved his capital from Delhi to Daulatabad and lost control of southern India.

c.1325 Native populations in the Little Colorado River Valley established the Kachina cult.

c.1325 The Aztecs settled on a marshy island in Lake Texcoco, Mexico, and founded the city of Tenochtitlán.

... FASCINATING FACT ...
For years before his great victory at Bannockburn in 1314, Robert Bruce was a fugitive from the English. On one occasion he had decided to give up while hiding in a cave, but was inspired to continue by the perseverance of a spider building a web.

▲ *Robert Bruce, King of Scotland.*

1326–1327 Queen Isabella invaded England. She arrested and later killed her husband King Edward II. Queen Isabella made her son Edward III the new king of England.

1328 Philip VI ascended the French throne and established the Valois dynasty. He continued efforts to centralize the state, but made concessions to the nobility and clergy.

127

1332–1338

▲ Ibn Battutah is regarded as one of the greatest Arab travellers from Medieval times. His travels began after he dreamed of setting off to the East, carried by a giant bird.

1332 Edward III of England drove out the Scottish king David II and appointed Edward de Baliol the king of Scotland. But David soon returned and war between England and Scotland began again.

*c.***1333** Drought, famine and the Black Death, a fatal disease, struck China.

*c.***1333** Arabian traveller and explorer Ibn Battutah came to India. His writings are an important source of information about the period. He spent 27 years travelling through Asia, Africa and Europe, covering a distance of 120,000 km. He wrote one of the most famous travel books, the *Rihlah*.

1333 In Japan, the Kamakura shoguns were removed from power and Emperor Go-Daigo restored power to the imperial line.

1335 The first public mechanical clock was erected in Milan, Italy.

1336 In Japan, a powerful warrior leader Ashikaga Takuji drove Go-Daigo out of Kyoto and set up another member of the imperial family as a puppet emperor. The Northern Court was established at Kyoto, and Go-Daigo, who had fled south, established the Southern Court at Yoshino.

1336–1614 The Vijayanagara Empire in south India extended over parts of present-day Andhra Pradesh and Karnataka. They had a rich architectural and sculptural tradition, traces of which can be seen in the ruined city of Hampi in Karnataka.

1337 The Hundred Years War started between England and France when Edward III invaded Flanders to stake his claim over the French crown.

1338 The new ruler of Japan's Northern Court, Emperor Komyo, appointed Ashikaga Takauji as shogun, thus restoring the unity of Japan and the power of the shoguns. The rule of the Ashikaga shoguns, who were based in the Muromachi district, is known as the Muromachi period.

129

1338–1348

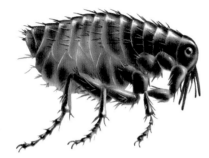

▲ *Plague is transmitted by the bite of the rat flea.*

1338 Friar Giovanni de Marignolli from Florence, Italy, travelled across Russia to Beijing.

1340 The English navy, led by Edward III, defeated a French fleet in the Battle of Sluys. The English established control over the English Channel and seized 200 ships from the French navy. The French suffered 30,000 casualities.

1340 The kimono, which was based on the Chinese court costume, was introduced in Japan.

1340 Alfonso XI of Castile crushed an army of Spanish and Moroccan muslims with the help of the Portuguese.

*c.***1343** The infectious disease, the Black Death, spread out of China.

*c.***1345** The Gothic cathedral of Notre Dame on the Seine in Paris was completed. The western front of the cathedral is divided into three stories and its doors are decorated with early Gothic carvings. Another striking feature of the dramatic cathedral are its three great rose windows.

1346 An English army of approximately 12,000 troops commanded by Edward III fought about 30,000 French troops in the Battle of Crécy. Although heavily outnumbered by the French, the English managed to win because of superior weaponry and tactics.

1346 Scotland's David II, an ally of Philip VI, invaded England, but was captured and imprisoned.

1347 Edward III captured the port of Calais in France and inflicted heavy losses to the French.

1348 The Black Death, which had already spread in Cyprus, reached Florence. It then spread to France and Scotland.

▼ *The Black Death plague originated in Central Asia and from there spread to Constantinople and Mediterranean ports. By the 14th century, the plague had reached Europe.*

1349–1360

1349 The Black Death spread to England. Nearly half of England's population was wiped out because of the disease, causing widespread social and economic problems. England was not in a position to continue its conflict with France and had to call a truce.

1349 The Black Death spread to Poland and Russia.

1350 The Pueblo Indians of the southwest of North America formed a few large settlements.

1350 Alfonso X of Castile died of the plague.

1350 Philip VI, King of France, died and was succeeded by his son John II.

1352 The Black Death spread back to India and China after claiming the lives of hundreds of Russians.

1354 After recovering from the Black Death, England continued the Hundred Years War by raiding Languedoc in southern France.

1356 France was defeated in the Battle of Poitiers by the Black Prince of Wales. King John II of France and several of his courtiers were captured and imprisoned in England. Charles, John's eldest son, was made regent of France, but was unable to prevent the civil war that followed, and eventually fled Paris.

1358 France was torn apart with a violent revolt by thousands of peasants.

...FASCINATING FACT...
In 1392 the French painter Jacques Gringonneur was commissioned to paint playing cards for the king of France. The pack of 52 cards contained four suits. The spades stood for soldiers, diamonds for craftsmen, clubs for farmers and hearts for the clergy.

▲ *Higher taxes were imposed by the state on the peasants of France. This, coupled with an increase of rents by landlords, led to a revolt in the country.*

1360 The English and the French signed a treaty, the Peace of Bretigny. Charles agreed to give England Calais, Guienne and Ponthieu as well as three million gold crowns as ransom money. King John of France was released but returned voluntarily to England when the money could not be raised.

1360–1372

1360 The Black Death returned to England, France and Poland, claiming the many lives. The plague was called the Black Death in England because of the black spots that appeared on the skin. Most people who caught the disease died in great pain after just three days.

▼ *It is estimated that nearly 25 million people in Europe died of the Black Death plague.*

1361 Murad I ascended the throne of the Ottoman Empire following the death of his father Sultan Orkhan. During his reign, the Ottoman Empire expanded to include Anatolia and the Balkans.

1364 Charles V became king of France.

1368 The Ming dynasty came to power in China, providing a boost to arts such as landscape and figure painting, ceramics and metalwork.

1368–1370 Waldemar IV, King of Denmark, was defeated by the powerful Hanseatic League, a group of trading cities. Waldemar was forced to sign the Treaty of Stralsund, which ensured that the League dominated trade along the Baltic coast.

1369 British poet Geoffrey Chaucer produced his first major work, *Book of the Duchess.*

1371 Ottoman sultan Murad I completed his conquest of the Balkan Peninsula with victory in the Battle of Chernomen.

1372 Tezozomoc became the ruler of Azcapotzalco, the most powerful city-state in Mexico. He brought Tenochtitlán under his control and crowned Acamapichtli its king.

▲ *Chaucer's* Canterbury Tales *is a collection of tales told by a group of fictional pilgrims on their way from Southwark to Canterbury in England.*

1372 France defeated England at La Rochelle and took control of the English Channel. They also won back Poitou and Britanny.

1372 John of Gaunt, Duke of Lancaster, led England's forces against France. He led his troops to Calais, from where they moved to Bordeaux.

135

1377 Richard II ascended the English throne. Born in 1367, he was the son of Edward the Black Prince and Joan, the Fair Maid of Kent. Richard was only ten years old when he succeeded his grandfather, Edward III.

1380 Tarot cards began appearing in Italy and France.

1381 In England, farm labourers and artisans revolted against the poll tax and low wages. Richard II agreed to abolish some taxes and reduce others, but later went back on his word.

1385 John I founded the Aviz dynasty in Portugal after defeating Castile in the Battle of Aljubarrota.

1389 The Ottoman Turks, led by Murad I, defeated the Serbians in the Battle of Kosovo. This victory consolidated Ottoman control of the Balkans. Murad was killed in the battle, being succeeded by his son Bayazid I.

◀ *Edward the Black Prince never ruled as king because of his early death at the age of 45.*

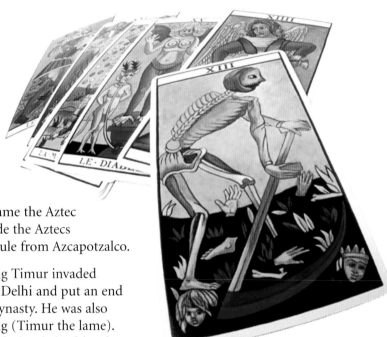

▶ *Tarot cards can be traced to the 14th century, though no one knows for sure where they originated.*

1391 In Mexico, Huitzilihuitl became the Aztec emperor. He made the Aztecs independent of rule from Azcapotzalco.

1398 Mongol king Timur invaded India. He sacked Delhi and put an end to the Tughluq dynasty. He was also called Timur Leng (Timur the lame). He was the son of a local chief, but he claimed in 1370 that he was a descendant of Genghis Khan. Timur's reign in India was short and he left to invade Georgia and Baghdad in 1400.

1399 Henry Bolingbroke, son of John of Gaunt, captured Richard II, King of England. The English Parliament appointed Bolingbroke as king in place of the corrupt Richard. He ascended the English throne as Henry IV and established the Lancastrian dynasty.

***c.*1400** Sri Lanka was divided into the Kotte, Kandy and Jaffna regions. The first two were Sinhalese kingdoms and the last was a Tamil kingdom.

1402-1407

1402 Mongol king Timur defeated the Ottoman sultan Bayazid I in the Battle of Ankara and took him prisoner. Timur then raided the port of Smyrna and killed many of its inhabitants.

1402 Yung-lo became emperor of China. The Ming dynasty reached the height of its power under his rule.

1403 A Welsh revolt against English rule, led by Owain Glyndwr, reached its peak, but was defeated in 1409.

1403 The world's first quarantine was declared by the doge (chief magistrate) of Venice to safeguard the city against the Black Death.

*c.*1404–1406 Malacca, in the Malay Peninsula, developed into an important trading centre in Southeast Asia.

*c.*1405–1407 Chinese admiral and diplomat Zheng He visited southern Vietnam, Thailand, Malacca, Java and Sri Lanka.

1405 The Mongol king Timur died, leading to the disintegration of the vast Mongolian Empire in Central Asia.

1406 Louis, Duke of Orléans, attacked English territories in France.

... FASCINATING FACT ...
The wild coffee plant was originally native to Ethiopia. In the 1400s, Arabs began cultivating the plant. Mocha in Yemen was the main centre of production of the qahwah seeds. The Turks imported these seeds and used them to make a strong drink called qahwe, which the visiting Italian traders loved. By the 1600s Italians introduced coffee to Europe.

*c.*1406–1420 In Beijing, China, Emperor Yung-lo of the Ming dynasty constructed the Forbidden City, a 72-hectare royal palace complex. It was called the Forbidden City because only the emperor could visit all parts of the palace complex.

▲ *The Forbidden City in Beijing contained about 9000 rooms.*

1407 The Chinese Ming dynasty took control of Vietnam.

1407 The Black Death killed several thousand people in London.

1410-1420

1410 The K'iche' Mayans of Central America expanded their kingdom to include a large part of the Guatemalan highlands and some parts of its Pacific coast, where cacao was grown.

1410 Polish and Lithuanian forces defeated the Teutonic Knights in the Battle of Tannenberg. This ended the latter's dreams of Baltic conquest and marked the beginning of their decline.

1413 Henry V became the king of England.

1413 Muhammad I, son of Bayazid I, became the ruler of the Ottoman Empire after a civil war following his father's death.

1415 An English army led by Henry V defeated the French in the Battle of Agincourt. Henry V's success over a much larger French army was due mainly to the superiority of the English longbow men over the heavily armoured French knights. This showed how outdated the French methods of warfare had become. The victory enabled the English to conquer much of France. The battle is the central scene of Shakespeare's drama *Henry V*.

1416 Henry V took over Caen, Bayeux, Lisieux, Alençon, Falaise and Cherbourg in France.

1416 The fleet of the Ottoman Turks was defeated by Venice at Dardanelles, off north-western Turkey.

1420 Henry V forced the French to sign the Treaty of Troyes, in which he was named heir to the French throne.

1420 Portuguese explorer João Gonçalves Zarco discovered the Madeira Islands near North Africa.

1420 Sesshu, the foremost Japanese master of ink painting called *suiboku*, was born. Sesshu was a Zen Buddhist priest and also known as Sesshu Toyo. It is believed that he may have studied under Shubun in Kyoto. He made a trip to China in 1467, visiting many Zen monasteries and studying the works of old masters. Adapting the Chinese style of landscape painting, he set the standard in ink painting.

▼ The French army suffered a disastrous defeat at the hands of the English in the Battle of Agincourt in 1415, in spite of having more men and superior armour.

1421 Ottoman sultan Mohammed I died and his son Murad II ascended the Ottoman throne.

1421 Murad II extended his empire into southeastern Europe. He defeated the Byzantine king Manuel II Palaeologus and forced him to pay tribute to the Ottoman Empire.

1422 In China, the Ming Empire moved its capital from Nanjing to Beijing. Local administration and governance as well as trade with the neighbouring countries improved.

*c.*1422 The Chinese fleet led by Admiral Zheng He made expeditions to new countries around the Indian Ocean.

1422 Henry VI became king of England. He was the only son of Henry V and Catherine Valois and became king of England when he was barely nine months old. When his grandfather, Charles VI of France, died,

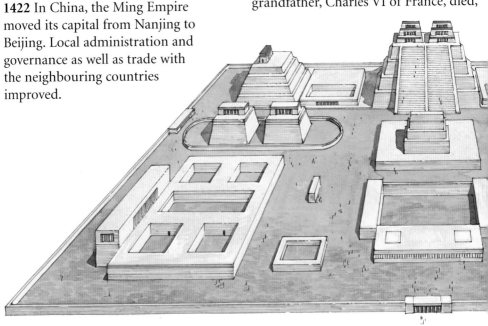

Henry was proclaimed king of France by the English, in accordance with the terms of the Treaty of Troyes. However, many Frenchmen refused to accept Henry and declared Charles' son to be King Charles VII. The English council attempted to protect English interests in France by crowning Henry king of France at Paris in 1431.

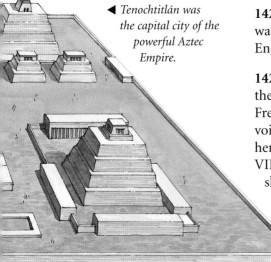

◄ *Tenochtitlán was the capital city of the powerful Aztec Empire.*

*c.*1425 In New Mexico, the pueblo people built multi-storied apartments built of stone and sun-dried bricks.

*c.*1427 In Mexico, Tenochtitlán, Tlacopan and Texcoco came together to form the Triple Alliance, which defeated the powerful city of Azcapotzalco and established the Aztec Empire. Tenochtitlán became the leading city of Mexico.

1428 Orléans in central France was surrounded and attacked by English forces.

1429 Joan of Arc freed Orléans from the English with the help of a small French army. Joan claimed to hear the voice of the Archangel Michael telling her to free France and return Charles VII to the throne. As a 16-year-old girl, she travelled to a nearby town and asked to join the French army. She was rejected, but returned one year later.

143

1429-1441

1429 In Florence, Italy, Cosimo de' Medici became the head of the Medici banking house. He was the richest man of his time.

1429 Charles VII was crowned king of France.

1430 The Order of the Golden Fleece was founded by Duke Phillip III of Burgundy to celebrate his marriage to the Portuguese princess Isabelle of Aviz. It was modelled on the English Order of the Garter, the highest order of English knighthood. There were initially 24 knights in the order, but the number increased to 30 in 1433 and 51 in 1516. Only Catholics could join the order.

1431 Joan of Arc was captured by the English and burned to death.

1431 Angkor, the capital of the Khmer Empire of Cambodia, was attacked and destroyed by people from Thailand. The Khmer Empire ended and Cambodia's new capital was established at Phnom Penh.

1431 Ottoman sultan Murad II attacked Constantinople, but could not break through the city's defences.

1438 In Peru, Emperor Pachacuti established and expanded the Inca Empire.

1439 Murad II conquered Serbia and made it a part of the Ottoman Empire.

...FASCINATING FACT...

By the Middle Ages, slavery was officially banned in most European cities, but Africans were still sold by their countries. Gradually, European countries began trading in these African slaves, who were eventually spread over parts of Europe, most of the Caribbean and North America. An estimated 12 million Africans were sold to European traders and 17 million were sold to the Arabians.

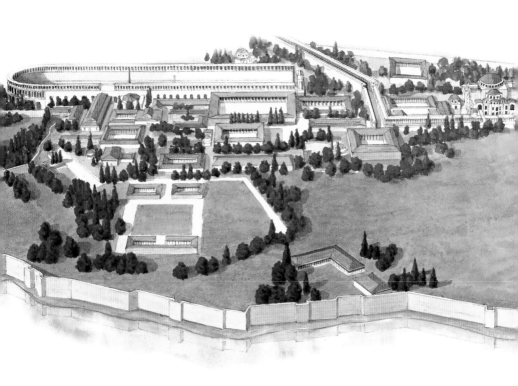

▲ *Constantinople was renamed Istanbul after it was captured by the Ottoman Empire.*

1439 Byzantine emperor John VIII Palaeologus offered to unite the Byzantine and Latin churches in return for military help against the Ottomans.

*c.*1441 In Central America, the Mayan city of Mayapán was destroyed in a fight among rival ruling groups and the region surrounding it was divided into six separate city-states ruled by individual chieftains. The Mayan culture was by now in serious decline.

145

1441-1450

c.1441 Portuguese traders and colonists first brought African slaves to Lisbon, where they were sold in the markets.

1442 The French reclaimed Gascony from the English.

1442 The first phase of the rule of Vlad II, Dracul, ended. He was the king of Wallachia, in present-day Romania. Vlad II returned to the throne just a year later and was given the duty of protecting trade routes between Transylvania and Wallachia. Vlad is believed to have murdered members of a rival royal family and is also thought to be the man on whom the mythical character Dracula was based.

1443 Poland, Hungary and Serbia came together to fight the Ottoman Turks. They had some early victories, but Ottoman sultan Murad II defeated them in the Battle of Zlatica, in the Balkans.

1444 The Ottoman Turks defeated the Hungarians in the Battle of Varna. The battle took place on November 10, 1444 near Varna in eastern Bulgaria. Sultan Murad II defeated the Polish and Hungarian armies and signed a ten-year truce with Hungary.

c.1446 Korean king Sejong proclaimed the Korean Hangul alphabet as the official script, replacing the Chinese script that had been in use until then.

1448 Portuguese navigator Dinís Dias discovered and named Cape Verde, the westernmost part of Africa.

1448 The Ottoman Turks defeated the Hungarians in the second Battle of Kosovo after a three-day struggle.

1448 France invaded the English territory of Maine and brought it under their control.

1450 The French defeated the English army at the Battle of Formigny and reoccupied Normandy.

▲ *The famous mythical character of Dracula is said to be based on King Vlad II, Dracul, of Wallachia. The character was created by the author Bram Stoker.*

1450-1460

1450 Jack Cade, also known as John Mortimer, led the Cade's Rebellion against Henry VI.

1451 The Ottoman sultan Murad II passed away and his son Muhammad II ascended the throne.

1452–1519 Leonardo da Vinci lived during this period. He was a talented Renaissance painter, sculptor and inventor, who was born in the town of Vinci near Florence. *Mona Lisa* and *The Last Supper* are two of his most famous paintings. He is also known for devising plans of a helicopter, an armoured tank and a submarine centuries before they were actually built. In addition, he helped advance the study of anatomy, astronomy, and civil engineering.

1453 Ottoman Turks led by Muhammad II defeated Constantine XI Palaeologus, the last Byzantine emperor, and captured Constantinople. This marked the end of the Byzantine Empire.

1453 The French defeated and killed John Talbot, the first Earl of Shrewsbury, who had invaded France with a small army to fight for the English cause. This was England's last effort at gaining French territory. The Hundred Years War ended with the French having reclaimed all their territories, except Calais, which remained with the English for another hundred years.

▲ *The red rose, the symbol of the House of Lancaster.*

148

1453 Ottoman sultan Muhammad II invaded Greece and Albania.

1455 The Duke of York led his forces against those of King Henry VI in order to claim the throne of England. York won the Battle at St Albans, thus starting a series of civil wars that became known as the Wars of the Roses. This war was fought between the House of York, represented by a white rose, and the House of Lancaster (which ruled England), represented by a red rose.

▲ *The white rose, the symbol of the House of York.*

1455 Johannes Gutenberg of Germany published the first book printed using fully moveable type – the Bible. He was a German metalworker and inventor, who achieved fame for his contributions to the technology of printing. His printing press was based on presses used in winemaking. Gutenberg's method of printing continued to be used without much change even in the 20th century.

1456 Ottoman Turks conquered the Balkans and Greece, but were defeated by the Hungarians at Belgrade. The setback proved to be only temporary and soon the Ottomans were advancing again.

1460 Yorkists defeated the Lancastrians and imprisoned King Henry VI. The king managed to flee with his family to Scotland. Henry returned to England in 1464 to attempt a Lancastrian revolt, but was captured again and kept in the Tower of London.

1461-1475

1461 Edward, the new duke of York, defeated the Lancastrians at Mortimer's Cross, and later at Towton. The English Parliament declared him king of England and he ruled as Edward IV until 1483.

1461 Charles VII, King of France, was succeeded by his son Louis XI. Louis XI greatly reduced the powers of French noblemen and clergy.

1462 Ivan III, also called Ivan the Great, became the grand prince of Moscow, Russia.

1463 High taxes levied on goods passing through the Ottoman Empire affected Venice's trade, forcing the Venetians to declare war.

1467–1477 In Japan, the Onin War broke out between two rival clans because of a succession dispute. In the century following the war, Japan went through a period of turmoil and violence, and feudal lords called daimyo rose to power.

1470 Portuguese king Fernão Gomes sent João de Santarem and Pedro de Escolar to explore the Gold Coast in Africa. The explorers established the port of San Jorge d'el Mina.

1470 In southern Guatemala, the Kaqchikel people established an empire with Iximché as their capital. The fortified capital city had ceremonial platforms, temples and ball courts.

...FASCINATING FACT...

The first English book to be printed was *The Recuyell of the Histories of Troy*, a set of stories about the Trojan War. The book was originally written in French by Raoul Lefèvre. William Caxton, an English printer, translated these stories and published them in 1475.

1471 Henry VI died in the Tower of London. Many people suspected that the former king was murdered by the new king, Edward IV, but this was never proved.

1471–1528 German painter and printmaker Albrecht Dürer lived during this period. He was well-known for his paintings and for prints made from woodcuts.

▲ *Introduction of the cannon and gunpowder revolutionized warfare. Cannons were used in the Hundred Years War.*

1475 After being dethroned for a brief period from October 1470 until April 1471, Edward IV of England invaded France. Edward, however, signed the Treaty of Picquigny with Louis XI before any fighting took place.

151

1475-1483

1475–1564 Italian artist Michelangelo lived during this period. He was a painter, sculptor, poet and architect. Some of his most famous works are the *Pietà* at the Vatican, the statue of *David* and the Sistine chapel paintings. When he finished work on the *Last Judgment*, Michelangelo was accused of indecency for painting naked figures inside the private chapel of the Pope. However, the Pope supported his work.

1476 Charles the Bold, of Burgundy, was defeated at Grandson and Morat by Swiss states supporting Louis XI of France.

1476 English publisher William Caxton established the first English press at Westminster. The first book known to have been printed there was *Dictes or Sayengis of the Philosophres* (Sayings of the Philosophers). The book was written by Earl Rivers, the king's brother-in-law.

1476 The Swiss army killed Charles the Bold in the Battle of Nancy.

▶ *This marble sculpture called* David *was made by Italian artist Michelangelo.*

1478 The growing power of the Tarascan and Aztec Empires in Central America resulted in wars in which the Aztecs lost about 20,000 men.

1480 Louis XI of France brought Anjou, Bar, Maine and Provence under direct royal control following the death of their leader René, the count of Anjou.

1480 Ottoman sultan Muhammad II invaded southern Italy and captured the town of Otranto.

1483 Richard III became the king of England. He was the last king of the House of York.

1483 Louis XI passed away and his son Charles VIII ascended the throne.

1483 The king and queen of Castile, Ferdinand and Isabella, appointed the Dominican monk Tomas de Torquemada to conduct the Spanish Inquisition to track down heretics.

1483–1495

▲ *A Welsh archer wielding the longbow. The longbow played an important role in the battles of Crécy, Poitiers and Agincourt.*

1483–1520 Italian painter and architect Raphael lived during this period. His most famous works include his paintings of Madonna and his large figure compositions in the papal apartments at the Vatican in Rome.

1485 Lancastrian Henry Tudor, Earl of Richmond, fought and defeated Richard III with the help of the Welsh army in the Battle of Bosworth.

1486 The Aztec king Ahuitzotl defeated the people of Guerrero and Oaxaca, and forced them to pay tribute to the Aztec kingdom.

1488–1576 Italian painter Titian lived during this period. He painted mythological and religious subjects as well as portraits, and was an inspiration to future generations of artists.

*c.*1490 In India, Guru Nanak Dev established a religion called Sikhism.

*c.*1490 In Mexico, more than 200,000 people inhabited Tenochtitlan and its neighbouring island city Tlatelolco. Most of the residents were craftsmen such as potters and stonemasons.

*c.*1490 Portuguese explorers discovered Congo and introduced Christianity to the Congo Empire.

1492 Italian-Spanish explorer Christopher Columbus landed on an island in the Bahamas and named it San Salvador.

1494 Christopher Columbus discovered the Caribbean islands of Jamaica, Guadeloupe, Montserrat, Antigua, St Martin, Puerto Rico and the Virgin Islands.

▲ *The Battle of Bosworth, fought near Leicester in England on August 22 1485, was the final battle in the Wars of the Roses. It helped establish the Tudor dynasty on the English throne.*

1495 The Portuguese king João II died and was succeeded by Manuel I who continued to encourage exploration, colonization and foreign trade.

155

1497 John Cabot, the English explorer, discovered Newfoundland. He was born Giovani Caboto and was an explorer of Italian origin. He changed his name when he made England his base of operations and is best known as John Cabot for his explorations made under the English flag. In 1497, he left Bristol on his ship, the *Matthew*, looking for a sea route to Asia. He ended up in North America, the first European to reach there since the Vikings.

1497–1498 Spanish explorer Amerigo Vespucci navigated an exploration of the North American landmass. He also led a second expedition to Guyana and the mouth of the Amazon. The Americas were been named after him.

◀ *The voyages of Portuguese navigator Vasco da Gama to India laid open the sea route to the East from Europe and helped Portugal establish a flourishing trade.*

1498 The Portuguese explorer Vasco da Gama arrived in India. His route took him round the Cape of Good Hope, past the easternmost point reached by explorer Bartolomew Dias in 1488. He then sailed up the east coast of Africa and across the Indian Ocean to Calicut in the southern part of India. This voyage opened up a way for Europeans to reach the wealth of the Indies, and out of it grew the Portuguese Empire.

1498 Louis XII was crowned the king of France.

1498 Christopher Columbus discovered Trinidad in the Caribbean Sea.

1498 Spanish colonists arrived in the Caribbean island Hispaniola, which was later divided into Haiti and the Dominican Republic. After killing the natives, the Spanish settled there bringing with them African slaves to carry out hard labour for them.

1499 A plague epidemic killed thousands of people in London.

1499 Venice again went to war against the Ottoman Empire, but was defeated.

1500 Portuguese explorer Pedro Álvares Cabral discovered Brazil and made it a Portuguese territory.

1502 The Islamic Safavid dynasty of Persia came to power in Azerbaijan.

...FASCINATING FACT...
In the Middle Ages, just as people were tried and punished, animals too were tried and tortured. Animals that were convicted of a crime were hung to death or had their heads or limbs cut off as punishment.

1502–1507

1502 Montezuma II became the Aztec emperor. His reign was marked by warfare, and he made enemies of neighbouring tribes and peoples. When Cortés arrived in Mexico he was able to gain allies among Montezuma's enemies. Montezuma thought the Spanish were descendants of a god and tried to coax them into leaving with rich gifts. Montezuma's name is linked to fabulous treasures that the Spanish stole from the Aztecs.

1502–1504 During his fourth voyage, Christopher Columbus discovered Honduras, Nicaragua, Panama, Costa Rica and Colombia. He had set sail hoping to find either Asia or Japan. Columbus reached Honduras in Central America and coasted southward encountering inhospitable shores. He and his crew suffered many hardships until they reached the Gulf of Darién. On his return, Columbus was shipwrecked in Jamaica. After his rescue, he was forced to abandon his hopes of finding Asia and had to return to Spain.

1504 Ferdinand V, King of Spain, defeated Louis XII of France and captured Naples.

1505 The first Portuguese trading post in Sri Lanka was established at Colombo.

1505 Ivan the Great, the grand duke of Moscow, died. He was succeeded by his son Basil III Ivanovich.

1505 In Poland, the national diet (parliament) took charge of running the country. The members of the diet were elected by Polish nobility.

1505 Francisco de Almeida of Portugal conquered the African kingdoms of Quiloa and Mombasa. He then went on to India and established forts at Calicut, Cannanore and Cochin on the east coast.

1506 Donato Bramante, the great Renaissance architect and painter, began the construction of Saint Peter's Basilica at Rome.

1507 Zafi in Morocco was captured by the Portuguese, who began to export Moorish, Berber and Jewish slaves from there.

1507 Muhammad Shaybany defeated the Timurid rulers of Khorasan and established the Shaibanid dynasty in the Transoxiana area of Central Asia.

▶ *Columbus and two of his men stepping ashore on the Bahamas, to be greeted by local people.*

1508-1511

*c.*1508 Spanish explorers arrived in Cuba and Puerto Rico and established colonies.

1508 Pope Julius II formed the League of Cambrai along with the Holy Roman emperor Maximilian I, Louis XII of France and Ferdinand V of Spain to fight against Venice, which had taken over papal lands on the Adriatic Sea.

1508–1509 Spanish explorer Juan Ponce de León colonized Puerto Rico.

1509 Henry VII died and his son Henry VIII ascended the English throne. In his youth Henry VIII was educated in the teachings of the Renaissance and became a skilled musician and sportsman. He was made prince of Wales in 1503 following the death of his elder brother Arthur. At that time he also received permission from the Pope to marry his brother's widow, Katherine of Aragon. The marriage took place after his accession and would later dominate English politics.

▲ *King Henry VIII of England waged fruitless wars against France and Scotland.*

1509 Spain led a crusade against the African Muslim kingdoms of Oran, Bougie and Tripoli.

1509–1510 Spaniards explored the South American landmass. They also ventured into Colombia and founded Darién on the Isthmus of Panama.

1510 Ismail Safavi of Persia extended his empire from the River Tigris to the River Oxus by defeating the Uzbeks and capturing Herat, Bactria and Khiva.

1510 The Portuguese conquered Goa on the Malabar Coast and took control of the spice trade in India. The Portuguese troops were led by Afonso de Alberquerque.

► *Map of the Americas. The exploration of the Americas by various European navigators opened the way for colonization of the continent. By the end of the 16th century, Spain and Portugal had successfully established colonies in America.*

1510–1511 The League of Cambrai collapsed and Pope Julius II formed the Holy League to fight Louis XII of France. The Holy League consisted of Venice, Switzerland, Emperor Maximilian I, Henry VIII of England and Ferdinand V of Spain.

1511 The Strait of Malacca and the port of Malacca were under the control of the Portuguese, who also offered the Thai kingdom of Ayudhya firearms and ammunitions in return for trading rights.

1511-1514

1511 African slaves were sent to Cuba to work as labourers as the native population of the island had reduced greatly due to deaths caused by disease and ill-treatment by the Spanish.

1512 The Ottoman sultan Bayazid II died and his son Selim I came to power.

1513 Spanish explorer Vasco Núñez de Balboa became the first European to reach the Pacific Ocean.

1513 Italian writer Niccolo Machiavelli wrote *The Prince*, a book about corruption in government.

1513 Mauritius and the Réunion Islands in the Pacific Ocean were discovered by the Portuguese.

1513 James IV of Scotland was defeated and killed by the English in the Battle of Flodden.

1513 The Portuguese were the first Europeans to reach China through the sea route.

1513 John I, King of Denmark, Norway and Sweden, died. His son Christian II ascended the throne of Denmark and Norway, but the Swedes refused to accept him as their king.

...FASCINATING FACT...

Frescoes are paintings done on plaster. There are two types of frescoes – *buon fresco* and *secco fresco*. In the *buon fresco* the surface has to be prepared with at least three layers of plaster, the last one usually made of marble dust. The painting is done with water-based pigments that are applied before the plaster dries, so that the colours dry along with plaster, making them last longer. A *secco fresco* is painted on dry plaster. In this technique colours are not very bright or long-lasting.

▲ *Henry VIII and Anne Boleyn (left) at the royal court.*

1513 English forces invaded France and captured the towns of Therouanne and Tournai.

1514 Henry VIII of England called off his war with Scotland and France, and returned Tournai to France.

163

1514–1519

1514 Ottoman sultan Selim I defeated the Safavid shah Ismail and captured the Persian capital Tabriz. He forced the Shia Muslims of Persia to accept the Sunni faith.

1515 Louis XII died and his nephew Francis I ascended the French throne. He resumed the Italian Wars, beginning his reign with the capture of Milan. A candidate for the Holy Roman emperor's crown, Francis I was eventually defeated by Charles V, King of Spain. In 1520, Francis tried to secure the support of Henry VIII of England against the emperor during a meeting that was called the Field of the Cloth of Gold because of the rich clothes worn by those attending. This scene was later captured as a famous painting, though the identity of the artist remains uncertain.

1515 France defeated the Swiss and Venetian forces of the Holy League in the Battle of Marignano.

1516 Ferdinand V of Spain passed away. He was succeeded by his grandson Charles I, who brought Valencia and Catalonia under direct royal rule.

1516 Ladislas II, King of Bohemia and Hungary, died leaving the thrones of both countries to his son Louis.

1516–1517 The Mamluk sultanate came to an end when Selim I, the Ottoman sultan, conquered Syria and Egypt. With Mecca under their control, the Ottomans undertook the construction of mosques, hospitals and public buildings in the area and organized annual pilgrimages to the holy shrine located there. This gave the Ottoman rulers immense prestige in the Muslim world.

◄ *In 1519 the Spanish conquistador Hernando Cortés led a group of 600 men into Mexico. They were able to conquer the Aztec Empire in less than two years.*

1517 Martin Luther, a German monk, began the Reformation movement in Wittenberg, Germany. He protested against the Roman Church's misuse of power. It was the beginning of a long period of religious conflict in Europe and led to the formation of Protestant churches. Luther was educated at the cathedral school at Eisenach and later at the University of Erfurt. In 1505 he completed his master's examination and began the study of law. He gave up his career in law and said his true calling was in religion.

1517 England was struck by an epidemic of the mysterious 'sweating sickness'. Its cause is still unknown.

1518 Swiss clergyman Huldrych Zwingli joined Martin Luther's Reformation movement.

1519–1521 Spanish conquistador Hernando Cortés arrived in Mexico. He attacked the Aztec's capital Tenochtitlán. Aztec king Montezuma II was captured during the attack.

165

1519–1521

1519 Charles I of Spain became the Holy Roman emperor upon the death of Maximilian I. Born at Ghent, Charles was brought up in Flanders by his aunt, Margaret of Austria, who was his regent in the Netherlands. Charles inherited a vast empire. It was made up of the Netherlands, Luxembourg, Artois, and the Free County of Burgundy. Aragón, Navarre, Granada, Naples, Sicily, Sardinia, Spanish America, and the kingship of Spain also came to him on the death of Ferdinand II.

1519–1521 Portuguese-born Spanish explorer Ferdinand Magellan set out to explore Asia. He arrived at the Philippine Islands after sailing across the Pacific Ocean. Magellan was killed by the Mactan people who lived in the Philippines. His ship later returned to Spain.

1520 The town of Panama was founded on the Isthmus of Panama with Pedro Arías as its first governor.

1520 Christian II, King of Denmark and Norway, defeated and killed Sten Sture the Younger, regent of Sweden, at Bogesund. Christian ascended the Swedish throne after putting down a peasant revolt.

1520 Ottoman sultan Selim I died. He was succeeded by his son Suleiman I, also known as Suleiman the Magnificent. Selim's reign is known as the 'golden age' of the Ottoman Empire. He waged war on the Christians for decades and massively increased the Ottoman Empire.

1521 Ottoman sultan Suleiman captured Belgrade and made it his base to raid deep into Hungary.

1521 Manuel I of Portugal passed away. His son João III succeeded him.

1521 Survivors of Magellan's expedition returned to Spain, bringing spices from the east. This was the first round the world expedition.

1521 Spanish conquistadors founded San Juan, the capital of Puerto Rico.

▲ *Ferdinand Magellan was the first navigator to sail across the Pacific from east to west.*

1522-1523

1522 Cuauhtémoc, the last Aztec ruler, was captured and killed by the Spaniards with the help of the Tlaxcalans, enemies of the Aztecs. The city of Tenochtitlán was destroyed and the Aztec Empire came to an end.

1522 African slaves in Hispaniola rose up in revolt. This is believed to have been the first slave revolt.

1522 French forces were driven out of Milan by the Holy Roman emperor Charles V, with the help of England, Florence, Mantua and the papal forces.

◀ *The cross of the religious military order known as the Hospitallers.*

...FASCINATING FACT...

The Incas of South America believed in life after death. The Incas had elaborate burials with clothes, food, water, ornaments and furniture. The servants and wives of the dead were also buried alive with them. Being buried with the dead was considered an honour! The dead Inca were buried in a sitting posture on low ornamental stools called *duhos*.

◀ *The Aztecs loved to play a game called tlachtli. The players had to get a small rubber ball through a stone hoop.*

1522 The Portuguese were expelled from China.

1522 Martin Luther and Huldrych Zwingli published new books to promote the Reformation movement.

1522–1528 Spanish settlers in Mexico wiped out all traces of the Aztecs by destroying their religious manuscripts, objects of art and temples. They built churches, monasteries and mansions on the ruins of Tenochtitlán.

1523 Danish noblemen drove out Christian II, King of Denmark. Frederick I, Duke of Holstein, was crowned the new king.

1523 Sweden freed itself from Denmark. Gustav I, who established the house of Vasa, was crowned king of Sweden.

1522 Ottoman sultan Suleiman drove out the Knights Hospitallers from the Greek island of Rhodes. The campaign saw 200,000 Turks attack 7000 Christians. The Christian Knights surrendered only after a seven-month siege and on condition they could peacefully move to Malta.

169

1523-1525

1523 Huayna Capac, ruler of the Peruvian Inca Empire, passed away. His kingdom was divided between his two sons, Atahualpa and Huáscar.

1523 In Zurich, Dutch priest Menno Simonsz and his followers broke away from the Catholic Church, forming a Protestant sect called the Mennonites.

1524 Italian navigator Giovanni da Verrazano was commissioned by the French to explore North America. He discovered an island off the eastern coast and named it Angoulême. The island is now known as Manhattan.

1524 Reformation preacher Thomas Münzer asked the peasants in Germany to rebel against their feudal rulers and all Catholics, resulting in violent fighting and great loss of life and property. The revolt ended with the execution of Münzer in the following year.

1524 Ismail Safavi, the shah of Persia, died. His son Tahmasp I was crowned ruler of Persia.

1524 Vasco da Gama was sent to India as the Portuguese viceroy, but died shortly after arriving in Goa.

1524 Tecum Uman, King of the Quiche Mayans of Gautemala, was killed by Spanish conquistador Pedro de Alvarado.

1524 Spanish conquistador Francisco Pizarro set out to search for a rumoured civilization in South America, the Incas.

1525 Spanish and German forces defeated France in the Battle of Pavia. Francis I, King of France, was taken prisoner.

1525 Albert von Brandenburg, the Grand Master of the Teutonic Knights, became a Protestant and declared himself owner of the lands of the Teutonic Knights with the title the Duke of Prussia. He thus established Prussia as a country.

▶ *The mountain city of Machu Picchu was a forgotten marvel, lost for 400 years.*

Later Middle Ages and Renaissance

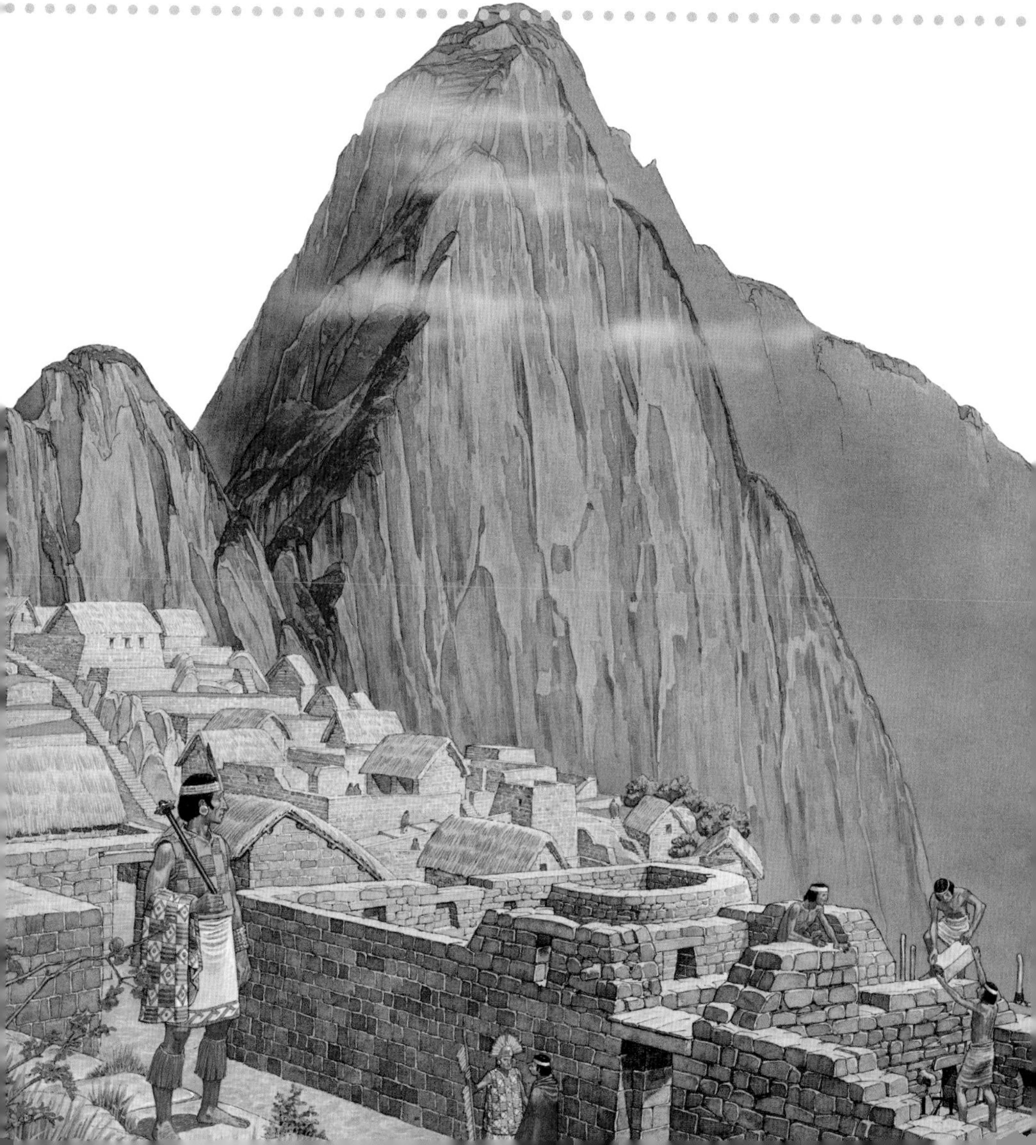

1526 In India, Babar, the ruler of Kabul, defeated Ibrahim Lodi, the sultan ruling over Delhi, in the first Battle of Panipat. Babar, who established the Mughal dynasty in India, was a descendent of Genghis Khan and Timur. Babar was also a good poet and lover of nature, and constructed many gardens. His memoir *Babar nameh* is a world classic of autobiography.

1526 After his defeat in war against the Holy Roman emperor, Francis I signed the Treaty of Madrid and gave up Burgundy and all claims to Flanders, Artois, Tournai and Italy. However, he later went back on his promise.

▲ *Babar founded the Mughal dynasty that was to dominate northern India for over 200 years.*

1525 Southern Athapaskan peoples of Canada migrated to the Southwest of North America. They later split into groups such as the Apache and Navajo.

1526 The Teutonic Knights formally broke away from the Roman Church and joined Martin Luther's movement.

1526 Ottoman sultan Suleiman killed Louis II of Hungary in the Battle of Mohács and took all his lands. The Ottoman Empire reached the height of its power during the reign of Suleiman. He completely reconstructed the Ottoman law system.

1526 Ferdinand, younger brother of Emperor Charles V, was crowned king of Bohemia. He faced rival claimants in Hungary and periodically fought against the Ottoman Empire.

1526 Spanish conquistador Francisco Pizarro discovered Peru. He left to return to Spain, but was determined to return with an army to conquer the new lands.

1527 Henry VIII of England and Francis I of France signed the Treaty of Westminster, agreeing to be allies.

1527 Pope Clement VII allied with France. The Holy Roman emperor Charles V raided and destroyed the city of Rome and had Pope Clement VII imprisoned in the castle of Saint'Angelo in Rome. The pope was released after a few months.

1528–1572 Christian missionaries arrived in Mexico and converted a large part of the native population.

▼ *Present-day Mexico is the site of such great civilizations as the Maya and the Toltec, and empires such as the one founded by the Aztecs in the 14th century.*

1528-1530

1528 The Reformation movement gained popularity in the Swiss states of Bern, Basel and a few others. Despite this, most of the country still remained strictly Catholic.

1528 Jacob Hutter, an Austrian preacher, established the Protestant sect of Hutterites. The Hutterites modelled themselves on the early church of Jerusalem. After facing opposition in Moravia and Tirol, they moved to Hungary and Ukraine.

1529 Emperor Charles V appointed the Spanish explorer Francisco Pizarro the governor of Peru.

1529 The Welsers, a business family of Augsburg, Germany, formed the colony of New Granada in South America. The territory was granted them by Charles V. It comprised areas that were later known as Venezuela and Colombia.

1529 A severe epidemic of 'sweating sickness' struck London and spread to Germany and Austria.

1529 Mughal emperor Babar defeated the Afghan chieftains ruling over the eastern Indian states of Bihar and Bengal. His empire stretched from Kabul in the west to Bengal in the east.

...FASCINATING FACT...

In medieval Europe, babies were wrapped tightly in cloth until they were six months old. It was considered unhealthy for them to move their hands and legs! Until the age of six, boys and girls were both dressed in frocks. Once a boy was six years old, he was given his first pair of breeches. 'Breeching' was an important occasion and called for celebration. A feast was arranged and family and friends got together to celebrate.

1529 The Ottoman Turks conquered Algeria and invaded Hungary. King John Zapolya now ruled Hungary as an Ottoman puppet.

1529 Francis I of France and the Holy Roman emperor Charles V signed the Treaty of Cambrai.

1529 Martin Luther's protest against the Catholic Church's ban on his teachings led to the Reformation movement being named Protestantism.

1530 Spanish conquistador Alvarado defeated the K'iche' and Kaqchikel Mayans and destroyed their cities.

▶ During the reign of Suleiman I, the Ottoman Empire reached its peak. It included most of the major Muslim cities and extended to the Balkans and Hungary.

175

1530-1534

1530 Mughal emperor Babar died and his son Humayun succeeded him.

1530 The Knights Hospitaller of Saint John settled down in the island of Malta, which was given to them by Charles V. They became known as the Knights of Malta.

***c*.1530** In Peru, Inca ruler Atahualpa defeated his brother Huáscar and later had him killed.

1531 Protestant princes and imperial cities of Europe came together to form the Schmalkaldic League against the Holy Roman emperor Charles V. The objective of the league was to protect the newly formed Lutheran churches from being attacked by Charles V and other Catholics.

1531 Huldrych Zwingli was killed in the Battle of Kappel between the Protestant state of Zurich and Catholic forces from other Swiss states. Zurich was defeated in the fight.

▲ *Anne Boleyn, the second wife of King Henry VIII of England and mother of the future queen, Elizabeth I.*

1533 England's Henry VIII married his mistress Anne Boleyn in a secret ceremony. The marriage followed Henry's divorce from his first wife, Katherine of Aragon. The divorce was not approved by the pope.

1533 Christian III became the king of Denmark and Norway, following his victory in the civil war known as the Count's War. His succession was opposed by many, but he was able to suppress the rebels. Christian made Lutheranism the state religion, and arrested the Catholic bishops who opposed him.

1533 Ivan IV (also known as Ivan the Terrrible) became the grand duke of Moscow and assumed the title of Tsar, meaning 'emperor'. He carried out a series of reforms, including a centralized administration and formation of the first national assembly. He brutally suppressed all opposition.

1533 Spanish adventurer Francisco Pizarro invaded Peru and had Inca ruler Atahualpa killed. The Inca retreated to the mountains and began a war that would last for generations.

1534 French explorer Jacques Cartier was sent by Francis I, King of France, on an expedition to North America.

▼ *Jacques Cartier was commissioned by the French king Francis I to explore North America with the chief aim of finding gold and spices.*

1534–1536

1534 The protestant form of Christianity was established in England when Henry VIII broke his ties with the Roman Church following the pope's refusal to recognize his second marriage. An Act of Supremacy established the king of England as the supreme head of the Church.

▼ *1539 saw the dissolution (closing down) of Roman Catholic monastries in England and Wales. The property was sold off to nobles, raising money for Henry VIII.*

1534 Ottoman sultan Suleiman I took over the Persian city of Tabriz and extended his kingdom to include Iraq.

1534 Ignatius Loyola founded the counter-Reformation Roman Catholic order of the Society of Jesus, or the Jesuits, in Paris. They served as a preaching, teaching and missionary society and soon spread worldwide.

1534 Ottoman Turkish forces conquered Tunis and Baghdad.

1535 Spanish conqueror Francisco Pizarro founded the town of Lima in Peru.

1535 Mexico, Central America, Florida and parts of the Southwest United States were brought together to form the viceroyalty of New Spain. Its capital was at Tenochtitlán, which was renamed Ciudad de México, and its first viceroy was Antonio de Mendoza. Spain slowly consolidated its rule over these lands.

1535 Wales was incorporated into the English legal and governmental systems by an agreement called the Act of Union. The act was passed during the reign of Henry VIII. The act was supported by many Welsh people, as it gave them equal rights and reformed local government. However, the act also made English the official language, meaning Welsh could no longer be used in legal, tax or government documents.

1535 The Sforza dynasty in Milan ended with the death of Francesco Sforza II. Milan came under the control of the Holy Roman emperor Charles V.

1536 Spain completed the conquest of the Inca and Aztec Empires.

1536 Reformist leaders and Anabaptists (reformers who held that only believing adults should be baptised) John of Leyden and Jacob Hutter were tortured and executed by the Catholic bishop of Munster.

1536-1540

1536 Jesuit priests were invited to conduct the Inquisition in Portugal to root out Protestantism.

1536 Amsterdam emerged as a major commercial centre in Europe.

1536–1598 Japanese shogun Toyotomi Hideyoshi lived during this period. He totally reformed Japanese government.

1536 Anne Boleyn, second wife of Henry VIII, was beheaded. Henry ordered her execution on the grounds of her alleged adultery, though the real reason was her failure to produce a son and heir.

1536 Francis I declared war against Charles V for the third time. French forces captured Turin in Italy. The war ended two years later and in 1539 they called a truce with the Treaty of Toledo.

1537 Spanish explorer Juan Salazar de Espinosa established the town of Asunción on the Paraguay River, in South America.

1538 The Ottoman Turks led by the admiral Khayr ad-din defeated the combined forces of Venice, the Holy Roman emperor Charles V and Pope Paul III in a naval battle, and took control of the Mediterranean. Khayr ad-din was known to Christians as Barbarossa and dominated the Mediterranean for 20 years.

1540 Hungary was split into three parts and thrown into confusion by the invasion of Ferdinand of Hapsburg, following the death of its king, John Zápolya. John II Zápolya, son of the dead king, ascended the throne, but was not very successful in bringing order and peace to the country.

1540 The Jesuit order was recognized by Pope Paul III and they were given an important role in spreading the Counter Reformation.

1540 The Spanish had brought most of the Mayan areas under their control. The natives rebelled weakly and unsuccessfully from time to time, but the revolts were put down by the Spaniards.

▲ *The* Mary Rose *sank after water poured through the gun-ports (holes for firing cannon)*
that had been cut into her hull.

...FASCINATING FACT...

The warship *HMS Mary Rose*, built between 1509 and 1511, fought
numerous battles for the English and was a favourite of Henry VIII.
Although the ship survived tough battles, its end came in an unexpected
way. In 1545, when the ship was brought in from the Portsmouth
dockyard to the Solent, a sudden gust of wind caused it to keel and its
cannons to break loose, sinking the ship into its watery grave.

1540-1542

1540 In India, Afghan king Sher Shah Suri defeated the Mughal emperor Humayun and drove him out of India. Sher Shah died in 1545, whereupon Humayun returned to Delhi and re-established the Mughal Empire that was to last for 300 years.

1540 Following pirate attacks, Spanish ships crossing the Atlantic sailed in large convoys protected by warships.

1541 Scots lawyer John Knox took the Reformation movement to Scotland. He was also the founder of the Presbyterian Church.

1541 After discovering the Gulf of Lawrence and founding a French colony in Canada, the French explorer Jacques Cartier explored much of North America and established a French colony at Quebec.

1541 Geneva became an important centre of Protestantism under the leadership of John Calvin, the Reformation leader.

1541 Spanish conquistador Pedro de Valdivia founded Santiago, the capital of Chile. He battled and defeated a large force of local warriors in the region. He later extended the Spanish rule south of the Bío-Bío River. He became the governer of Chile in 1549. He also founded Concepción in Chile.

1541–1614 Spanish painter El Greco lived during this period. He was the first great master of Spanish painting.

1542 Spanish explorers discovered California, and the areas around the Mississippi and Amazon. In Yucatán, Mexico, they established the town of Mérida.

1542 Henry VIII, King of England, was crowned king of Ireland, a title that had long been vacant.

1542 Henry VIII defeated James V of Scotland in the Battle of Solway Moss. The Scottish king died soon thereafter and was succeeded by his infant daughter, Mary Queen of Scots.

▲ *French navigator Jacques Cartier made three voyages to North America wherein he explored much of the continent. He is said to have discovered the St Lawrence River.*

1543-1548

▲ *A learned and religious woman, Catherine Parr was the sixth and last wife of Henry VIII.*

1543 Henry VIII married Catherine Parr after having had his fifth wife, Catherine Howard, beheaded.

1543 Portuguese sailors from China arrived on the island of Tanegashima in Japan. They established trade through the port of Nagasaki, supplying firearms and tobacco among other things from the west.

1543 Polish astronomer Nicolaus Copernicus published theories that stated that the Earth and other planets rotated on their own axes and revolved in orbits around the Sun. This is generally termed as the heliocentric (or 'Sun-centred') system.

1544 French forces led by Comte d'Enghien defeated Charles V in the Battle of Ceresole, in Italy.

1545 Spanish colonies in Cuba and New Spain were struck by a terrible epidemic of typhus that claimed a large number of lives.

1546 The Holy Roman emperor Charles V led Catholic forces to victory against Protestant forces of the Schmalkaldic League in the Battle of Mühlberg.

1547 Francis I, King of France, died and was succeeded by his son Henri II. He made several reforms and suppressed Protestants. He also continued the war against Charles V.

1547 Henry VIII of England passed away and was succeeded by Edward VI, his son by his third wife, Jane Seymour.

1547 The English forces defeated the Scottish army in the Battle of Pinkie. It was the last battle fought between the Scottish and the English Royal armies. The English army occupied Scottish towns and castles for several years, until a peace was agreed.

▲ *Copernicus' theory about the Sun as the centre of the solar system refuted the traditional theory that placed the Earth at the centre of the Universe.*

1548 Poland's Catholic king Sigismund I died and his son Sigismund II ascended the throne. The Protestant Reformation gained popularity in Poland during his reign. He also incorporated Livonia and Lithuania into Poland by a treaty.

185

1549–1555

1549 Christianity gained popularity in Japan due to the efforts of the Jesuit priest Francis Xavier.

1550 England and France signed a peace treaty at Boulogne.

1550 In North America, the Mohawk, Oneida, Onondaga, Cayuga and Seneca tribes came together to form the League of the Iroquois.

◀ *Lady Jane Grey was crowned queen in 1553, but within nine days was forced from the throne by the supporters of the rightful heir, Mary Tudor. Jane was imprisoned and beheaded in the Tower of London 1554, aged 16.*

...FASCINATING FACT...

The Olmecs first grew cocoa between 1500BC and 400BC. The cocoa bean was used to make a bitter and strong beverage that was laced with chillies to improve its taste. Chocolate was a popular drink among wealthy Mayans and Aztecs. In AD1544, chocolate came to Spain, where it was sweetened with sugar and flavoured with vanilla, cinnamon and other flavouring agents. Nearly 100 years later, chocolate was used to make rolls, cakes and truffles and only in AD1847 was the first chocolate bar manufactured in England.

1551 France began its war against Holy Roman emperor Charles V yet again by capturing Toul, Metz and Verdun in the Lorraine region.

1552 Maurice of Saxony joined Henri II of France in his war against Charles V. Charles V was defeated by Henri II at Metz and Maurice captured Augsburg.

1552 Ivan IV, the Tsar of Moscow, expanded his kingdom by capturing the Tatar city of Kazan. He then proceeded to invade Astrakhan, a city in southern Russia.

1553 Edward VI, King of England, passed away. Mary Tudor succeeded him. She married King Philip II of Spain, son of Charles V, and re-established the Roman Catholic church in England.

1553 English traders arrived in southern Nigeria and began trading in gold, ivory and pepper.

▶ *Edward VI, King of England and Ireland, had an uneventful reign and eventually died as a minor, apparently due to tuberculosis.*

1553 Mary, Queen of England, suppressed a revolt led by the supporters of Lady Jane Grey, who had been appointed the legal heir to the English throne by the dying King Edward VI. Lady Jane was imprisoned, and executed the following year.

1555 German Catholics and Protestants ended their fight with the Religious Peace of Augsburg, according to which each state had the freedom to decide on the religion it would follow.

187

1555–1559

1555 The ousted ruler Humayun conquered Delhi and re-established the Mughal Empire in India.

1555 Emperor Charles V retired after appointing his brother Ferdinand as his successor. Charles also gave the Netherlands, Spain, Milan and the Spanish colonies to his son Philip.

1556 Mughal emperor Humayun was succeeded by his son Akbar. Akbar reorganized the administration of his empire and encouraged arts and literature. He was said to be the greatest Mughal emperor. He expanded his empire by conquering Gujarat, Bengal, Kashmir and Deccan. Several Sanskrit classics were translated into Persian during his reign.

1557 The Portuguese colonized Macão off the Chinese coast, from where they began to conduct trade with the Chinese mainland.

◀ *Mughal emperor Humayun remained ousted from the throne for 15 years before he could re-assert his authority.*

1557 João III, King of Portugal, died and was succeeded by his infant grandson, Sebastian. Sebastian was very religious and died in 1578 fighting in a Crusade against Muslims in Morocco. After his death, many of his followers founded a faith called Sebastianism.

1557 Spanish forces drove the French out of Italy after defeating them in the Battle of St Quentin.

1558 England's ambitions to conquer France came to an end when the French reclaimed Calais, the last English territory in France.

1558 Mary Tudor, Queen of England, died. Elizabeth, daughter of Henry VIII and Ann Boleyn, ascended the English throne. Her reign is considered the 'golden period' of English history, a time when art and literature flourished. Elizabeth's Protestant faith was to cause friction with Catholic states.

▲ *Elizabeth I, Queen of England.*

1559 Spanish colonists arrived in Florida, but were driven out by North American Indians to Port Royal Sound in South Carolina.

1559–1564

1559 Christian III, King of Denmark and Norway, died. He was succeeded by Frederick II.

1560 English forces defeated French troops supporting Mary Stuart's claim to the English throne at Leith, in Scotland. The Treaty of Edinburgh ended French interference in Scotland.

1560 Gustavus I stepped down from the throne of Sweden and was succeeded by his son Eric XIV. In 1561, Eric also became the ruler of Estonia.

1560 Francis II of France died and his brother Charles IX ascended the French throne. Charles IX's mother Catherine de' Medici dominated the early part of his reign. His reign was marked by conflicts between Catholics and Protestants, called Huguenots.

1562 Civil war broke out in France following the mass murder of several Huguenots by François, the duke of Guise.

1563 The conflict between French Catholics and the Huguenots was temporarily ended when Catherine de' Medici, the queen mother, signed the Peace of Amboise, which granted liberty of conscience to the Huguenots. However, celebration of religious services was confined to the households of the nobility, and only to a limited number of towns.

1563 The Church of England (or the Episcopal Church) was founded on the basis of guidelines called the Thirty-nine Articles.

1564 Maximilian II became the Holy Roman emperor. He advocated religeous tolerance and worked for the reform of the Roman Catholic Church.

1564–1616 English poet and playwright William Shakespeare lived during this period. *Macbeth, Othello, Romeo and Juliet* and *A Midsummer Night's Dream* are some of his most popular plays.

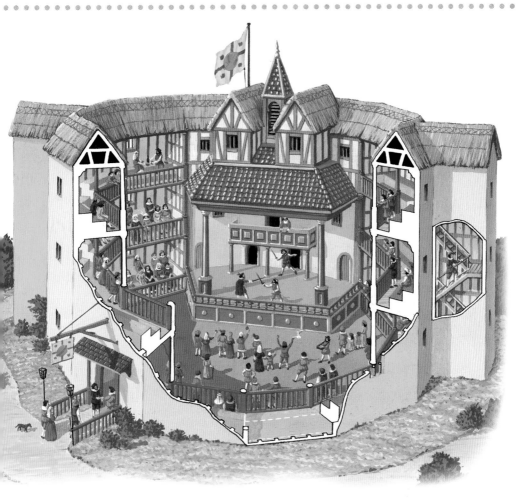

▲ *The original Globe Theatre in London was the venue for Shakespeare's stage plays after 1599. In 1613 the theatre was destroyed in a fire mishap during a performance and was later rebuilt.*

1565-1568

1565 The Spaniards established the first permanent European colony in North America at St Augustine in Florida.

1565 Cebu in the Philippines was colonized by Miguel Lopez de Legazpe from New Spain.

1565 In India, the Bahmani sultans, ruling princely states in the Deccan, raided and destroyed the south Indian Vijayanagar kingdom.

1565 English naval commander and slave trader John Hawkins introduced tobacco from Florida to England for the first time.

◀ *The life of Mary, Queen of Scots ended tragically. The English secret service uncovered a Catholic plot and claimed that Mary was involved. She was beheaded at Fotheringay Castle in February 1587.*

1566 Suleiman the Magnificent died and his son Selim II ascended the Ottoman throne. Selim was a weak drunk, but his ministers ensured that Ottoman power increased in the Mediterranean during his rule.

1567 The Portuguese killed French colonists in Brazil and founded the city of Rio de Janeiro.

1567 Scottish noblemen forced Mary Queen of Scots to step down from the Scottish throne.

1567 Catholics and Huguenots in France went to war for the second time. It ended with the Peace of Longjumeau in 1568, an agreement between Catherine de' Medici and the Protestants.

1568 Eric XIV of Sweden was removed from power and his brother John III was made king of Sweden.

1568 In Japan, Oda Nobunaga suppressed his rival *daimyo*s, or local lords, and took control of Kyoto, thereby ending the rule of the Ashikaga shogunate in Japan. He battled the fanatical religious Ikko sect, defeating them in Osaka in 1580. Nobunaga allowed the Jesuits to establish a church in Kyoto in order to weaken the strength of the Buddhists.

FASCINATING FACT

In 16th-century Florence there was a revival of the ancient Greek theatre style, in which long monologues or dialogues were accompanied by orchestral music. This popular style of musical drama (which came to be known as 'opera') was initially written and composed by amateurs. It was through the efforts of Claudio Monteverdi, the Late Renaissance musician, that opera came into its own and developed into an impressive theatrical presentation.

1568–1572

1568 In France the Catholic Cardinal of Lorraine tried to have Protestant Huguenot leaders, the prince of Condé and Gaspard de Coligny (admiral of France), abducted. They avoided capture and managed to escape to the fortress of La Rochelle.

1569 In France, Catholic forces defeated Huguenot forces in the Battle of Jarnac. The Catholic troops under Marshal Gaspard de Tavannes surprised and defeated the Huguenots, who were being led by Gaspard de Coligny and the prince of Condé. The prince of Condé was executed after the battle. Coligny escaped by reorganizing his troops and retreating to the south. He was defeated at Moncontour the same year.

1569 Flemish cartographer Gerardus Mercator introduced the *Meracator Projection* map, which revolutionized and simplified navigational chart making.

1570 Ivan the Terrible, tsar of Moscow, captured the great city of Novgorod in northwestern Russia. He destroyed many of the buildings in the city and killed thousands of its citizens.

1570 The Huguenots ended their third religious war against the Catholics of France with the Treaty of St Germain. The treaty recognized four Huguenot strongholds: La Rochelle, Cognac, La Charite and Montauban.

1570 The Ottoman Turks led by Selim II defeated the combined naval forces of Spain and Venice, and captured Cyprus.

1570 Panama became an important trading post. Gold from the Andes was brought there to be sent to the Caribbean ports, from where it was shipped to Spain.

1570 In Granada, Spain, the Morisco Rebellion was put down after two years of fighting between the Christians and Moriscos. The Moriscos were former Muslims who had promised to become Christians. They were forced to leave Granada and settle in small groups in different parts of Castile.

1571 The combined naval forces of Spain, Venice, Genoa and Malta defeated the Ottoman fleet in the Battle of Lepanto. The battle was fought near the Gulf of Patras off the port of

◄ *Lepanto was the last great battle between fleets of galleys – warships powered by huge banks of oarsmen.*

Lepanto, Greece. The combined fleet had 250 galleys carrying about 30,000 men. Nearly 15,000 Turks were killed or taken prisoners along with 200 ships. The victors lost over 7000 men. The battle ended Turkish control of the Mediterranean.

1571 German astronomer Johannes Kepler was born in this year. He won a scholarship to the University of Tübingen where he studied to be a Lutheran priest. It was here that he was first introduced to the ideas of the astronomer Copernicus, which put the Sun, not the Earth, at the centre of the solar system. Kepler is famous for his laws of planetary motion. He was also the first to investigate the formation of pictures with a pin hole camera, and to formulate different eyeglass designs for nearsightedness and farsightedness.

1572 Thousands of Huguenots were killed by the Catholics of France on the orders of King Charles IX, in the Massacre of St Bartholomew. The religious wars began again in France.

1573–1580

1573 Henry of Valois, brother of Charles IX of France, was elected king of Poland. In 1575, Henry of Valois gave up the Polish throne and returned to France when his brother Charles IX died. He became Henry III of France.

1574 Sultan Selim II died and his son Murad III became ruler of the Ottoman Turks.

1576 The English explorer Sir Martin Frobisher discovered Baffin Island off North America while trying to find a shorter route to China.

1576 In Spanish-ruled Netherlands, 17 Protestant provinces came together to form the Pacification of Ghent, in their war against the Spanish Inquisition (a formal office set up by the Catholic monarchs of Spain to deal with Jews and Muslims accused of heresy).

1576 The Catholics of France formed a Holy League with the support of Philip II of Spain to fight against the Huguenots. Henry III, King of France, made himself the head of the League and banned Protestantism.

1577 Swiss mathematician Jost Burgi invented the minute hand. Burgi's invention was part of a clock made for an astronomer who needed an accurate clock for his stargazing.

1577 Flemish painter Peter Paul Ruebens was born. He was well educated as he came from a wealthy lawyer's family. After school, he served as a page in the royal court at Antwerp. Ruebens went on to become the leading artist of his time and influenced many artists.

1578–1606 In the Philippines, Manila developed into an important trading town and a centre for Spanish Catholic missionaries.

1580 The English explorer Francis Drake returned to Portsmouth after having set out on a trip around the world in 1577. He was the first Englishman to have made such a trip.

1580 Spain defeated Portugal in the Battle of Alcantara and Philip II of Spain was crowned the king of Portugal (as Philip I).

▲ *Martin Frobisher's route (red) to Baffin Island.*

1581 In Britain, Jesuit priest Edmund Campion was tried for distributing pamphlets against the Anglican Church. He was executed.

1581 African slaves sent by the Spanish king Philip II arrived at St Augustine in Florida. They were the first African slaves to arrive on American shores.

1582 Ivan the Terrible of Moscow was defeated by Stephen Báthory of Poland in the Livonian War. Later, in a fit of temper, Ivan killed his eldest son.

1582 Pope Gregory XIII introduced the new, more accurate, Gregorian calendar, replacing the older Julian calendar. Though Roman Catholic countries in Europe adopted the new calendar, many Protestant countries continued to use the Julian version.

◀ *Elizabeth I ruled England with great authority and helped the country become a major power in Europe.*

1582 Ivan the Terrible made agreements of peace with Poland and Sweden. He also allowed the Russian Orthodox Church to establish links with the Roman Catholic Church.

1582 After the death of Japanese Taira noblemanToyotomi Oda Nobunaga, his general Hideyoshi took control of all of Oda's territory.

1584 English navigator Sir Walter Raleigh founded the Virginia colony on Roanoke Island in North America. Raleigh is also remembered in anecdotes as having once laid his cloak on a muddy puddle so that Queen Elizabeth wouldn't get her shoes dirty.

1584 Ivan the Terrible died. He was succeeded by his feeble-minded son Fyodor Ivanovich.

1585 English explorers discovered the Chesapeake Bay and Davis Strait in North America.

1585 Civil war broke out in France after the sudden death of Francis of Alencon made Huguenot leader Henry of Navarre heir to the French throne.

1585 Spanish forces captured Antwerp and expelled all Protestants. Southern Netherlands, Flanders and Brabant were also brought under Spanish control.

. . . FASCINATING FACT . . .

In Medieval Europe, peasants spun linen or woollen yarn, dyed it, wove the fabric and made clothes for themselves. The clothes were usually coarse and since the peasants could afford only one set, they were hardly ever washed. When the clothes wore out they were patched and used till the fabric fell apart, and even then the fibres were mixed with fresh wool to spin new yarn that could be used again.

1586-1589

1586 The English explorer and privateer Sir Francis Drake attacked the Spanish colonies of San Domingo, Cartagena and St Augustine. He looted the towns and forced them to pay ransom.

1586 Hideyoshi was made the prime minister of Japan by the Japanese emperor Goyozei.

1586 Polish king Stephen Báthory died. His son John III of Sweden succeeded him on the Polish throne as Sigismund III.

1587 Mary Queen of Scots was executed by Elizabeth I of England after she plotted to kill Elizabeth and seize her throne. She was born Mary Stuart and became queen after her father's death, when she was only six days old. At one time, she claimed the crowns of Scotland, France, England and Ireland. Although she was renowned for her beauty and kind heart, she lacked the political skills to rule Scotland with success. Her second marriage raised criticism and ended in murder and scandal. After her third marriage she was forced to abdicate in favour of her infant son James I. She fled to England hoping that her cousin Elizabeth I would help her. But Elizabeth was afraid that Mary would take over the English throne with help from the Catholics. Mary was imprisoned, and Elizabeth ordered that all Mary's possessions be burned. Eventually, Mary was beheaded for treason. Upon Elizabeth's death in 1603, Mary's son became king of England.

1587 Hideyoshi defeated the Japanese feudal rulers (*daimyo*s) and brought them under his control.

1587 In Persia, the Safavid ruler Abbas I came to power. He is considered the greatest of the Safavid rulers. During his reign, art and architecture flowered; administration of the country was reorganized; and foreign trade was encouraged.

1588 The English defeated the Spanish Armada. King Philip II of Spain had sent the 130-ship Armada to conquer Protestant England and make himself king of England.

1588 The Danish-Norwegian king Frederick II passed away and was succeeded by his son Christian IV.

1589 Huguenot leader Henry of Navarre ascended the throne of France as Henry IV.

▼ *The ill-fated Spanish Armada suffered a decisive defeat at the hands of the English army and had to also battle storms on the way back to Spain.*

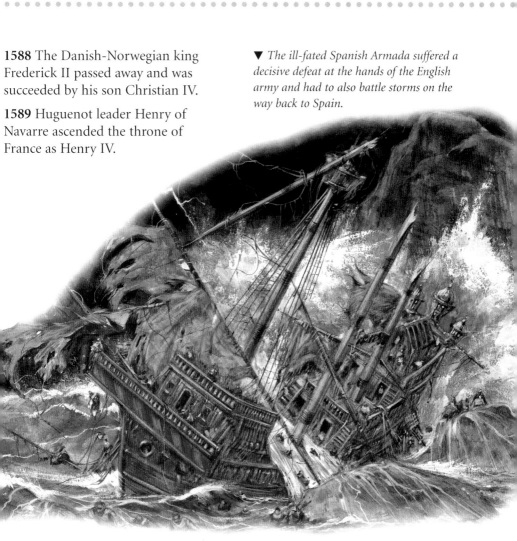

1590-1595

1590 Henry IV of France defeated the Catholic League in the Battle of Ivry, fought in Normandy. The battle was to be a decisive victory for Henri, who led Huguenot forces against the League. Henri's forces went on to lay siege to Paris, where they were defeated. Despite this setback, Henri IV became the legitimate successor to the throne after the death of his cousin, Henri III of France. The new king was unpopular in the south, and not trusted by many in the army. The rest of the country refused to recognize him as king as he had been excommunicated by the Pope.

1590 Ottoman sultan Murad III ended the 12 year war between the Ottomans and the shah of Persia. He extended the Ottoman Empire by conquering Georgia, Azerbaijan and Shirwan.

1590 Prime Minister Hideyoshi unified Japan by conquering the northern part of Honshu Island.

1591 French mathematician François Viète, known as the father of modern algebraic notation, began the use of letters to represent unknown quantities and coefficients in algebra.

1592 John III of Sweden passed away. He was succeeded by his son Sigismund IV, King of Poland.

1592 Having made himself Shogun of all Japan, Hideyoshi invaded Korea, but was driven out by Chinese forces and Korean guerrillas.

1593 Henry IV of France converted from Protestantism to Catholicism, making himself eligible for the French throne. The French people wanted only a Catholic ruler as king.

1595 The Dutch began trade with Asia, and Dutch colonies were established on the African Guinea coast and in the East Indies.

1595 The Ottoman sultan Murad III died. His eldest son Mohammed III succeeded him. His accession and weak rule marked the beginning of the downfall of the Ottoman Empire.

1595 Henry IV of France defeated Spain and conquered Burgundy.

▼ *Modern-day Tokyo, Japan. The unification of Japan was achieved by Hideyoshi towards the end of the 16th century.*

1596–1600

1596 Ottoman sultan Mohammed III defeated Hungarian forces in the Battle of Keresztes.

1596 Hideyoshi invaded Korea for the second time, but the invasion came to a sudden end with his death.

1597 The first-ever opera was written. The word 'opera' is a Latin word meaning 'works'. It is the plural of *opus* since it combined solo and choral singing, drama and dancing in a staged spectacle. The earliest work considered an opera is *Dafne*, written by Jacopo Peri.

1598 Spaniards colonized Pueblo (American Indian) territory in the Southwest of North America.

1598 The king of France, Henry IV, issued the Edict of Nantes, giving Protestant Huguenots equal political rights with Catholics and permitting them to practice their religion in certain French cities. The edict permitted public worship in most of the kingdom, except Paris.

1598 Fyodor I, the Tsar of Moscow, died. The last of the Riurikovich Tsars, Fyodor was born mentally challenged and was appointed as a figurehead on the throne. When he became tsar, Russia had already been devastated by the excesses of his father, Ivan the Terrible. Russia entered into a further decline under Fyodor's reign. His failure to produce an heir to the throne

...FASCINATING FACT...

In medieval Japan, warriors called samurai began the practice of ritual suicide or hara-kiri (*seppuko*). A samurai committed hara-kiri by cutting open his stomach. Hara-kiri was committed for a number of reasons, including proving one's loyalty to one's master, expressing sorrow, as a method of punishing oneself, or to prevent oneself from being captured.

▲ The Japanese warrior caste Samurai held bravery, honour and loyalty to one's master even above life.

1598 Henry IV and Philip II ended the war between France and Spain by signing the Treaty of Vervins.

1598 Spain's Philip II passed away. He was succeeded by his son Philip III, during whose reign the Spanish economy suffered. Agricultural production declined and unemployment and poverty increased.

1600 The British East India Company was formed. The company was popularly known as John Company, and was founded by a Royal Charter of Elizabeth I. Over the next 250 years, the East India Company became one of the most powerful commercial enterprises of its time. Most of its business was based in India, where it gained governmental and military authority. India was often referred to as the 'Jewel in the Crown'.

brought an end to the dynasty that had ruled Russia for centuries. Russia then entered the Time of Troubles. Fyodor was also known as Fyodor the Bellringer because of his tendency to travel the land and ring the bells at churches.

1600 Tokugawa Ieyasu established himself as ruler of Japan after defeating other rivals for the throne in the Battle of Sekigahara.

205

1602–1605

1602 The Dutch East India Company was formed. It had its headquarters at Batavia (now Jakarta) in Indonesia.

1602 The English East India Company's fleet, led by James Lancaster, arrived in Sumatra. There, they captured a Portuguese ship and traded its cargo for pepper.

▼ *Guy Fawkes was just one of the people accused of the murder plot. The leader was said to be Robert Catesby.*

1602 New England, Cape Cod and the islands of Martha's Vineyard and Cuttyhunk were discovered by the English navigator Bartholomew Gosnold.

1603 The plague ravaged London yet again and claimed nearly 33,000 lives.

Guy Fawkes

1603 Queen Elizabeth I died and her great nephew, King James VI of Scotland, who was the son of Mary Queen of Scots, ascended the English throne as James I.

1603 The Ottoman sultan Mohammed III was succeeded by his son Ahmed I.

1603 After the death of Toyotomi Hideyoshi, the Japanese emperor made Ieyasu Tokugawa the new Shogun, or military ruler. The Tokugawas ruled Japan till 1867, a period during which the country was peaceful and prosperous.

1604 French explorer Samuel de Champlain explored the Atlantic Coast of North America and established a colony at Nova Scotia.

1604 Charles IX (also called Karl IX) ascended the throne of Sweden after ousting Sigismund IV and killing dozens of noblemen. He was the youngest son of Gustav I of Sweden and Margareta Lejonhufvud. Charles's short reign was characterized by uninterrupted warfare. His wars in Poland and Russia kept him occupied in two overseas contests for the possession of Livonia and Ingria. Charles's designs on Laponia led him to start a war with Denmark in the last year of his reign. He had no notable success in any of these campaigns.

1605 A group of Roman Catholic rebels plotted to blow up the Houses of Parliament in London. The 'Gunpowder Plot' was discovered and Guy Fawkes, one of the main conspirators, was arrested. He had served for years as a soldier in the army of Archduke Albert of Austria in the Netherlands. He also fought against the Protestant United Provinces in the Eighty Years' War and in the war that captured Calais. While he was in service, Fawkes gained considerable expertise with explosives. After the plot, the Protestant government ordered a crackdown on English Catholics.

1605–1608

1605–1606 Spanish explorers discovered the southwestern Pacific islands in Vanuatu, and sailed in the waters between Australia and New Guinea.

1605 The Mughal emperor Akbar the Great passed away and was succeeded by his son Jahangir.

1605 Fyodor II became the Tsar of Russia.

1606 The first Union Flag was designed as a mix of the flags of England and Scotland. The flag was used by the United Kingdom of Great Britain as the national flag. It is commonly known as the Union Jack, or more properly the Union Flag, as it only becomes a jack when flown at sea.

▶ *A Spanish galleon. The name 'galleon' was derived from the word 'galley', which means 'war vessel'.*

1606 The Treaty of Zsitva-Török ended the tradition of Austria paying Hungary tribute and Transylvania, which was originally under Hungarian rule, was given to the István Bocskay.

1606 Australia had her first European visitors when a Dutch expedition arrived at the Cape York Peninsula. They were driven away by the natives.

1606 The London Company and the Plymouth Company were established to develop English colonies in North America, as a result of the Virginia Charter granted by James I of England.

1606 Rembrandt van Rijn, the famous Dutch painter who specialized in portraits and biblical scenes, was born.

1607 The first successful British colony in North America was established in the Chesapeake Bay area.
It was named Jamestown after the king of England, James I. In 1608, the fort at Jamestown, Virginia, was destroyed by fire and several colonists died of starvation and disease.

1608 The first English East India Company ship to reach India arrived in Surat, Gujarat.

... FASCINATING FACT ...
Pocahontas, the character made famous by the Disney cartoon with the same name, was the daughter of Powhatan, an Indian chieftain who ruled over nearly 30 tribes in Virginia. Pocahontas was kidnapped by starving Jamestown colonists who wanted chief Powhatan to give them food in return for her safety.
She converted to Christianity during her captivity and changed her name to Rebecca. In 1614 she married John Rolfe of Jamestown and died in England in 1617, at the age of 22.

1608-1610

1608 Matthias took over the leadership of the Hapsburg House from his mentally unstable brother Rudolf II, the Holy Roman emperor.

1608 Samuel de Champlain founded a French settlement at Quebec, Canada.

1609 Portuguese monopoly on trade with Japan ended when Japanese Shogun Ieyasu invited the Dutch to establish a trading post at Hirado in western Japan.

1609 Henry Hudson of the Dutch East India Company discovered the area around present-day New York City and declared it a Dutch colony.

1609 Philip III of Spain expelled 275,000 Moriscos (Moors converted to Christianity) for practicing Islam secretly. The Moors had contributed greatly to the development of Spanish art, architecture, literature and culture. The Spanish economy suffered a serious short-term decline.

1609 Spain's economy transformed as agriculture was replaced by sheep farming and instead of importing silver and gold from the Americas, the country was exporting olive oil, wool and wine in exchange for food.

1609 Johannes Kepler discovered that planets move around the Sun on elliptical paths and at different speeds. Kepler initially believed that celestial objects moved in perfect circles. This theory was in keeping with observations by Plato that the sphere was the perfect shape. After spending 20 years doing calculations with data collected by Tycho Brahe, Kepler came to the conclusion that the circular model of planetary motion was inconsistent with that data. Kepler was able to formulate three laws of planetary motion, now known as Kepler's laws. These laws state that planets move in ellipses, not circles.

1609 Japan and Korea established friendly relations through artistic, cultural and political exchanges, ending decades of warfare.

1610 Christianity spread through the interior of South America when the Jesuits established missions in Paraguay, Argentina and Brazil.

1610 Henry IV of France died. His young son Louis XIII succeeded him, although real power lay with Henry's widow Marie de Medici.

▼ *The Alcazar Fortress was originally built by the Moors, who introduced Islamic architecture in Spain.*

1610-1612

▲ *The Cathedral of St Basil the Blessed on Red Square, Moscow, was built between 1554 and 1560 by Tsar Ivan IV the Terrible.*

1610 Grand duke of Moscow Basil IV was removed from power by Sigismund III of Poland. Moscow was thrown into confusion in the fight for succession between Sigismund's son Ladislav IV Vasa and other rivals who were claming the throne.

1610 English mariner Henry Hudson explored the northernmost part of North America, hoping to locate a shorter route to China, Japan and the eastern countries. Hudson was able to locate only the northern straits and a shallow bay on the western side of the continent, both of which were named after him. Hudson died on the voyage.

1611 English forces drove Hugh O'Neill, the rebellious earl of Tyrone, out of Ireland and annexed Ulster to the British kingdom.

1611 Sir Thomas Cole, governor of Jamestown in Virginia, ended communal farming by giving each settler three acres of farm land and permission to keep or sell most of what they grew on their land.

◀ *After his unsuccessful uprising against the English forces, Hugh O'Neill, earl of Tyrone, spent the rest of his life in Rome.*

1611 With permission from King James I, the Church of England published an official English Bible for the first time.

1612 Mughal emperor Jahangir gave the English East India Company permission to trade in India after two of their ships defeated four Portuguese galleons at Surat.

1612 King of Hungary and Bohemia and archduke of Austria, the Holy Roman emperor Rudolf II, died. He was succeeded by his brother Matthias.

1612 England established Londonderry in Northern Ireland. Plantations of 3000 acres each were given away to English and Scottish Protestants, and to Irishmen who were supporters of the English throne.

1611 Denmark and Sweden went to war, ending 40 years of peace. The war ended when Sweden signed the Peace of Knared, giving up Finland.

1611 Charles IX of Sweden passed away and was succeeded by his son Gustavus II Adolphus. The new king increased the powers of the Swedish Council and gave it a more important role in running the country.

1613–1617

◀ *Cervantes'* Don Quixote *relates the tale of an elderly knight who sets out to seek adventure in the company of his squire and his horse.*

1613 Russian noblemen, or boyars, elected Mikhail Romanov (the first of the Romanov rulers) as the Tsar of Russia. His election ended eight years of political chaos in Russia.

1613 The rule of the Catholic king, Gabriel Báthory of Transylvania, came to an end and Bethlen Gábor came to power. Gábor established Protestantism in Transylvania.

1614 Gustavus II Adolphus of Sweden defeated the Russians and captured the city of Novgorod.

1615 Part II of Cervantes' *Don Quixote* was published. The author was 58 years old. *Don Quixote* was an enormous and immediate success. A fake Part II was published earlier in 1614. This probably forced Cervantes to complete work on the book the following year.

1616 The English East India Company established trade with Persia from its trading post at Surat.

1616 Baffin Bay in the North Atlantic Ocean was discovered by the English explorer William Baffin.

1616 Japan's shogun Tokugawa Ieyasu died and his son Hidetada succeeded him.

1616 Manchurian forces led by Nurhachi invaded China. Nurhachi laid the foundations of the later Ch'ing dynasty that later replaced the Chinese Mings.

1616–1622 Dutch traders explored the west coast of Australia. They discovered only desert and abandoned hope of establishing a colony.

1617 Philip III sent Don García de Silva y Figueroa as Spanish ambassador to the Safavid court at Isfahan, Persia, establishing diplomatic links between Christian and Muslim countries for the first time.

1617 Mustafa I succeeded his brother Ahmed I to the Ottoman throne. He was deposed the very next year by the elite troops for his mental problems, but was restored to the throne in 1622.

...FASCINATING FACT...

Japanese *Kabuki* theatre was born in 1603, when a woman called Okuni performed this dance-drama style for the first time at the Kitane shrine in Kyoto. This brilliant and unusual art form is a mix of drama, singing, miming and dancing. The plays are based on social issues and historical events, and the actors encourage audience participation by speaking to them during the play. In 1629 the shogunate banned women from performing in public, and ever since, men have carried on the tradition, playing both male and female roles.

1618-1621

1618 Sir Walter Raleigh returned to England after an unsuccessful expedition to the Orinoco River in South America. He was arrested and executed by James I of England after King Philip III of Spain demanded Raleigh's death as a condition for peace.

1618 An epidemic of smallpox killed nearly 9000 of New England's 10,000 European inhabitants. The disease then spread to the indigenous peoples, killing thousands.

▼ *The historic* Mayflower *ship carried the English Puritans from England to America.*

1618 Roman Catholics of Bohemia shut down Protestant chapels, violating the rights given to them by the late Holy Roman emperor Rudolf II. Angry Protestants threw two of Prague's governors from a window in Hradcany Palace. This incident, which is referred to as the 'Defenestration of Prague', led to the Thirty Years War between France, Sweden, Spain and the Holy Roman Empire, among other countries.

1618 Abbas the Great of Persia took control of Georgia and Azerbaijan from the Ottoman Turks.

1619 Holy Roman emperor Matthias died. He was succeeded by Ferdinand, who was earlier the king of Bohemia.

1619 African slaves were brought to Virginia. The Africans were hired on contract to work on tobacco, rice and indigo plantations, but by the 1660s the contracts were cancelled and their employers held them as slaves.

1620 The ship *Mayflower* completed its journey from Southampton to America. A large number of the passengers were Puritans belonging to the English Separatist Church. The Puritans founded the Plymouth colony, a place where they could practice their religion freely.

1620 In the third year of the Thirty Years War, Frederick V of Bohemia was defeated by the Catholic League in the Battle of the White Mountain. Maximilian of Bavaria and the Holy Roman emperor Ferdinand II took away all the lands and the powers of the Bohemian nobility, ending Czech independence for 300 years.

1621 Gorée Island off the coast of Senegal became a Dutch trading post, where slaves and gold were sent to Europe.

1621 The Dutch West India Company was founded and within the next 15 years the Dutch colonized parts of northeastern Brazil and the island of Curacao, establishing themselves as a threat to Spanish and Portuguese traders.

1621-1624

1621 Philip III of Spain died. He was succeeded by his son Philip IV, who left the administration of the country in the hands of his prime minister Gaspar de Gusman.

1622 Native Americans attacked several settlements in Virginia and killed more than 300 colonists.

1622 James I of England dissolved the English Parliament and imprisoned some members of the House of Commons for speaking against him. His relations with the English Parliament were stormy from the beginning because of his belief in the concept of divine right of monarchy. This concept held that kings received their authority from God and, hence, could not be held accountable to parliament.

1622 Persian Safavid ruler Abbas gained control of trade in the Persian Gulf with the help of the British East India Company. They drove out the Portuguese, who had previously controlled the area.

1622 The Protestants defeated the Catholics in the Battle of Wiesloch. The Thirty Years War continued without a decision, but with losses on both sides.

1622 Abbas of Persia defeated the Ottoman Turks and captured Baghdad, Mosul and Mesopotamia.

1623 Japanese shogun Hidetada stepped down to let his son Iemitsu take his place. The shogunate reached its peak under Iemitsu, who further reduced the privileges of the emperor.

1623 The English East India Company's trade in Southeast Asia and Japan came to an end with the Massacre of Amboina. Agents of the Dutch East India Company tortured and killed ten English traders along with ten Japanese and a Portuguese.

1624 Dutch settlers bought Manhattan from local tribes and renamed it New Amsterdam. According to legend, the island was bought from the natives in exchange for beads and other trinkets.

218

New York County (of which Manhattan is a part) is named in honour of the Duke of York, who was later to become King James II of England.

1624 Brazil was invaded by Dutch naval troops and the capital city of Bahia (now Salvador) was captured by them.

▶ *The Hopi are a Native American tribe based in northeastern Arizona in the United States. They are the descendants of the larger Pueblo Indian group.*

219

1625 Sir William Courteen founded the first English colony on the island of Barbados in the Caribbean.

1625 About 40,000 people died of plague in the city of London.

1625 James I of England died. His son Charles I succeeded him. Charles appointed the Duke of Buckingham as chief minister. Buckingham proved to be incompetent and Parliament asked for him to be replaced. Charles refused, beginning his conflict with Parliament.

1625 The Huguenots of France rose in revolt against the Catholic government. Charles I of England sent ships to France to help Louis XIII fight against the Huguenots.

1625 The Netherlands and England signed the Treaty of Southampton, agreeing to join forces against Spain.

▼ *In 1653, Oliver Cromwell became Lord Protector. Here, Bible in hand, he makes a rousing speech to his Roundhead troops. Both sides in the English Civil War believed that they were fighting for God, and prayed that He would bring them victory.*

...FASCINATING FACT...

In 17th-century Japan, artists thrived as it became fashionable to decorate homes with paintings. However, they were expensive and only a few people could afford to buy originals. Wood block printing or *ukiyo-e* made it possible to produce several low cost prints of a painting. *Ukiyo-e* prints were made by tracing a painting and transferring it on to a block of wood. The wood was then carved and used to make several impressions of the painting. Prints made in this manner were of such high quality that *ukiyo-e* developed into an art form in itself.

1626 French colonizers settled in Madagascar and began to drive out the Hovas who had been on the island for 600 years.

1626 Spain, France and the papacy called for a truce and signed the Treaty of Monzon. According to the treaty, Spain would not block the Valtelline and would let France use the Alpine passes to move troops.

1626 The Thirty Years War continued with Catholic forces winning the Battle of Dessau. The defeated Danish forces fled to Hungary.

1627 The Catholic forces led by Albrecht von Wallenstein, general of the Holy Roman emperor, and Baron von Tilly, general of the Catholic League, conquered Holstein, Schleswig, Jutland, Mecklenburg and Pomerania in northeastern Germany.

1627 Korea was invaded by the Manchurians of China and brought under their control. The invaders withdrew only after they were granted certain concessions. However, in 1636 the Manchurians captured the capital Seoul.

1627-1629

1627 In central India, Shivaji Bhonsle founded the Maratha kingdom, which was very powerful in north and south India during the 17th century.

1627 The Mughal emperor Shah Jahan succeeded his father Jahangir. For the last five years of his life Shah Jahan was imprisoned by his son Aurangzeb, with only his eldest daughter Jahanara Begum by his side. His room had a direct view of the Taj Mahal, a funeral monument he built for his wife. Shah Jahan was being punished for supporting Dara Shikoh, Aurangzeb's older brother, in the fight for succession.

1628 Huguenot power in France ended when they surrendered at La Rochelle, after the town had been surrounded and continuously attacked by French Catholic forces for 14 months.

1628 Dutch forces regained Malacca from the Portuguese and established themselves as the main European power in Java.

1629 The Italian architect Gian Lorenzo Bernini was given the task of completing St Peter's Basilica in Rome.

1629 The Holy Roman emperor Ferdinand II issued the Edict of Restitution, lifting the ban on Protestant institutions in Europe.

1629 Abbas, the shah of Persia, died and was succeeded by his grandson Safi I. He had most of his relatives killed, so there could be no claimant to the throne. Meanwhile, the Uzbeks captured Kandahar, the first capital of Afghanistan.

1629 The English Parliament was dissolved by Charles I, who for the following 11 years ruled without calling a Parliament.

1629 The Holy Roman emperor Ferdinand II and Christian IV of Denmark called a truce and signed the Treaty of Lübeck. According to the treaty, Denmark got back the duchy of Holstein and promised to keep out of Germany.

1629 Sweden and Poland agreed to end enmity with the Truce of Altmark.

▼ *From the beginning of its construction in 1506, St Peter's Basilica in Rome took over a century to be completed. Until 1989, it was the largest church in Christendom.*

1630–1631

▲ According to legend, Shah Jahan cut off the hands of the craftsmen involved in the construction of the Taj Mahal so that they could not make such a monument again.

1630 England called off its war against France and Spain.

1630 Venice was devastated by an epidemic of plague.

1630 New settlers arrived in North America and founded the towns of Boston, Roxbury, Lynn, Dorchester, Mystic and Watertown, in an area called the Massachusetts Bay Colony.

1630 The Diet of Segesovar elected George Rákóczi I to succeed Bethlen Gábor of Transylvania.

1630 Ottoman emperor Murad IV captured and destroyed the city of Hamadan after defeating the Persians.

1631 The Mughal emperor Shah Jahan built the Taj Mahal at Agra, India, in the memory of his wife Mumtaz Mahal.

1631 Cardinal Richelieu, the chief minister of France, sent troops to fight against the Hapsburgs of Germany as part of the Thirty Years War. France was unsuccessful and had to end the war by signing the Treaty of Barwalde.

1631 In the Thirty Years War, Catholic forces invaded the German Protestant town of Magdeburg, killed most of the population, and set fire to the place. The atrocity shocked Europe and led to demands for war to be fought according to an agreed set of rules.

1631 Swedish Lutherans defeated the Catholic League in the Battle of Breitenfeld. In late August that year, the Imperial Commander invaded Saxony in the hope of forcing the ruler of Saxony John George I to abandon an alliance he planned to conclude with the king of Sweden. The king responded by uniting his army with the elector's forces, hoping to fight the commander and force him to leave Saxony.

1631 The shipbuilding industry developed in North America due to the availability of cheap lumber. American ships were made at the shipbuilding yards in Boston as well as other coastal towns in Massachusetts, at half the cost of those made in England.

1631 Johannes Kepler became the first astronomer to predict the planetary passage of Venus.

1631 French mathematician Pierre Vernier invented the vernier scales for measuring lines and angles accurately.

1632 Maryland in North America was colonized by the Englishman Lord Baltimore. An agriculturally rich area close to the sea, Maryland attracted a lot of new settlers.

1632 French settlers colonized eastern Canada and named it Acadia, now Nova Scotia.

◀ *Built as a flagship and equipped with superior firepower, Swedish king Gustavus II's two-decker* Vasa *sank as she embarked on her first voyage in 1628. After over 300 years, the ship was recovered and placed at the Vasa Ship Museum in Stockholm, Sweden.*

1632 Sigismund III Vasa, King of Poland, died and was succeeded by his son Ladislas IV. The new king had to almost immediately deal with a Russian invasion.

1632 In the Thirty Years War, Gustavus II Adolphus of Sweden defeated the Catholic League led by General von Tilly. Tilly died and Gustavas captured Munich.

1632 Swedish forces led by Gustavus II Adolphus defeated the Catholics in the Battle of Lützen. Protestant Gustavus II Adolphus was killed at battle, as was Gottfried Heinrich, count of the Catholic Pappenheim.

1633 The Dutch trading post of Hartford was founded at the mouth of the Park River, a tributary of the Connecticut River in North America. The first settlement was established in 1635.

1633 Ladislas IV of Poland drove out Russian invaders attacking the Polish town of Smolensk.

1633 Italian astronomer Galileo Galilei was tried and tortured by the Inquisition in Rome for defending Polish astronomer Copernicus' theory about the Sun being the centre of the Universe and the Earth revolving around it.

... **FASCINATING FACT** ...

The first calculator was invented in 1640 by the French mathematician, physicist and philosopher Blaise Pascal. He was 19 years old when he invented a device called the Pascaline that could add and subtract, using wheels that were numbered 0 to 9 and a toothed wheel for the 1 in numbers greater than 9. Pascal invented the calculator to help his father, who was a tax collector in Rouen.

1634-1636

1634 Lake Michigan and the Wisconsin region of North America were discovered by the French explorer Jean Nicolet.

1634 Massachusetts Puritans founded the towns of Windsor and Wethersfield in Connecticut. The word 'Puritan' was applied to a number of Protestant churches from the late 1500s to the early 1700s. Puritans did not use the term for themselves, and the word described a type of religious innovation, rather than a particular church. The closest analogy in the present day to the meaning of 'Puritan' in the 17th century would be 'fundamentalist'.

1634 Poland and Russia called off their war with the Treaty of Polianov, according to which Russia gave up all the Polish territories that it had captured and Ladislas IV of Poland gave up his claim to the Russian throne.

1634 Kandahar was once again made part of the Mughal Empire when Shah Jahan defeated the Uzbeks of Central Asia and drove them out of Afghanistan.

1634 Dutch forces drove out the Spaniards from Curaçao and the French and English from St Eustatius, and established their control over these Caribbean islands.

1635 The Zaydi imams, who had been driven out of Yemen by the Ottoman Turks, restablished themselves as rulers of Yemen.

1635 Saxony withdrew from the Thirty Years War after signing the Peace of Prague with the Holy Roman emperor Ferdinand II. However, the war continued between the Hapsburgs of Germany and the combined French and Swedish forces.

1635 Ottoman sultan Murad IV invaded Persia and captured the towns of Erivan and Tabriz.

1635 The Portuguese monopoly over the sugar industry in Brazil ended when the Dutch established colonies and sugar plantations in northern Brazil.

1636 Sugar cane was introduced in Barbados by a Dutch planter. It slowly replaced cotton, ginger, indigo and tobacco to become the chief crop of this Caribbean island.

▼ *Widespread sugar cultivation in the Caribbean led to a rise in the African slave trade.*

1636-1637

1636 The Japanese people were forbidden from travelling abroad by the country's shogun. This began an increasing policy of isolation by the Japanese that would last over 200 years.

1636 The English colony of Providence was founded on Rhode Island by clergyman Roger Williams.

1636 The first North American institution providing higher education was established in Cambridge, Massachusetts. It later became Harvard College. Today Harvard University is the richest university in the United States. In 2004, it received $22.4 billion dollars in donations, nearly twice as much as its closest competitor, Yale.

1636 Dutch colonists established the town of Haarlem on Manhattan Island.

1636 Spanish forces in the Netherlands invaded northwestern France. The French halted the invasion and a lengthy war began.

1637 The French established trading posts along the Senegal River in Western Africa.

1637 The New Sweden Company was formed on the order of the Swedish queen Christina to establish colonies in North America.

1637 The Dutch drove Portuguese colonists out of Costa Rica and established forts along the coast.

1637 Ferdinand III was crowned Holy Roman emperor after the death of his father, Ferdinand II. He hoped to make peace with France and Sweden, but the war dragged on for 11 more years. It finally ended with the Peace of Westphalia and the Treaty of Münster with France and the Treaty of Osnabrück with Sweden. Ferdinand married three times. His first wife was his cousin, the Infanta Maria Anna of Spain, by whom he had two sons. Ferdinand IV, his eldest, died before his father, while Leopold succeeded him.

1637–1709 A series of weak rulers led to the decline of the Safavid dynasty. Its end came when the Ghalzai Afghans invaded Persia and occupied the city of Kandahar.

▲ *Founded in 1636, Harvard University is the oldest American institution for higher education.*

1637-1640

1637 Japanese shogun Iemitsu Tokugawa suppressed a revolt by the Christian peasants of Kyushu Island.

1637 North American tribesmen attacked and burned down the English town at Fort Mystic in Massachusetts.

1637 The first opera house, *Teatro San Cassiano*, opened in Venice. Most Venetian opera houses of the time were named after the nearest church. The *Teatro di San Cassiano* was no exception. Before the opening, most performances took place in the homes of the wealthy and the aristocracy. As its popularity grew, the Venetian nobility rented the box seats, while the public was admitted to the lower-level seating at a cheaper price. The theatre was owned by the Tron family.

1638 Mauritius was colonized by the Dutch and named after John Maurice of Nassau, the Dutch governor in Brazil.

1638 The New Sweden Company established Port Christina, now known as Wilmington, on the Delaware River.

1638 Ottoman sultan Murad IV defeated the Persian Safavids and regained Baghdad. Murad IV of Turkey was only five years old when his father died. He ascended the throne after the second dethronement of his insane uncle Mad Mustafa I. Over the next few years his mother Sultana Kösem ruled, but power was also held by the civil aristocracy and the military, who were mainly interested in their own advancement.

...FASCINATING FACT...
In 1621 the first Thanksgiving was celebrated in New England. A feast was organized with cod, sea bass, wild turkey, duck and goose. The Native Americans who participated in the feast brought popcorn, which the colonists had never eaten before.

1638 Growing mistrust of the king, Charles I, and the increasing influence of his ideas on the Scottish Church caused the Scottish Presbyterians to rise in protest.

1639 American-English settler Stephen Day printed and published *The Whole Book of Psalms Faithfully Translated Into English Metre*. It was the first book to be printed in New England.

1639 Charles I of England broke up the Scottish forces that had occupied Edinburgh Castle without any bloodshed, but the newly formed Scottish Parliament refused to accept English-influenced reforms to the Scottish Church.

1640 Ottoman sultan Murad IV died. His brother Ibrahim I succeeded him.

▼ *Edinburgh Castle is also the home of the one o'clock gun. It is fired every day at precisely 1:00 p.m., except on Sunday.*

1640-1642

1640 Thomas Wentworth, lord lieutenant of Ireland, gained the support of the Irish Parliament and led Irish troops against Scotland, in support of the English cause.

1640 Scottish forces defeated English forces loyal to King Charles I, captured the towns of Newcastle and Durham, and forced him to sign the Treaty of Ripon, whereby English taxes would be used to pay for the maintenance of the Scottish army.

1640 King Charles I freed the imprisoned members of Parliament and called for the English Parliament to meet again to approve new taxes.

1640 Portugal declared independence from Spain and elected João da Braganza as its ruler, while Spain was busy trying to put down a revolt in Catalonia.

1641 The English Parliament had the Archbishop of Canterbury, William Laud, imprisoned in the Tower of London for having used the Court of High Commission and Court of Star Chamber to harass and torture Presbyterians and Calvinsts. These special courts were also abolished.

1641 A peasant revolt in Ireland against their English landlords turned into a fight between the Catholics and Protestants, in which hundreds of Protestants lost their lives.

1641 The Dutch drove out the Portuguese from Malacca for the second time and established flourishing trade in the East Indies.

1641–1652 Buryat Mongols from Lake Baikal were defeated and brought under the control of the Russians.

1642–1643 The Pacific islands of New Guinea and New Ireland had their first Dutch visitors, led by Dutch explorer Abel Janszoon Tasman.

1642 Tibet was formed as a religious state under the leadership of Ngawang Lobsang Gyatso, the fifth Dalai Lama.

▲ *A map of Portugal and Spain. Portugal won independence from Spain in 1640 with French support, ending the so-called Sixty-Years Captivity.*

1642–1643

1642 Paul de Chomedey founded the French colony of Ville Marie, now known as Montreal, on the St Lawrence River in North America.

1642 Dutch explorer Abel Janszoon Tasman discovered Tasmania and named it Van Diemen's Land, after Anton Van Diemen, the governor-general of the Dutch East Indies.

1642 Abel Janszoon Tasman discovered New Zealand.

1642 Safi I, shah of Persia, died. He was succeeded by his son Abbas II.

1642 Civil war broke out in England. The issues were complex, but broadly the Anglican clergy, the landlords and the peasants supported Charles I, and the merchants, the noblemen and the middle classes supported Parliament.

1642 The chief minister of France, Cardinal Richelieu, died. He had dominated Louis XIII and ruled the country by proxy for 18 years. French bureaucracy at the time was populated by office-holders who had bought their positions to benefit from the social status attached. Called *noblesse de robe*, they were notorious for ignoring their duties. Richelieu replaced or bypassed many of these officials – primarily the tax officials – with intendants, who were paid directly by the crown and could be easily fired.

1642 The English Parliament ordered the closure of theatres, putting an end to the tradition of Elizabethan and Jacobean theatre in England.

1643 Louis XIII of France passed away and his son four-year-old son, Louis XIV, ascended the French throne.

1643 French forces defeated a combined force of Spanish, Dutch, Flemish and Italian soldiers in the Battle of Rocroi. France became the dominant military power in Europe.

1643 The English settlements of New Haven, Plymouth, Massachusetts and Connecticut came together to form the New England Confederation.

▲ *New Zealand (shown in the map) was called Aotearoa by the native Maori. Aotearoa means 'land of the long white cloud'.*

1643-1647

1643 Italian mathematician Evangelista Torricelli invented the barometer.

1644 Ming emperor Chongzhen committed suicide when Li Dzucheng, a bandit, captured Beijing. Li was eventually killed by the Ming general Wu San-kuei with the help of the Manchus.

1644 The Manchurians established the Ch'ing dynasty, the last great Chinese dynasty. They later extended the boundaries of their kingdom to include Tibet, parts of Mongolia, Nepal and Turkistan.

1644 In England, parliamentary forces led by Oliver Cromwell defeated the Cavaliers of Charles I in the Battle of Marston Moor.

1645 The English Civil War continued with Oliver Cromwell's parliamentary forces defeating the Cavaliers once again in the Battle of Naseby.

1645 In Europe's Thirty Years War, Swedish forces defeated an imperial army led by Count Matthias Gallas at Magdeburg, and won battles in Bohemia, Moravia and Bavaria.

▼ *The soldiers of the parliamentary side during the English Civil War were called Roundheads.*

▲ *English general Oliver Cromwell.*

1645 Russian Tsar Mikhail Romanov passed away and was succeeded by his son Alexis Mikhailovich.

1645 Ottoman Turks invaded Crete and captured it from the Venetians.

1646 Oliver Cromwell's parliamentary forces defeated the final army of Cavaliers, forcing King Charles I to surrender to the Scots and put an end to the Civil War in England.

1647 The Scots handed Charles I to the English Parliament, but he soon fled to the Isle of Wight and signed a secret treaty with the Scots. He promised to bring back Presbyterianism to Scotland in return for their help in defeating the English Parliament. Charles hoped to regain power in England, winning the civil war at the last moment.

····FASCINATING FACT····

In the English Civil War the soldiers on the parliamentary side were called Roundheads. The name was used by those on the king's side to describe their Puritan rivals who had closely cropped hair, instead of the court fashion of long curly locks. The king's soldiers were called Cavaliers, which denoted brave knights on horseback. The royalists retained this name until 1679, when it was replaced by the term Tory.

239

1647-1649

1647 English clergyman George Fox, who was unhappy with Puritanism, founded a religious group called the 'Friends of Truth' at Leicestershire. The members of this group were later called the Quakers.

1648 Several hundred Ukrainian Jews were killed by peasants belonging to the Greek Orthodox Church, for refusing to convert to Christianity.

1648 The Peace of Westphalia ended the Eighty Years' War between the Spaniards and the Dutch and the Thirty Years War between Germany, France and Sweden. A third of the population of Germany died.

1648 Polish king Ladislas IV died. He was succeeded by his brother John II Casimir.

1648 Civil war broke out in England for the second time. Scottish forces invaded England to support King Charles I and his cavalier forces. Oliver Cromwell defeated the Scots in the Battle of Preston.

1648 Charles I was arrested by the English Parliament for having signed a secret treaty with the Scots. He was tried for treason against England, found guilty, and beheaded the following year.

1648 The French nobility rose in revolt against Cardinal Mazarin, the prime minister of France. However, the uprising, which was called the Fronde, was badly organized and dragged on inconclusively for several years.

1648 Ottoman sultan Ibrahim was killed at Constantinople by the Janissaries, a special force belonging to the Ottoman army. They crowned Ibrahim's son Mohammed IV as the new Ottoman sultan.

1648 Nitric acid, widely used in making explosives, was invented by Dutch scientist Johann Glauber.

1649 Following the execution of Charles I, England became a republic and Oliver Cromwell was made the Lord Protector of the Commonwealth.

Oliver Cromwell came from a landowning class often called 'the gentry', which dominated the social and political life of the country. Until 1640, he played only a small role in local administration, with no major part in national politics.

◄ *Following the defeat of his Scottish supporters in the second Civil War, Charles I was tried for treason and condemned as a traitor. The execution was carried out on a scaffold.*

241

1649–1651

1649 Rebellions by Irish forces in Drogheda and Wexford were brutally put down by Oliver Cromwell.

1649 A new Fronde rebellion in France was led by the Duke of Beaufort, but Cardinal Mazarin, prime minister of France, defeated Beaufort.

1650 A bad harvest in Sweden resulted in one of the worst food shortages in the country's history.

1650 English forces defeated the Scottish royalist earl of Montrose, who had come from Europe with the intention of avenging Charles I's death. The English Parliament sentenced him to death by hanging. Montrose had signed the National Covenant in 1638, as part of an uprising to defend the Presbyterian Kirk against King Charles' attempts to impose Archbishop Laud's Prayer Book in Scotland.

1650 Charles II returned from Europe, where he had been hiding since Cromwell's election, and proclaimed himself king of England and Scotland with the support of the Scots. However, Oliver Cromwell defeated him in the Battle of Dunbar.

1650 The Portuguese were driven out of the trading port of Muscat, after occupying it for nearly 150 years, by Sultan bin Saif al-Ya'rubi. He was the founder of the Ya'rubid dynasty that ruled Oman until 1749.

1650 Following the arrest of the Great Condé, Duke of Beaufort and other Frondeurs, rebellion broke out yet again in France, aided by an army from the Spanish Netherlands. However, the rebels were defeated in the Battle of Blanc-Champ.

1650 Abbas II of Persia captured Kandahar from the Mughals.

1651 Charles II was crowned king of Scotland at Scone in Scotland, and then marched into England to claim the throne of that country. He was defeated by Oliver Cromwell in the Battle of Worcester. Charles was forced to flee to France in disguise.

1651 Fort St James was built by the English on the River Gambia to develop trade with areas in the interior of western Africa.

◀ *Oliver Cromwell led the charge on the rebellious forces in the battle at Drogheda, Ireland. It was marked by large-scale massacre of the town's inhabitants, estimated at over 3000.*

1651-1654

1651 Cardinal Mazarin was dismissed and had to flee the country, but he returned later in the year with German troops to defeat the Great Condé and his rebels.

▼ France was the fashion trend-maker in 17th-century Europe.

1651 Ietsuna succeeded his father Iemitsu as the shogun of Japan. He ruled for 29 years and ruined the country's economy.

1651 The English Parliament passed the Navigation Act, forbidding ships belonging to other countries from docking in English ports and conducting trade in England. This angered the Dutch and led to the Anglo-Dutch War.

1652 The Dutch East India Company colonized Cape Town in South Africa.

1652 France was in political chaos due to the fight between the parliamentary Frondeurs led by the Great Condé and the royalists. Anne Marie Louise d'Orléans, duchess of Montpensier, helped the rebels enter Paris and establish a government, but the peasants helped Louis XIV to enter the city.

1653 Albemarle was founded by English settlers from Virginia in the area now known as North Carolina.

1653 The French Fronde was suppressed by the royalists and Cardinal Mazarin returned to Paris.

1653 The Instrument of Government was drawn up to lay down the guidelines by which the English Commonwealth would be administered and ruled. Oliver Cromwell was formally proclaimed Lord Protector of the Commonwealth of England, Scotland and Ireland.

1654 The English defeated the Dutch and ended the two-year Anglo-Dutch War with the Treaty of Westminster.

1654 Queen Christina of Sweden resigned from her post and joined the Catholic Church in Rome. She was succeeded by her cousin Charles X Gustavus. Earlier, in 1648, as commander of the Swedish army in Germany, Charles had participated in the last phase of the Thirty Years War. The war was concluded in 1948 with the signing of the Peace of Westphalia.

. . . FASCINATING FACT . . .

As early as the 16th and 17th centuries, European fashion followed examples set by the French court. Styles popularized by Louis XIII and Louis XIV were adopted by all French subjects and even in England. Louis III could not grow a long beard, so he began the style of a small chin tuft. It soon became popular and replaced the long stiff beards that had previously been fashionable. Louis XIV used tall and elaborate wigs to increase his height and this too became fashionable, replacing the long natural locks both men and women used to wear earlier.

1654-1657

1654 Russia declared war on Poland in order to gain control over Ukraine. Alexis I Mikhailovich, Tsar of Russia, captured Smolensk.

1654 Portugal regained its colonies in Brazil, which the Dutch had captured from them.

1655 Catholics and Anglicans were suppressed by the Puritan government of Cromwell. England was divided into 12 districts that were placed under harsh military forces to keep law and order.

1655 Charles X Gustavus of Sweden invaded Poland and captured Polish areas along the Baltic Sea.

1655 England occupied Jamaica to use it as a centre for their slave trade and as a base from where they could attack and raid Spanish colonies and ships.

1656 In the First Northern War, Swedish forces defeated Poland at the Battle of Warsaw.

1656 João IV of Portugal died and was succeeded by his son Afonso VI Braganza.

1656 Portuguese colonists in Sri Lanka were driven away by the Dutch.

1656 The first pendulum clock was invented by Christian Huygens, the Dutch mathematician-physicist. He was inspired by Galileo's study of pendulum movement in the cathedral of Pisa, famous for its leaning tower.

1657 Thousands of people died in a great fire that destroyed the Japanese capital city Edo. Fire was so frequent here that it was called 'Flower of Edo' or *Edo no hana*. The fires swept through the city, erasing vast tracts. Districts in Nihonbashi were destroyed by fire three times during the Meiji period. Companies of fire fighters were formed whose primary mission was to starve the fire of fuel. They would pull down houses and open up fire lanes to prevent the fire from spreading. In the late Edo period when the city had about a million residents, there were around 14,000 professional firemen.

◄ *The Leaning Tower of Pisa's uneven setting caused it to lean 4.5 m from the perpendicular.*

1657 Swedish king Charles X Gustavus was driven out of Poland by the combined forces of the Holy Roman emperor Ferdinand III and Poland.

1657 The Holy Roman emperor Ferdinand III died. He was succeeded by his son Leopold I.

1657 Charles X Gustavus of Sweden invaded Denmark to increase his control over the Baltic coast, but he was defeated and driven out.

1658 The combined forces of English and French troops defeated Spanish support to the Fronde in the Battle of the Dunes at Dunkirk.

1658 Oliver Cromwell, the Lord Protector of the Commonwealth of England, Scotland and Ireland, died. He was succeeded by his son Richard Cromwell.

1658 Aurangzeb took over the Mughal throne and imprisoned his father Shah Jahan. He was a Sunni Muslim and did not tolerate other religions. Mughal literature and arts declined during his reign.

1659 Richard Cromwell broke up the new English Parliament on the orders of the army, but he was forced to resign

◀ *Charles II claimed the crown of England after years of exile during the Puritan movement.*

by the Rump Parliament, a smaller group of parliamentary members. Civil war threatened to break out in England as the rivalry between royalists and parliamentarians began once again.

1659 France and Spain signed the Treaty of the Pyrenees, according to which the fortresses of Flanders and Artois and parts of Rousillon, Contans, Cerdagne, Hainault and Luxembourg became French territory. It was also agreed that Princess Maria Theresa of Spain would be engaged to Louis XIV of France.

1660 Charles X Gustavus of Sweden died. He was succeeded by his son Charles XI. The new king ended Sweden's war with Denmark by signing the Treaty of Copenhagen and the Northern War against Poland was ended with the Treaty of Oliva.

▲ *Samuel Pepys, a confidante of Charles II and later also of James II, is best known for his* Diary. *It relates the life and times of London during Charles II's reign.*

1660 Charles II was crowned king of England after agreeing to accept key concessions to Parliament. England returned to peace as a constitutional monarchy.

1661-1665

◀ *Louis XIV, also known as Louis The Great and The Sun King ruled France for 72 years. It was he who transformed Versailles into a grand and extravagant royal palace.*

1661 Louis XIV gained complete control of France after the death of Cardinal Mazarin, his dominating prime minister. Thereon the king decided not to appoint a new prime minister.

1662 The marriage of Charles II of England and Catherine of Braganza, Princess of Portugal, led to the two countries forming a strong and long-lasting partnership. The Portuguese colonies of Tangiers and Bombay were given to Charles.

1662 Following the death of Shun Chih, founder of the Manchurian Ch'ing dynasty in China, his son Hsuan Yeh came to power. The new king was friendly towards Christian missionaries and deeply interested in the cultural development of his kingdom.

1662 English philosopher and scientist Robert Boyle formulated the famous Boyle's Law, which stated that the volume of a gas is inversely proportional to its pressure.

1663 The English Parliament passed the Second Navigation Act, whereby English colonists could no longer trade with other European countries and all ships carrying European goods had to be unloaded and repacked in England. This meant that they were forced to pay export duties.

1663 Amsterdam was struck by a terrible epidemic of the plague.

1664 England gained control of New Netherlands, which was renamed New York.

1665 English colonist Philip Carteret founded New Jersey and made Elizabethtown its capital.

1665 London was struck by its last big epidemic of plague, known as the Great Plague. About 15 per cent of the population died.

1665 The second Anglo-Dutch war began when the Royal Navy defeated a Dutch fleet off Lowestoft.

...FASCINATING FACT...

In the 1600s medical science was rudimentary and most people could not afford to go to hospitals or doctors, so they just went to witches or quacks (unqualified doctors) for treatment. Some of the remedies suggested by these 'doctors' were bizarre. The bite of a mad dog could be treated if the patient held the key to a church door. A dead mole hung on the neck could prevent toothache, while wearing shoes lined with tansy leaves and eating a pill made of spider's webs was said to cure malaria.

1665-1667

1665 Philip IV, King of Spain, died. His young son Don Carlos ascended the Spanish throne. As Charles II, the new king proved to be an ineffective ruler, he was the last Habsburg ruler of Spain.

1666 The city of London was destroyed in a great fire. The fire started in the house and shop of Thomas Farynor, King Charles II's baker in Pudding Lane. Farynor forgot to douse the fire in his oven the previous night and sparks that fell on the firewood stacked nearby caught flame. Three hours later, the house and shop were on fire. Farynor, his wife and daughter and one servant escaped by climbing through an upstairs window. A maid who was too scared to climb out became the first victim of the fire.

1666 The English colonies at Antigua, Montserrat and St Kitts in the Antillean Islands were captured by the French. They had joined with Holland, Brunswick, Brandenburg and Denmark, and declared war against England.

1666 English mathematician and Cambridge University professor Isaac Newton formulated calculus, a branch of mathematics used when the values being calculated keep varying. Calculus is used to solve engineering problems and astronomical calculations.

1666 Isaac Newton devised the law of gravity.

1667 The French professor of science and mathematics, Jean Baptiste Denis, attempted blood transfusion in humans for the first time when he transferred lamb's blood into the veins of a sick boy. The patient was said to have been cured.

1667 Russia and Poland ended their war with the Treaty of Andrussovo, which gave Smolensk to Russia.

1667 The second Anglo-Dutch war ended with the inconclusive Treaty of Breda.

1667 France began the War of Devolution with Spain to gain control of the Spanish Netherlands.

1667 Shah Abbas II of Persia passed away and was succeeded by his eldest son Suleiman I.

▼ *The Great Fire of London is recorded as the worst fire in the city's history. The four-day blaze ravaged a large part of the city.*

1668-1672

1668 Jesuit missionaries from France founded Sault Sainte Marie between Lake Superior and Lake Huron. It was the first permanent European settlement in Michigan, North America.

1668 Poet, playwright and critic John Dryden became England's first literary personality to be honoured with the title of Poet Laureate.

1668 The War of Devolution ended with Spain and France signing the Treaty of Aix-la-Chapelle. France gained Lille, Tournay, Oudenaarde and other provinces in the Spanish Netherlands.

1668 John II Casimir of Poland resigned. Michael Wisniowiecki of Lithuania succeeded him to the Polish throne.

◄ In 1668, architect Louis Le Vau began to reconstruct the Palace of Versailes

1669 The Hanseatic League held its last meeting. This association of 150 trading cities collapsed due to internal disputes in Germany and rivalry from Britain and Holland.

1669 Three million people died during a famine in Bengal, India.

1670 Frederick III of Denmark died. His son Christian V ascended the Dutch throne. He was a popular ruler and continued his father's practice of allowing Danish commoners into state service.

1670 Charles II of England and Louis XIV of France signed the Treaty of Dover. It was an agreement stating England's support to France against the Dutch in return for a secret French subsidy ending Charles II's financial dependence on the Parliament.

1672 Puritans from Bermuda founded Charleston, South Carolina. It was named after Charles II, King of England.

1672 In the West Indies, Grenada came under French rule. Grenada remained under French rule until 1762, when it was captured by British forces.

...FASCINATING FACT...

The Janissaries were a special army belonging to the Ottoman Turkish Empire. The members of this army were chosen at a young age from Christian families in the Balkans. Once chosen, they had to break ties with their families and undergo strict training. Their influence grew during the 15th and 16th centuries, and by the 17th century their power had increased so much that they practically controlled the Ottoman throne. In 1826 the Janissary army was wiped out when Sultan Mahmud II bombarded their barracks in Constantinople.

1672-1675

1672 An army of 100,000 French troops invaded Holland with the help of the English Navy. The Dutch fleet were defeated at Southwold Bay.

1672 Ottoman Turks and Polish forces began a four-year war for the control of Ukraine.

1673 Louis XIV of France was prevented from capturing Amsterdam when Dutch nobleman William III of Orange came to the rescue of the city.

1673 New York and Delaware were regained by Dutch forces, only to be returned to the English the next year, under the Treaty of Westminster.

1673 A French mission arrived at the Ayudhya court in Thailand with letters from Pope Clement IX and Louis XIV, requesting permission to send missionaries.

1674 Louis XIV invaded the Palatinate in Germany, causing the Holy Roman Empire and Spain to join the Netherlands in the war against France.

1674 Following the death of the Polish king Michael Wisniowiecki, Poland's general John Sobieski ascended the throne. Sobieski had defeated the Ottoman Turks the previous year. In 1683 he signed a treaty with the Holy Roman emperor Leopold I. He defeated the Turkish army at Vienna, but his campaign for liberating Moldavia and Walachia from Turkish rule failed. Rebellion within his own family considerably weakened the Polish Empire and later led to its downfall.

1675 English scientist, designer and astronomer Christopher Wren was appointed to construct a new St Paul's Cathedral in London to replace the earlier structure that had been burned down in the Great Fire of 1666.

1675 The French East India Company established its first trading post at Surat, in India, and in the following year their second post was established at Bombay.

1675 The French forces defeated the Dutch at Turkheim.

▼ *Designed by Christopher Wren,*
St Paul's Cathedral in London took
40 years to build.

1675-1677

1675 Swedish forces invaded Brandenburg in support of King Louis XIV, but were defeated by Frederick William, elector of Brandenburg, in the Battle of Fehrbellin.

1675 Native tribes in New England led by King Philip – whose original name was Metacomet – raided 52 settlements and killed nearly 600 colonists in a revolt against being forced to pay an annual tribute (tax).

1675 Dutch microscopist Antonie van Leeuwenhoek became the first person to observe bacteria and protozoa with the help of his simple microscope. He also observed blood corpuscles, capillaries and the structure of nerves and muscles.

1676 Philip Carteret, founder of New Jersey, gave the western part of the New Jersey settlement to English Quaker immigrants.

1676 Alexis, the Tsar of Russia, died. Fyodor III ascended the throne. Although he was partially paralyzed since birth, he proved to be an able ruler.

1676 Poland had to end its war with the Ottoman Turks by signing the Treaty of Zuravno, according to which the Ottomans got a large part of Podolia and the Polish Ukraine.

▼ *Antonie van Leeuwenhoek made simple and small hand-held microscopes that let him observe objects magnified over 275 times.*

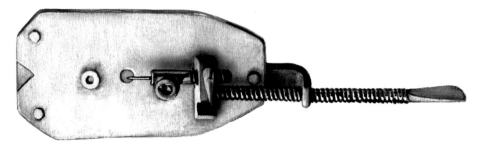

▶ *The Royal Greenwich Observatory was originally founded by King Charles II of England.*

1676 The death of King Philip (Metacomet) ended the war in New England. Philip was beheaded and his head was on display for 25 years. Most of the surviving Wampanoag people were sold off as slaves.

1676 Increasing enmity between the Native Americans and the Virginia colonists led to attacks on tribesmen. Jamestown colonist Nathaniel Bacon organized the attacks and many of the tribesman were forced to flee. 'Bacon's Rebellion' was not condoned by the governor of Virginia, and ended when Bacon died.

1676 The Observatory at Greenwich, England, was established to study the position of planets and develop a standard system of calculating time.

1677 French forces took control of the Dutch trading posts in Senegal and the island of Gorée, which was an important centre for the slave trade.

1677–1681

1677 Colonists in North Carolina protested against the English Navigation Acts under the leadership of John Culpeper. These acts restricted their freedom of trade.

1678 French Franciscan missionary Louis Hennepin discovered the Niagara Falls. They are situated on the United States-Canadian border, divided by Goat Island into the Horseshoe Falls and the American Falls.

1678–1679 The Franco-Dutch war was ended by the signing of the Treaties of Nijmegen. In the treaty, the French agreed to suspend the anti-Dutch tariff of 1667 and to return Maastricht. France also gained certain regions from Spain that strengthened its northeastern border.

▼ *A Franciscan missionary called Louis Hennepin discovered the Niagara Falls in the 17th century. The word Niagara means 'thunder of waters'.*

1680 Franciscan missionary Father Hennepin and French explorer Sieur de La Salle established the colony at St Anthony's Falls in the upper Mississippi Valley. It is now known as Minneapolis.

1680–1692 The Pueblos of New Mexico, North America, revolted and drove out nearly 2500 Spanish colonists.

1680 The peasants of Bohemia joined in a major revolt against the feudal system. The troops of Hapsburg emperor Leopold I suppressed the rebellion and the leaders were executed.

1680 Ietsuna, the Japanese Tokugawa shogun, died. He was succeeded by his brother Tsunayoshi, who promoted Neo-Confucianism in Japan. His reign is considered one of the most prosperous and peaceful periods in Japanese history.

1681 Pennsylvania was founded by William Penn, with the permission of Charles II, King of England. Penn was a Quaker and therefore encouraged European Protestants such as the Amish *(see page 270)*, Baptists, Mennonites and Quakers to immigrate to his colony in North America.

1681 The Ch'ing dynasty under Emperor K'ang-hsi established their control over the entire Chinese mainland by defeating the last three feudal states that had held out against them. K'ang-hsi also checked Russian expansion by signing the Treaty of Nerchinsk.

1681 Tartar provinces beside the Volga River were captured by the Russians and their inhabitants were forcibly converted to Christianity.

1681-1683

◄ *The sedan chair was carried on a pair of poles. In the 17th and 18th centuries, the sedan became an object of luxury in England, France and Italy.*

1681 The Languedoc Canal was constructed in France to connect the Atlantic Ocean with the Mediterranean Sea.

1681 Louis XIV moved the French court to the grand palace he had built in Versailles. The move completed the process begun by Louis XIII in 1624 which gave absolute power to the king. Nobles had to live at Versailles in return for position and wealth, so the king could control them.

1682 English colonist William Penn founded the city of Philadelphia.

1682 Frenchman Sieur de La Salle explored the Mississippi Valley and claimed it for France. He named the entire territory Louisiana, after King Louis XIV.

1682 Fyodor III of Russia passed away. His mentally handicapped brother Ivan became the Tsar of Russia.

1682 Austria and Poland went to war against the Ottoman Turks to free Hungary from their control.

1682 Peter I, also known as Peter the Great, was crowned the joint Tsar of Russia with his 16-year-old brother, Ivan. Because Peter was ony nine years old, his 25-year-old sister Sophia became regent for the brothers and ruled on their behalf.

1683 The Ch'ing dynasty took control of the island of Taiwan, making it part of Chinese territory. After the establishment of Ch'ing rule in Taiwan, immigration from Chinese mainland into Taiwan increased greatly.

1683 The 'Rye House plot' to assasinate Charles II of England was foiled and its conspirators were executed. The plot was named after the Rye House at Hoddeston, Hertfordshire, where Charles was supposed to be killed. His unexpected early departure foiled the plot. The main plotters were Lord William Russell, Algernon Sidney, James Scott, Arthur Capel, Robert Ferguson, Lord William Howard and Sir Thomas Armstrong.

1683 Spain and the Holy Roman emperor Leopold I joined Holland and Sweden in their war against Louis XIV.

. . . **FASCINATING FACT**. . .

Manchu women celebrated New Year's Eve by going for walks with groups of friends. The ritual of 'walking away sickness' was done in the belief that this could prevent illness in the New Year. The walk was also an opportunity to show off their new clothes and beautifully embroidered shoes. The silk shoes were stitched on to wooden platforms to prevent them from getting dirty.

1683–1685

1683 Afonso VI of Portugal died. Afonso's brother Pedro II ascended the Portuguese throne having already grabbed power in a coup.

1683 An Ottoman attack on Vienna failed due to German and Polish troops coming to the aid of the city. Viennese bakers invented a new pastry to celebrate: the croissant.

1683 Germantown, the first German settlement in America, was founded in Philadelphia by Mennonites from Germany. Development of handicraft industries such as weaving, tanning and wagon building led to prosperity.

1684 The English East India Company established their first trading post in China at Canton, after having traded in Chinese goods for nearly 80 years through Java.

1684 Louis XIV and the Holy Roman emperor Leopold I declared truce and Louis XIV was allowed to keep all the territories he had captured until then.

1684 French explorer Sieur de La Salle set sail from France with a fleet of four ships to establish a colony at the mouth of the Mississippi River. He was unable to locate Mississippi and landed in Matagorda Bay, Texas.

1685 Louis XIV of France issued the Edict of Fontainebleau, which cancelled the Edict of Nantes. The new edict ordered the destruction of Huguenot Churches and closing of Protestant schools.

1685 The king of England, Charles II, died, after converting to the Catholic faith on this deathbed. His Catholic brother James II succeeded him.

1685 James, duke of Monmouth, laid claim to the English throne with the help of Baroness Wentworth, the Earl of Argyll and other supporters. Monmouth was an illegitimate son of Charles II and a firm Protestant. He was defeated in the Battle of Sedgemoor and executed.

1685 More than 50,000 French Huguenot families left France and settled in Holland, South Africa, North America, Denmark, the Protestant German states and England. The economic dislocation this caused in France badly affected government finances.

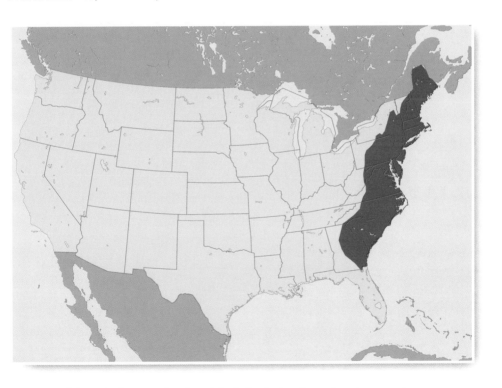

▲ *A map of the United States after the original 13 colonies, shown in red, were redrawn.*

1686–1689

1686 Holy Roman emperor Leopold I, Carlos II of Spain, Charles XI of Sweden and the electors of Bavaria, Saxony and the Palatine came together to form the League of Augsburg to fight against France. The War of the League of Augsburg started in 1688, when the elector of the Palatine died. Louis XIV claimed that he should rule the Palatine, but Leopold I disagreed and mobilized his armies. French forces crossed the river Rhine and captured key German towns.

1686 In India, the city of Calcutta (now Kolkata) was founded by Job Charnock, an administrator in the East India Company.

1687 Religious freedom was granted to the English and Scots through the Declaration of Liberty of Conscience, issued by James II. Despite this, James secretly laid plans to make his kingdoms firmly Catholic.

1687 Charles of Lorraine defeated the Ottoman Turks in the second Battle of Mohács. This victory allowed Leopold I of Austria to take over Hungary, a kingdom his family had inherited 150 years earlier.

1687 Venetian troops took control of the Peloponnesian islands and Athens from the Ottoman Turks.

1687 Following defeats by Christian states, Ottoman sultan Mohammed IV was imprisoned by his elite troops, the Janissaries. His brother Suleiman II ascended the Ottoman throne. During his reign the Turks successfully opposed an Austrian advance into Serbia and crushed an uprising in Bulgaria.

1688 England's 'Glorious Revolution' led to the removal of James II from power. The move replaced Roman Catholic rule in England with Protestant rule when they invited James' daughter Mary and her husband William of Orange to occupy the English throne. The new monarchs introduced important democratic reforms.

1688 Austrians drove the Ottoman forces out of Belgrade after a 21-day attack. The Ottomans, however, captured back the city in 1690.

1689 The French colony of Fort Prudhomme near Hatchie River in Tennessee, USA, was destroyed by Native Americans.

1689 William III of England joined forces with the League of Augsburg in its fight against Louis XIV.

▼ *Mary II and her Dutch husband, William III.*

1689–1691

▲ *James II's attempt at winning back the English throne was repelled at the Battle of the Boyne.*

1689 William and Mary of England were invited to accept the Scottish throne. The Jacobite party revolted against the new king under the leadership of the Viscount of Dundee. The Jacobite threat was ended with the killing of Dundee. They wanted to see the exiled James II and his descendants restored to the throne.

1689 Russia and China declared a truce and Russia returned all the Chinese territories it had captured, according to the terms of the Treaty of Nerchinsk.

1690 Mennonite clergyman William Rittenhouse set up North America's first paper mill at Germantown in Pennsylvania.

1690 French forces defeated the English fleet in the Battle of Beachy Head. On land, the prince of Waldek was defeated by the French in the Battle of Fleurus.

1690 William III of England landed in Ireland and fought the exiled James II in the Battle of the Boyne. The battle was fought on the banks of the river Boyne. William III's 35,000 troops defeated the 21,000 troops of James II, forcing him to flee the country.

1690 Bulgaria, Serbia, Transylvania and Belgrade were recaptured by the Ottoman Turks from the Austrians.

1691 French troops led by Marshal Louis-Francois de Boufflers beseiged the Spanish-occupied town of Mons in the Low Countries. The city later surrendered.

1691 William III's troops defeated the Jacobite Earl of Lucan, established control over Limerick, the only province that had resisted the Protestant army after the Battle of Boyne. The Irish rebellion was finally ended with the Treaty of Limerick.

1691 Ottoman Sultan Suleiman II died, and his brother Ahmed II succeeded him. His reign was marked by continuous war with the Holy League comprising Austria, Poland and Venice.

1691 The Ottoman Turks were defeated by Louis of Baden in the Battle of Szcelankemen.

...FASCINATING FACT...
The popular French bakery roll, the croissant, owes its origins to the Ottoman attack on Vienna in 1683. It is believed that Viennese bakers baked this light and delicious crescent-shaped roll, resembling the crescent on the Turkish flag, to celebrate Austria's victory over the Turks.

1692–1694

1692 A combined English and Dutch fleet defeated the French fleet at the Battle of La Hogue. France lost 15 powerful ships of the line in the battle.

1692 France defeated England in the Battle of Steenkirk.

1692–1693 Spanish forces suppressed the Native Americans of the New Mexican pueblos and took control of the area once again.

1693 French naval forces defeated an Anglo-Dutch fleet off Cape St Vincent and defeated a British fleet in the Battle of Lagos.

1693 Swiss Mennonite bishop Jakob Ammann founded the Amish sect, which settled in Pennsylvania in the 1700s. After 1850, they split into Old Order and New Order. The Old Order Amish spread in Ohio, Indiana, Kansas, Illinois and Iowa.

1694 The Bank of England was established in London and was given the status of the most important financial institution in England.

Often called the 'old lady of Threadneedle Street', the bank started with a capital of 12 million pounds. In exchange for the loan of its entire capital to the government, the bank received the right to issue notes and a monopoly on corporate banking in England. The bank introduced reforms that gave England the world's first modern finance sytem, and thus was more stable than most others.

1694 The French ports of Dieppe, Le Havre and Dunkirk were bombed by the Royal English Navy.

1694 Suleiman, the shah of Persia, died and his son Hussein ascended the Persian throne.

1694–1778 French writer Francois Voltaire lived during this period. He is considered to be one of the greatest French writers. *Candide* is his best-known work.

1694 Mary II, Queen of England and Scotland, died of smallpox. She had no children, so the throne passed to her husband, William III.

▲ *Sovereign-weighing machines at the Bank of England. Sovereigns are gold coins valued at 20 silver shillings.*

1695-1698

1695 The war between the League of Augsburg and France continued with France destroying Brussels, and England capturing Namur from the French.

1695 Ottoman sultan Ahmed II died and his nephew Mustapha II ascended the throne. He renewed the war against Christian Austria.

1696 The English parliament passed a new Navigation Act, forbidding English American colonies from exporting directly to Ireland or Scotland.

1696 John III Sobieski, King of Poland, died. Frederick, the elector of Saxony, was elected to the Polish throne the following year. He assumed the name of Augustus II and ruled for 37 years. Augustus' invasion of Livonia started the Second Northern War. During his reign, Poland declined from the position of a major European power to a protectorate of Russia.

1696 Spaniards established a colony at Pensacola in Florida.

1697 Charles XI of Sweden died. His son Charles XII succeeded him. He promoted important domestic reforms. His disastrous invasion of Russia, however, marked the end of Sweden's status as a major power.

1697 The Ottoman Turks, led by Sultan Mustafa II, faced a crushing defeat in the Battle of Zenta against Austria. This victory made Austria the leading power in central Europe.

1697 The War of the League of Augsburg ended after 11 years with the Treaty of Ryswick. France surrendered Freiburg, Breisach and Philippsburg to Germany. Spain was given Catalonia and the fortresses of Mons, Courtrai and Luxembourg. Louis XIV recognized William III as the king of England and promised to provide no further assistance to the exiled James II.

1698 The London Stock Exchange was established. Although other European cities like Antwerp had organized trading houses, the exchange at London was the first of its kind in the world.

▲ *The London Stock Exchange became a public limited company in 1991.*

1698 The first steam engine was designed and made by English engineer Thomas Savery. The engine was made to pump out water from coal mines, though the idea was later adapted to other purposes.

1699-1700

1699 Sikh leader Guru Gobind Singh formed the Sikh army, the Khalsa, to protect Sikhs from Mughal emperor Aurangazeb's cruelty.

1699 Christian V of Denmark died. He was succeeded by his son Frederick IV.

1699 The Swedish Empire was divided between Denmark, Russia, Poland and Saxony according to the Treaty of Preobrazhenskoe.

▲ *Although French missionaries managed to settle in parts of North America, French colonization of the region was not a success.*

1699 The Ottoman Empire ended its war against the Holy League of Austria, Poland, Russia and Venice with the Treaty of Carlowitz. The Turks had to surrender most of Hungary, Transylvania, Croatia, Slavonia, Dalmatia and some parts of Ukraine.

1699 Middle Plantation (now Williamsburg) was made the new capital of the Virginia colony, in North America, after Jamestown was destroyed in a fire the preceding year.

1699 French missionaries founded Cahokia, the first permanent settlement in Illinois.

1699 English adventurer and explorer William Dampier explored the west coast of Australia and discovered the Pacific island of New Britain.

1700 Carlos II died in Spain without leaving any children. Philip of Anjou, grandson of Louis XIV, claimed the Spanish throne. However, the throne was also claimed by Charles of Austria and Joseph of Bavaria. The War of the Spanish Succession between the three men divided Europe and lasted for 11 years.

1700 In India, the Mughal Empire under Aurangzeb's reign was weakened by continuous rebellions.

1700 Russia, Poland and Denmark came together to put down the powerful state of Sweden. Charles XII of Sweden forced Denmark to give up the fight by signing the Treaty of Travendal.

...FASCINATING FACT...

Although popularly considered to be Japanese in origin, the martial art karate developed in the 17th century on the island of Okinawa, a part of the Ryukyu Islands to the south of Japan and very close to China. It was, in fact, the island's location that led to the development of karate. Throughout its history, the island was attacked by the Chinese and the Japanese. Since ordinary people were not supposed to carry weapons, the people of Okinawa developed a new martial art to defend themselves.

275

◀ *Queen Anne, who reigned over England from 1702 until 1714, was the last Stuart monarch. Her reign was marked by conflicts in parliament and the War of the Spanish Succession.*

1701 England, Denmark and the Holy Roman emperor Leopold I opposed the succession of Philip V to the throne of Spain. They formed the Grand Alliance, and gathered a large army in the Netherlands to invade France.

1701 James II, the deposed king of England, died. His son claimed to be James III, but never occupied his throne. He was known as the Old Pretender.

1701 English agriculturist and inventor Jethro Tull revolutionized farming by the invention of the horse-drawn hoe and seeding drill. He also stressed the use of manure and the importance of breaking up the soil into small particles.

1702 William III of England died. His sister-in-law Anne succeeded him. She was the last Stuart monarch.

1701 The French fort of Pontchartrain was established, at the site that is modern-day Detroit. This was to prevent the English taking control of the Great Lakes region of North America.

1701 Frederick I, elector of Brandenburg, enlarged his territories and obtained a treaty from Emperor Leopold I that promoted him to the position of king of Prussia. Through this treaty, Prussia was obliged to support Austria in military and imperial matters.

1702 English and American colonists fought against the French, the Native tribes and the Spanish in Queen Anne's War, an extension of England's war against France in the War of the Spanish Succession.

1703 English clergyman John Wesley, the co-founder of Methodist church, was born.

1703 Peter the Great, tsar of Russia, founded the fort at the city of St Petersburg. The city remained the capital of Russia for two centuries. The city has been renamed thrice since its founding. It was renamed Petrograd in 1914 and Leningrad in 1924. Its original name was restored in 1991, six months before the breakup of the Soviet Union. Its grand palaces and cathedrals make St Petersburg one of the most beautiful cities in Europe.

1704 North America's first newspaper, *The Boston News-Letter*, was published.

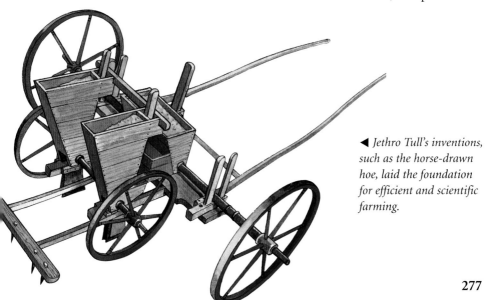

◄ *Jethro Tull's inventions, such as the horse-drawn hoe, laid the foundation for efficient and scientific farming.*

277

1704-1711

▲ *One of the first cast-iron bridges was built by using Abraham Darby's technique.*

1704 The Duke of Marlborough led the Grand Alliance to victory over French forces in the Battle of Schellenberg.

1704 Peter the Great of Russia defeated the Swedish led by Charles XII and conquered Narva.

1706 In the Great Northern War, Charles XI of Sweden defeated Augustus of Poland and Saxony. Charles forced him to sign the Treaty of Altranstadt, whereby Augustus gave up the Polish throne, though he returned in 1709.

1706 In the War of the Spanish Succession, forces led by the Duke of Marlborough defeated the French in the Battle of Ramillies and occupied the Spanish Netherlands.

1707 The Act of Union amalgamated the kingdoms of England and Scotland to form Great Britain.

1708 Combined British, Hanoverian, Prussian and Dutch forces, led by John Churchill, duke of Marlborough, defeated the French, led by Marshal Louis-Joseph, in the Battle of Oudenaarde. The battle was fought between the allied army of 80,000 men and 85,000 French troops. The French troops were caught off guard while trying to seize Oudenaarde. The allied army crossed the Schelde river and attacked the French forces. About 6000 French forces were killed and wounded, and 9000 captured. The allied army lost about 4000 men.

1709 The English trading post at Thanlyin, Burma, was established.

1709 Englishman Abraham Darby discovered that iron ore could be smelted using coke, to produce pig iron. Coke was superior in cost and efficiency by establishing furnaces that were much larger than is possible with using charcoal as fuel. The iron from his establishment was later used for building a cast-iron bridge and for the first locomotive with a high-pressure boiler. Iron became much cheaper to produce and became a key factor in the Industrial Revolution.

1709 The Swedish army's invasion of Poltava was crushed by Peter the Great of Russia. Charles XIV of Sweden fled to Moldavia. His infantry was completely destroyed, and his cavalry surrendered to the Russians.

1711 The Russians and Turks signed the Treaty of Pruth, which saw Russia return land around the Black Sea.

1711 North American tribes and North Carolina planters fought the Tuscarora Indian War.

1711 The War of the Spanish Succession saw all sides exhausted by the fighting and peace talks began.

▼ *British inventor Thomas Newcomen's (1663–1729) steam engine, which used atmospheric pressure, was a forerunner of James Watt's engine.*

279

◀ *The celebrated* Gulliver's Travels *by Jonathan Swift (1667–1745) depicted the voyages of its hero, set amid fantastical settings. It is regarded as a masterpiece of parody.*

1713 The Russian capital was shifted to St Petersburg from Moscow.

1714 The War of the Spanish Succession and the Queen Anne's War were ended with the Peace of Utrecht. France signed treaties with Britain, Prussia, the Dutch Republic, Portugal and Savoy, and was forced to surrender several territories, including some in Canada, to Britain. France also recognized Queen Anne of Britain, Frederick I and Victor Amadeus II of Sicily. Spain gave Gibraltar to Britain and also gave the British the exclusive right to supply African slaves in Spanish colonies for 30 years. French nobleman Philip of Anjou became king of Spain.

1712 Swiss-French philosopher Jean-Jacques Rousseau was born. His *Confessions* is one of the most famous autobiographies.

1713 Frederick William I became the king of Prussia. He built a strong army and carried out economic reforms. He freed serfs from compulsory labour, centralized his administration, encouraged industry and made primary education compulsory.

1714 The mercury thermometer was invented by the German physicist Daniel Gabriel Fahrenheit.

1714 Queen Anne of England died. George I, elector of Hanover and grandson of James I, was crowned king of England, Scotland and Ireland.

1715 The Jacobite Revolt, led by the earl of Mar, aimed to put the exiled James III, the Old Pretender, on the throne of Britain, instead of George I. It was suppressed in the Battle of Sheriff Muir. This revolt became known as 'The 15'.

1715 Louis XIV died and Louis XV ascended the French throne. Since the new king was only five years old, Philippe II, duke of Orléans, ruled the country as his regent. The reign of Louis XV was marked by setbacks in foreign and military missions.

1717 The seventh Dalai Lama was appointed by the Chinese emperor and Tibet was brought under Chinese rule.

1717 In South America, Santa Fe and Quito were brought together under the viceroyalty of New Granada.

. . . FASCINATING FACT . . .

Tattoos were a popular form of body art even as far back as the Egyptian civilization. Later too, several kings and queens such as Harold II, Edward VII, Peter the Great and Catherine the Great had decorative designs and royal emblems tattooed on themselves. Different methods were used to apply tattoos. The Maoris of New Zealand used a tiny bone adze (bladed tool); in Arizona and Malaysia people used thorns; in Japan needles were used; and in some parts of Africa the skin was cut with a knife and pigment was rubbed into the cuts to make the design.

1719-1727

1719–1748 During the reign of Mughal emperor Muhammad Shah, the empire lost its power as local rulers became more independent. However, art and architecture flourished under his patronage.

1721 The Great Northern War between Sweden and Russia was ended by the Treaty of Nystad. Russia was allowed to keep Livonia, Estonia, Ingria, part of Carelia and many of the Baltic islands.

1722 Dutchman Jacob Roggeveen discovered Easter Island and passed by Samoa while on a voyage in search of Australia.

1722 The Safavid capital Isfahan was captured by the Ghazlai Afghans and Iran was thrown into chaos following the defeat of the Safavids. The unstable conditions of the country led to the loss of Darba and Baku to the Russians, and Azerbaijan to the Ottoman Turks.

1723–1790 Scottish philosopher and economist Adam Smith's lived during this period. He was the author of

An Inquiry into the Nature and Causes of the Wealth of Nations, an important work in the field of economics.

1724 Hyderabad broke away from Mughal rule and Asaf Jah Nizam al-Mulk declared himself Nizam, or ruler, of this new princely state in the Deccan.

1725 Tahmasp II Safavi regained the Persian throne with the help of Nadir Quli of the Afshar tribe, who also helped him regain the territories lost to the Russians and the Turks.

1725 Peter the Great of Russia died. His wife Catherine I, empress of Russia, ascended the throne.

1727 George II, elector of Hanover, ascended the throne of Great Britain after the death of his father George I.

1727 Peter II, grandson of Peter the Great, ascended the Russian throne. Within three years he died and was succeeded by Anna Ivanova, niece of Peter the Great.

▶ *During the Georgian period, red-brick houses were built in English cities.*

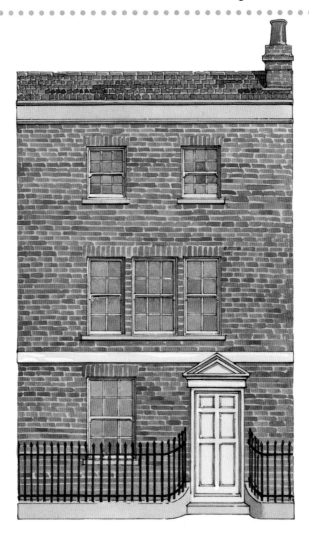

1727-1740

1727–1788 English artist Thomas Gainsborough lived during this period. He specialized in landscapes and portraits, and often combined both themes in his paintings.

▲ *Maria Theresa played a key role in the political affairs of Europe in the 18th century.*

1733 Russian explorers set out on the 'Great Northern Expedition' to study the Arctic and North Pacific coasts. The idea was conceived by Peter the Great to map the northern sea route to the east. The expedition was successful in mapping a large section of the Arctic coast of Siberia. However, ice and harsh weather made the route impracticable for ships.

1733–1738 The War of the Polish Succession was fought between France and Spain on the one hand and Austria and Russia on the other, following the death of Augustus II, king of Poland. The war was won by Russia and Austria.

1735 Englishman John Harrison invented the chronometer, a device used by navigators to measure time and longitude.

1736 Nadir Quli ascended the Persian throne after the death of Abbas III and established the Afsharid dynasty, taking on the title Nadir Shah.

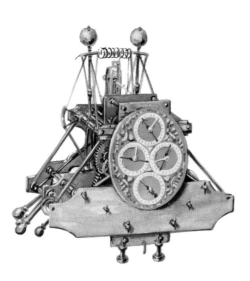

◄ After inventing his first chronometer, John Harrison designed three more instruments, each smaller and more accurate than its predecessor.

committee of the House of Commons. Captain Jenkins alleged that Spanish Coast Guards had cut off his ear after boarding his ship in the West Indies in 1731.

1740 Frederick II (or Frederick the Great) ascended the throne of Prussia after the death of his father Frederick William I.

1740 Maria Theresa, daughter of the late Holy Roman emperor Charles VI, was made archduchess of Austria and queen of Hungary and Bohemia, moves opposed by several countries.

1740 English clockmaker and inventor Benjamin Huntsman discovered a process for making good-quality steel more cheaply and in larger quantities than before.

1739 Nadir Shah invaded the Mughal capital of Delhi and raided the city. Among the great treasures that he took away to Iran were the famed Peacock Throne (studded with gold and gems) and the Kohinoor Diamond.

1739 British and Spanish forces in colonial America fought the War of Jenkins' Ear. The reason for the war was public opinion against the Spanish following an accusation made by Captain Robert Jenkins before a

▲ *The Tower of London was still being used as a state prison and a place of execution during the 1700s.*

1740 Ivan VI ascended the Russian throne. Within a year, Elizabeth, daughter of Peter the Great, got rid of Ivan and crowned herself empress.

1740 Frederick the Great of Prussia invaded Silesia, sparking off the Austrian War of Succession.

1741 In the Austrian War of Succession, Charles VII of Bavaria claimed the Austrian crown, invaded Bohemia and captured Prague. Prussians defeated Austrian forces in the Battle of Mollwitz.

1741 Muhammad ibn 'Abd-al-Wahhab, founder of the Islamic Wahhabi sect, combined forces with local chieftain Muhammad ibn Sa'ud to conquer the Arabian Peninsula, establish the Sa'udi dynasty and spread the Wahhabi faith.

1742 Charles VII, elector of Bavaria, was crowned Holy Roman emperor. He ruled until his death in 1745 and was succeeded by Francis I, duke of Lorraine.

1743 George II of Britain led a combined English, Hanoverian and Austrian force to defeat the French in the Battle of Dettingen.

1744 British and Spanish colonies fought the King George's War in America, a part of the Austrian War of Succession.

1745 Combined Dutch, British and Hanoverian forces, led by the duke of Cumberland, were defeated by the French in the Battle of Fontenoy. Britain withdrew from the Austrian War of Succession.

1745 Francis I, duke of Lorriane and husband of Maria Theresa of Austria, was elected the Holy Roman emperor following the death of Charles VII of Bavaria.

1745 Frederick II of Prussia ended his war with Austria with the Treaty of Dresden.

...FASCINATING FACT...

The origins of the Kohinoor, a huge uncut diamond originally weighing 191 carats, are not clearly known. It may have been given to Humayun by an Indian king and remained with the Mughals until Nadir Shah took it in 1739. After Nadir Shah's death it fell into the hands of the Durranis of Afghanistan, from whom it was taken by Ranjit Singh, the ruler of Punjab. When Punjab came under British rule, the Kohinoor became part of Queen Victoria's crown jewels and was later incorporated in the state crown made for Elizabeth II.

1745–1755

1745 Charles Edward Stuart, also known as Bonnie Prince Charlie, led the second Jacobite revolt. Although initially successful in capturing the English towns of Carlisle, Preston and Manchester, he was defeated in the Battle of Culloden. The uprising is known as 'The 45'.

1747 The Ashrafid dynasty of Persia began to decline with the death of Nadir Shah. Nadir Shah's sons succeeded him, but were slowly driven out of Isfahan.

▼ *The Battle of Culloden, which lasted only about 40 minutes, was a decisive reverse for the Jacobites led by Charles Edward.*

1748 The Treaty of Aix-la-Chapelle ended the War of the Austrian Succession. According to the treaty, France gained Louisbourg in Nova Scotia and Madras, in India, went to Britain. The treaty preserved Maria Theresa's right to the Austrian lands.

1749 Ahmad ibn Saiid, Ya'rubid governor of Suhar in Oman, established himself as the ruler of Oman, Zanzibar, Pemba and Kilwa.

1749–1832 Johann Wolfgang von Goethe lived during this period. He was one of Germany's most outstanding writers. *The Sorrows of Young Werther*, *The Elf King* and *Faust* are some of his best known works.

1750 The British Parliament passed the Iron Act to restrict the iron industry in America and support the British iron industry. According to the act, iron could be exported to Britain duty-free. The act prohibited the colonists from producing finished iron goods and exporting iron to any other country.

1751 The British Parliament banned the issuing of currency notes in New England by passing the Currency Act.

1751 Pennsylvania hospital, the first hospital in the United States, was opened following a charter granted by the Pennsylvania legislature to Benjamin Franklin and Dr Thomas Bond.

1755 The Church of Sainte-Geneviève in Paris (later called the Pantheon) was designed by the French architect Jacques-Germain Soufflot. Soufflot was a leader in the Neo-Classical style of architecture.

1755 British and French colonial forces fought the Battle of Monongahela, part of the wars for supremacy in America. French forces defeated the British in this battle.

1756-1758

1756 Maria Theresa of Austria formed an alliance with France, Russia and Saxony against Prussia. Frederick II of Prussia captured Saxony and began the Seven Years War.

1756–1791 Austrian composer Wolfgang Amadeus Mozart lived during this period. He is considered one of the greatest composers of all times.

1757 Frederick II of Prussia invaded Bohemia and fought the Austrians in the Battle of Prague. The Prussian army consisted of 65,000 men, while the Austrian army comprised 62,000 men. The Austrians were defeated in the battle. Later in the year, the Austrians defeated Frederick II in the Battle of Kolin.

1757 In India, Bengal came under British rule when forces of the East India Company, led by Robert Clive, defeated Siraj ud-Daula, the Nawab of Bengal, in the Battle of Plassey. The British had 3000 troops, while the nawab had an army of 50,000 men.

The British won the battle with their superior artillery and also because Clive had bribed the nawab's troops through Mir Jaffer, the general of the nawab. The battle marked the first stage in the British conquest in India.

1757 The Prussians defeated the Austrians in the Battle of Leuthen. The Prussian army comprised 39,000 men and 167 cannons, while the Austrians had 58,500 men and 210 cannons.

1757 French forces defeated German forces led by the Duke of Cumberland in the Battle of Hastenbach, and forced him to sign the Treaty of Kloster-Zeven.

1757–1827 English poet, painter and engraver William Blake's lifetime. He is considered one of the most important contributors to the Romantic style.

1758 In the Seven Years War, Frederick II of Prussia defeated the Russians in the Battle of Zorndorf and the Germans defeated the French in the Battle of Crefeld.

1758 In the French and Indian War, the British colonial forces won their first victory against the French at Louisborg in Canada.

1758 The British forces faced a crushing defeat against the French at Fort Ticonderoga in Canada.

▼ *The Battle of Plassey set the stage for establishing British rule in India. The British forces won the day despite being vastly outnumbered.*

1759-1763

1759 Russian forces defeated the Prussians in the Battles of Paltzig and Kunersdorf, and captured Dresden, during the Seven Years War.

1759 British colonial forces led by James Wolfe defeated the French and captured Quebec in the Battle of the Plains of Abraham.

1760 In the Seven Years War, British colonial forces led by Sir Eyre Coote defeated French colonial forces led by Count de Lally at Wandiwash in south India, reducing their power in India considerably.

1760 British colonial forces led by Sir Eyrie Coote surrounded the French colonial town of Pondicherry and defeated the French army. The British East India Company was established as the foremost colonial power in India.

1760 King George III became the king of Great Britain and Ireland. His efforts to raise funds through taxation of the American colonies would later lead to the American Revolution.

1761 The Bridgewater Canal was designed and constructed by Englishman James Brindley to carry coal from Worsley to Manchester. It was later extended to Mersey, putting Liverpool on the canal route. This was the world's first entirely artificial waterway.

1762 Following the death of the Russian empress Elizabeth, her son Peter III ascended the throne, but he was unpopular. He was forced by the nobles of Russia to make way for his wife Catherine II, also known as Catherine the Great. She reorganized administration and law and expanded Russian territory.

1762 Russia withdrew from the Seven Years War when Peter III of Russia, an admirer of Frederick II of Prussia, signed the Treaty of St Petersburg.

1763 After several victories and losses on both sides, Prussia won the Seven Years War, which ended with the Treaty of Hubertusburg, establishing Prussia as a major European power.

▼ To capture Quebec in 1759, British troops climbed up the cliffs to take the French by surprise. James Wolfe (1727–1759), commander of the British army, died in the battle.

1763-1767

1763 North American tribes destroyed several British forts near Niagara, and surrounded the British colony at Detroit, attacking the inhabitants. The Native Americans were defeated near Pittsburgh.

1763 George III of Britain ordered that British colonies be established in the eastern parts of North America and that all colonies west of the Appalachians should move east.

1763 The French and Indian War in America ended with the Treaty of Paris. Canada went to the British, Florida and the area to the east of the Mississippi went to the French, and the area west of the Mississippi went to Spain.

1764 The British Parliament passed the Sugar Act to raise revenue from their American colonies. The act enforced new duties on sugar imported into the North American colonies from non-British Caribbean sources. North American merchants objected to this act and some even agreed not to import British goods.

◄ *James Watt's steam engine vastly improved upon the efficiency of the device built earlier by Newcomen. The Watt engine began to be used – in mills and canals, and later in steamboats and locomotives.*

1764 Scottish inventor James Watt designed his first steam engine. He then worked on his design to improve its efficiency. In 1781, Watt replaced the up-and-down action of the original engine with rotary motion. In 1782, he patented his double-acting engine. He also invented a pressure gauge in 1790. Used together, these made steam engines far more powerful and reliable.

1765 Joseph II succeeded his father Francis I as the Holy Roman emperor. He abolished serfdom, established religious equality before the law, and granted freedom to the press. Joseph angered the Roman Catholic Church by attempting to impose state control over it.

1765 The British passed the Stamp Act and Quartering Act in their American colonies.

1766 The British established themselves in Baghdad, an important trade centre in the Middle East.

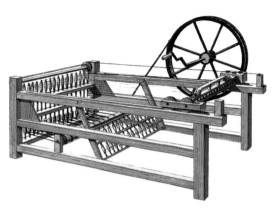

▲ *The hand-powered multiple spinning jenny developed by James Hargreaves.*

1767 English inventor James Hargreaves developed the spinning jenny, a hand-operated spinning machine that vastly increased the amount of thread each worker could produce. It is recognized as one of the first mass-production industrial machines.

1767 The South Pacific island of Tahiti was discovered by English explorer Samuel Wallis, while Pitcairn Island was discovered by Philip Carteret, a member of Wallis' expedition.

1767-1769

1767 The Townshend Revenue Acts passed by the British Parliament imposed several new taxes on colonists in America. The four acts imposed duties on the import of paint, glass, paper, lead and tea. The acts also established a board of customs commissioners to enforce collections. Like many of the earlier acts, these too were repealed because of widespread protests by colonists.

1767 The Burmese captured Ayudhya, forcing the Thai royal family to flee to Cambodia.

1767 The English architect John Wood the Younger made the Royal Crescent, a housing complex, at Bath. The first of its kind, it was considered a fashionable building and was widely imitated.

1768 Philip Astley founded the first modern circus in England. Astley built stands around his performance ring and opened Astley's Amphitheatre. One of his performers went on to establish the Royal Circus.

1768 English naval captain and explorer James Cook set out on the first of his Pacific expeditions, during which he visited New Zealand and discovered the Great Barrier Reef off Australia.

1769 Sir Richard Arkwright invented the 'water frame' to spin stronger cotton yarn. Arkwright later installed water frames at Crompton Mill, Derby, making it the world's first industrial factory. He later opened several factories equipped with machines for textile manufacturing.

1769 San Francisco Bay was discovered when Gaspar de Portolá, governor of the Spanish colony of Upper California, set out on an expedition from Velicatá in Lower California to find the Monterey Bay.

1769 The Portuguese were expelled from their last trading post in Morocco. The Moroccan ruler encouraged Dutch, English, French and Swedish traders to take their place.

1769 Nicolas-Joseph Cugnot, a French military engineer, invented the first automobile, a steam-powered tricycle. The tricycle drew a carriage carrying artillery, but proved less reliable than horses and was soon abandoned.

1769 Hundreds of thousands of people were killed in a famine in Bengal, in India.

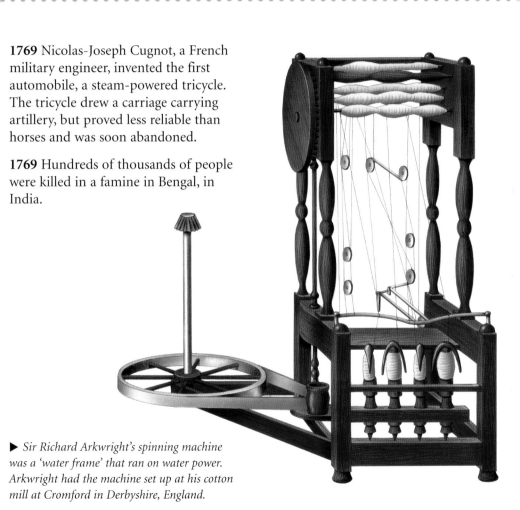

▶ *Sir Richard Arkwright's spinning machine was a 'water frame' that ran on water power. Arkwright had the machine set up at his cotton mill at Cromford in Derbyshire, England.*

1770–1775

1770 Following the killing of five colonists and the injuring of six more during a mob attack on British soldiers posted at Boston, Massachusetts, the troops were removed to nearby islands.

1770–1827 German Classical composer Ludwig van Beethoven lived during this period.

1772 British explorer James Cook began his second voyage to the Pacific and crossed the Antarctic Circle in the following year.

1772 Prussia, Austria and Russia signed a treaty agreeing to divide Poland among themselves. Thus, Russia got Belorussia, Prussia got Royal Russia and Great Poland, and Austria got Little Poland, western Podolia and Galacia. Weak and disunited, Poland did not resist.

1773 Phillis Wheatley became the first African-American woman to publish a book.

◀ *In 1773 colonists disguised themselves as Native Americans and boarded British ships anchored in Boston harbour. They threw the cargoes of tea into the sea. This protest against taxation was nicknamed the 'Boston Tea Party'.*

1774 The British Parliament passed a number of acts called the Coercive Acts. They restricted the freedom of American colonies and increased Britain's domination over them.

1774 Louis XV, King of France, died. His grandson Louis XVI ascended the French throne. By this date France was economically weak and the government faced bankruptcy.

1775 George Washington was appointed the general and commander-in-chief of the Continental Army, the joint army of the British colonies in North America.

1775 French scholar and philosopher Denis Diderot completed his *Encyclopedia*, which reflected his views on philosophy and science.

...FASCINATING FACT...

During the American Revolution, several Americans risked their lives for the honour and independence of their country. Among these were a few brave women. One of the most well-known women patriots was Mary Hays, who kept up a continuous supply of drinking water during the Battle of Monmouth Court House in New Jersey. This earned her the name 'Mollie Pitcher'. When her husband William Hays collapsed in exhaustion, Mary manned the cannon and kept firing at the enemy.

1775-1776

1775 The American War of Independence began with a fight between the British forces and the local militia at Concord in Massachusetts.

1775 British troops captured military stores at Lexington. Two months later, 15,000 colonial troops assembled near Bunker Hill in Boston to prevent the British from occupying that area. The colonists withstood an attack from British ships and a later attack by British troops, but were eventually forced to retreat. The British suffered about 1000 casualties.

1775 Fort Ticonderoga in New York was captured by the Americans and the arms and weapons stored there were taken to Boston.

1775 Benjamin Franklin was appointed as Postmaster-General of the newly established American Post Office.

1776 American forces based at Fort Moultrie in South Carolina repelled a British naval attack and severely damaged their fleet.

1776 The viceroyalty of La Plata was established in Spanish South America, and Buenos Aires was made its capital.

1776 Spanish Franciscan missionary Silvestre Vélez de Escalante explored western Colorado, rediscovered the Grand Canyon and travelled to Utah in his search for a route from Santa Fe in New Mexico to Monterey in California.

1776 The Declaration of American Independence, drafted by Thomas Jefferson and others, was approved by the Congress. The document announced the separation of 13 North American colonies from Britain.

1776 British naval explorer Captain James Cook set out on his third and final voyage in search of a northwestern passage around Canada. The expedition was unsuccessful and Cook was killed by the natives of Hawaii.

1776 In Brooklyn, New York, American forces led by George Washington suffered a severe defeat against British forces led by General

Howe in the Battle of Long Island. This battle initiated the British campaign to capture New York, isolating New England from the rest of the rebellious colonies.

▼ *Silvestre Vélez de Escalante rediscovered the Grand Canyon in 1776. It is located in the Colorado Plateau in Arizona. The huge canyon is cut by the Colorado River and runs a winding course of about 446 km.*

1776-1778

1776 George Washington's American colonial army defeated British forces in the Battle of Harlem Heights in Manhattan.

1776 An American fleet was almost completely destroyed by the British in the Battle of Valcour Bay on Lake Champlain. This battle is regarded as the first naval battle fought by the United States navy.

1776 The Americans lost Fort Washington in Manhattan, and Fort Lee in New Jersey to the British.

1776 American forces recovered from their losses by winning against a force of Hessians fighting for the British at Trenton in New Jersey.

1777 The industrial centres of the English Midlands was connected to the ports at Hull, Liverpool and Bristol by the Grand Trunk Canal.

1777 The United States Congress adopted the United States flag, which had 13 stars and 13 stripes in red and white.

1777 American troops defeated the British in two separate encounters at Princeton and Ridgefield. The Americans were defeated at Fort Ticonderoga.

1777 American militiary and troops from Massachusetts together defeated a joint British-Hessian army in the Battle of Bennington.

1777 American troops had their first major victory against the British in the Battles of Saratoga. The first battle was fought between British troops led by John Burgoyne and the continental army under Horatio Gates. The British failed to break the American lines. At the second battle, Burgoyne faced a counterattack by General Benedict Arnold. The British were forced to surrender at Saratoga.

1778 America signed treaties with France, in which France recognized the independence of the United States and assured military support in their war against England. Spain joined the fight on America's side the following year.

▲ *The national flag of the United States features 50 stars representing the 50 states and 13 stripes for the original 13 states.*

1778-1780

▲ *Many Native Americans sided with the British in the American War of Independence.*

1778 Iroquois tribesmen, encouraged by the British, raided American frontier settlements and destroyed Cobleskill in New York. Many more attacks followed.

1778 Benjamin Franklin was appointed the American diplomatic representative in France.

1778–1829 British chemist Sir Humphry Davy lived during this period. Davy made significant discoveries in chemistry and experimented with electricity.

1778–1779 Austria and Prussia fought the War of the Bavarian Succession. This followed Frederick II's opposition to the succession of Joseph II, son of Francis I and Maria Theresa, to the position of elector of Bavaria. The war ended with the Peace of Tetschen, which gave Bavaria to a nobleman.

1779 American forces defeated a combined force of Native Americans and Americans loyal to the British at Elmira in New York, destroying nearly 40 Native American villages.

1779 Englishman Samuel Crompton invented the spinning mule, a completely automated spinning machine that combined the ideas of Arkwright and Hargreaves to produce yarn in bulk.

1780 British forces captured Charleston and crushed the American army in the south.

1780 General Cornwallis and his troops defeated the Americans in South Carolina, killing 900 men and capturing 1000.

1780 Peruvian Indian nobility lost their power and wealth due to the harsh steps taken by the Spanish government to put down a revolt led by Tupac Amaru II. Native governors were appointed to maintain law and order.

1780 Unhappy with the new taxes imposed upon them by the Spanish government, the residents of New Granada staged the Comunero rebellion, in which natives, people of Spanish descent and people of both European and Indian descent participated.

...FASCINATING FACT...

Punch and Judy, the famous English puppet show, was in fact born in Italy in the 14th century. The hook-nosed and humpbacked comic character of Polichinelle first came to England in 1660, where his name was changed to Punch, and he was used in glove puppet performances along with his wife Judy. By the late 1800s, travelling performers were taking the *Punch and Judy* show all over England, to carnivals, fairs, holiday resorts and the streets of London.

1781–1784

1781 British naval forces were defeated by a French fleet just off Yorktown in South Carolina, after which the American army led by George Washington forced General Cornwallis and his troops to surrender Yorktown.

1782 The first American commercial bank, the Bank of North America, was opened. It was succeeded by the First Bank of the United States.

1783 The American Congress declared the end of the War of Independence and the Continental army was disbanded.

1783 The Treaty of Paris was signed by the United States and Great Britain, concluding the American Revolution. Britain recognized the independence of 13 colonies in North America. Britain also signed treaties with Spain and France. By these terms, Britain ceded Minorca and East and West Florida to Spain, and Tobago and Senegal to France.

1783 Shahin Girai, ruler of Crimea and the last descendant of Genghis Khan, was defeated by Catherine the Great of Russia and Crimea became part of the Russian Empire.

1783 British industrialist Henry Cort developed a method called the 'puddling' process by which pig iron could be converted into wrought iron. He also obtained a patent for producing iron bars economically and quickly in a rolling mill with grooved rolls. His inventions provided a major boost to the British iron-making industry and iron production increased significantly.

1783 French brothers Joseph-Michel Montgolfier and Jacques-Étienne Montgolfier developed the first hot-air balloon. Their balloon rose to a height of 1000 m and remained aloft for ten minutes. Next, they sent a sheep, a rooster and a duck as passengers. The first manned flight took place on November 21 the same year.

1783 French inventor Claude-François-Dorothée, the Marquis de Jouffroy d'Abbans, invented the first steamboat, the *Pyroscaphe* (meaning 'fire boat'). The vessel was driven by a horizontally mounted engine that drove two sidewheels, each equipped with eight paddles.

1784 The United States began trade with China.

1784 The first Russian settlement in America was founded on Kodiak Island in Alaska. The colony was established by Siberian fur merchants G I Shelikhov and Ivan Golikov.

◀ *The Montgolfier brothers devised the first hot-air balloon. They burnt straw and wool beneath the balloon to fill it with heated air.*

1784–1789

1784 John Adams went to England as the first American ambassador to Great Britain.

1785 Aqa Muhammad Khan of the Qajar tribe in Persia took control of the northern provinces, declared himself shah and established his capital at Tehran. Over the next 15 years, he defeated all the other tribes, including the Zands of northern Persia, and brought all of Iran under his control.

1785 English clergyman Edmund Cartwright invented the first powered loom to weave cloth, and in 1789 he patented a wool-combing machine.

1786 The War of Independence had exhausted the United States of America and reduced its money reserves severely. This led to poverty, unemployment and revolts by farmers who were deep in debt.

1786 Frederick William II ascended the throne of Prussia after the death of his uncle Frederick the Great.

1787 The Northwest Ordinance was passed by the United States Congress. This established rules to make the northwestern territories into states, defining the rights of citizens and limited slavery. The American Constitution was drafted and approved by the members of the Congress.

1788 Scottish miller and inventor Andrew Meikle developed the first functional threshing machine.

1788 British naval captain Arthur Philip arrived with the First Fleet at Botany Bay and established the convict colony of New South Wales, the first European settlement in Australia.

1789 Captain William Bligh, commander of the HMS *Bounty*, was faced with a mutiny aboard his ship. He was abandoned with 18 of his crew members in a longboat in the middle of the Pacific, near Tonga. After two and a half months, the boat reached a Portuguese settlement on Timor in the East Indies.

▶ *Edmund Cartwright was inspired to devise his powered loom after a visit to Sir Richard Arkwright's cotton mill at Cromford. Cartwright himself set up a weaving and spinning factory in Doncaster, England.*

1789-1792

1789 Unhappy with the monarchy, the poverty in the country and the unequal class system in France, the middle class elected radical reformers to the National Assembly.

1789 King Louis XVI of France called French troops to surround Paris and Versailles, and sacked the prime minister Jacques Necker. Frenzied mobs demonstrated in front of the palace and broke into the Bastille, a prison in Paris.

▲ *The cornerstone of the Capitol, seat of the Congress in Washington, DC, was laid by George Washington on September 18, 1793.*

1789 The French National Assembly made Marquis de Lafayette commander of the National Guards and Jean-Sylvain Bailly the Mayor of Paris. The 'Declaration of the Rights of Man and of the Citizen' was made by the National Assembly to set out equal rights to all Frenchmen. Many areas of France collapsed into violent anarchy.

1789 The National Assembly took control of all Church lands and distributed them among poor peasants, and divided France into districts.

1789 George Washington and John Adams were elected the first president and vice president, respectively, of the United States by the House of Representatives and the Senate.

1790 President Washington chose a site near the River Potomac to establish the new national capital of the United States.

1791 Louis XVI tried to flee France with his family, but he was caught at Varennes and imprisoned.

1791 James Hoban was commissioned to build the White House in Washington, DC, the official residence of the president of the United States.

1792 France declared war against Prussia and Austria following their attempts to interfere in the French Revolution.

1792 After several initial defeats, French forces defeated the Prussians at Valmy. The French National Assembly then dethroned Louis XVI and declared a republic. Dozens of noblemen were convicted of opposing the new regime and executed.

...FASCINATING FACT...

The guillotine was used to execute prisoners in France for the first time in 1792. Joseph-Ignace Guillotin, a doctor and a member of the National Assembly, said that all sentences of death should be carried out by a machine, so that death by beheading would not be confined to nobles and executions would be as painless as possible. The last execution by the guillotine was in 1977, after which France abolished capital punishment.

1792–1794

1792 George Vancouver, the English navigator, surveyed the Pacific coast from San Francisco to British Columbia and later published detailed maps and descriptions of his voyage.

▼ *The painting collection of the Louvre Museum in Paris is one of the richest in the world.*

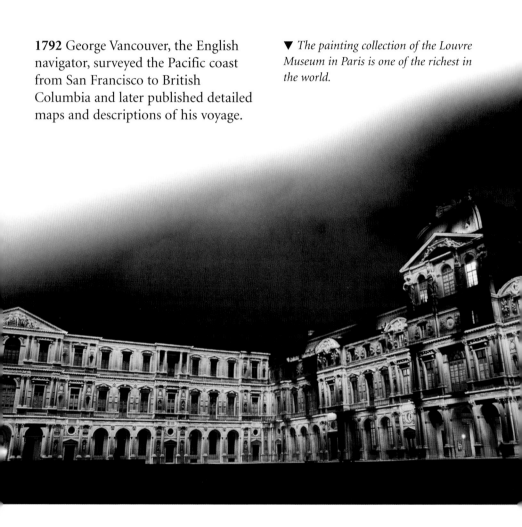

1792 The Coinage Act was passed in the United States. This act established the United States Mint. It was the first building of the federation raised under the Constitution. In 1799, the mint was made an independent agency and the Coinage Act of 1873 made it a part of the Department of the Treasury.

1793 Alexander Mackenzie, a fur trader from Scotland who had emigrated to America, became the first European to travel the length the Mackenzie River, named after him.

1793 Louis XVI of France and his wife Marie Antoinette were accused of supporting foreign enemies of the new French Republic. They were tried, found guilty and executed.

1793 French revolutionary forces were defeated in several encounters and the European powers threatened to invade Paris, where the moderate Republican party of Girondins was replaced by the Montagnards, supported by shopkeepers, craftsmen and labourers.

1793 Poland was partitioned for the second time, with extensive border areas going to Russia and Prussia.

1793 American engineer and inventor Eli Whitney invented the cotton gin to clean raw cotton. Its invention played an important role in the development of textile technology. He introduced the concept of mass production of interchangeable parts. He also proposed mass-producing identical parts for muskets, which led to the development of the American System of manufacture.

1793 The Reign of Terror started in France during which thousands of people were declared enemies of the Revolution and executed. At least 17,000 people were executed during this period.

1793 A museum was established at the Louvre Palace in Paris and opened to the public. It was called the Central Museum of the Arts.

1794 French forces defeated the Austrians and reoccupied Belgium.

1794-1797

1794 Around 1000 American troops led by General Anthony Wayne confronted over 2000 troops of the northwestern Indian Confederation, who were supported by the British. The Native Americans were forced to flee after the British abandoned them. The defeat in the Battle of the Fallen Timbers forced the Native Americans to sign the Treaty of Greenville.

1794 In France, Maximilien Robespierre, the Jacobin leader behind the Reign of Terror, was executed. Civil war and revolts continued in France.

1795 France occupied Utrecht in the Netherlands.

1795 Russia and Prussia put down a Polish revolt against the partitioning of their country. The remaining parts of Poland were then divided between Russia and Prussia.

1796 British surgeon Edward Jenner developed the vaccine against smallpox. He showed that people who contracted the relatively harmless disease, cowpox, became immune to smallpox.

1796 Corsican artillery officer in the French army, Napoleon Bonaparte was made the commander-in-chief of the French army in Italy. He set up a republican government at Lombardy, and later in other parts of Italy.

◄ *The 18th-century French Revolution lasted over a decade.*

▶ *The guillotine comprises a heavy triangular blade suspended between two upright posts. The device was used for executing people during the French Revolution.*

1796 Catherine the Great of Russia died. Her son Paul ascended the Russian throne. He reversed many of Catherine's policies and angered the nobles and the army because of his inefficient rule. Russia went to war against France during his reign.

1797 George Washington retired after his third term as the president of the United States and Federalist John Adams was elected to succeed him. Thomas Jefferson was elected vice president.

1797 Napoleon Bonaparte defeated the Austrians and the war ended with the signing of the Treaty of Campo Formio. France gained a number of Austrian territories through this treaty.

1797–1860 Christian missionaries in Polynesia destroyed the religious idols of the natives and persuaded them to convert to Christianity.

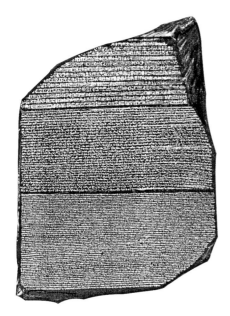

▲ *The Rosetta Stone from ancient Egypt was found to be inscribed with various languages and scripts.*

1797 Aqa Muhammad Khan, shah of Persia, was killed. He was succeeded by his nephew Fath Ali Shah. The new king quelled a rebellion in Khorasan, but failed to defeat the European powers. He also warred against Russia.

1798 In Ireland there was an unsuccessful rebellion against the British.

1798 French general Napoleon Bonaparte conquered Malta and Egypt, but the following year he was defeated at Acre, in Syria, by joint British-Turkish forces and driven back.

1798 The technique of lithographic printing was developed by Aloys Senefelder of Germany. In this method, a stone with a calcium carbonate base was taken on which a design was drawn with greasy ink. The stone was wetted with water and after various steps it was brushed with oily ink. The stone retained the ink only on the design and this inked surface was then printed.

1799 George Washington, one of the greatest figures in US history, died.

1799 The Rosetta Stone, the key to deciphering the hieroglyphic writings of ancient Egypt, was discovered by Napoleon's troops near the town of Rosetta, northeast of Alexandria.

1799 The Directorate of France was forced to resign and the Consulate was established with Napoleon Bonaparte as First Consul. The new government was effectively a military dictatorship.

1800 Bone china was invented by the British potter Josiah Spode.

1801 Thomas Jefferson was elected the third president of the United States. Aaron Burr was sworn in as vice president.

1801 Paul, Tsar of Russia, was murdered by noblemen angered by his weak rule. His son Alexander I ascended the Russian throne.

▲ *Napoleon Bonaparte, French general and later emperor, remains one of the most celebrated figures in Western history. He is noted for his military victories in the western and central mainland of Europe.*

...FASCINATING FACT...

The Aborigines of Australia lived a nomadic life until the first European settlers came in 1788. Aborigines did not have homes, nor did they take part in planting and farming or rearing animals. They moved constantly, hunting and gathering food. There were hundreds of tribes and languages, but their customs and beliefs were broadly similar and many groups worshipped the same totem – symbol of their ancestors. They believed that their ancestors made the world and turned good plants and animals into human beings and bad ones into rocks and mountains.

1801-1804

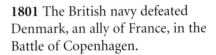

▼ *Richard Trevithick's steam locomotive had its first run in 1804, hauling 10 tonnes of iron and 70 men along a 17-km stretch.*

1801 The British navy defeated Denmark, an ally of France, in the Battle of Copenhagen.

1801 The Act of Union was passed, which united Great Britain and Ireland under the name of the United Kingdom. The flag created by the merger, the Union Flag (or Jack), still remains the flag of the United Kingdom. The upright red cross on the flag represents England. The blue background represents Scotland, while the diagonal red cross represents Ireland.

1801 British engineer William Symington developed a steam-driven paddle, which was used in one of the first functional steamboats, the *Charlotte Dundas*.

1802 The British crown won complete control over Sri Lanka by the Treaty of Amiens, which was signed by Britain, France, Spain and Batavia during the Napoleonic Wars.

1802 Marie Tussaud moved to Britain from France with her collection of wax models and established the famous Madame Tussaud's museum of wax figures. During the Reign of Terror, she made death masks from heads severed by the guillotine. Wax statues of several important personalities are kept in the museum, which had branches throughout the world by the turn of the 21st century.

1802 Port Philip was established by the British in the New South Wales colony in Australia.

1803 The United States of America bought Louisiana from the French for $15 million. Louisiana covered all North America west of the Mississippi River to the Rocky Mountains. The addition of Louisiana doubled the area of the United States. The purchased territory contained such modern states as Arkansas, Minnesota, Missouri, Iowa, Nebraska and Oklahoma.

1803 British engineer Richard Trevithick invented the first high-pressure railway steam engine. He later modified his engine to be used in an iron-rolling mill and to power a barge.

1803 The British colony of Hobart was established in Van Damein's Land, now Tasmania. It was moved to its present site in Sullivan Cove the following year.

1804 Frenchman Joseph-Marie Jacquard invented the Jacquard loom, which could weave textiles with elaborate patterns, and revolutionized the textile industry.

1804 Napoleon Bonaparte became emperor of France. Earlier, in 1802, Napoleon had instituted a new constitution whereby he secured the position of First Consul for life.

1804–1830 The Black War was fought between the Aborigines of Tasmania and European settlers and soldiers. Most of the Aborigines were killed by the time the war ended.

1805 Napoleon's troops fought Russia and Austria in the Battle of Austerlitz. The French army comprised about 73,000 soldiers, while the combined Russian-Austrian army had over 89,000 troops commanded by Russian general Kutuzuv and Austrian general von Weyrother. The French forces were victorious and the Treaty of Pressburg was signed by France and Austria.

◄ *Lord Nelson's full title at the time of his death was Vice Admiral of the White The Right Honourable Horatio, Viscount Nelson, Knight of the Most Honourable Order of Bath.*

1805 In the Napoleanic Wars, a British fleet led by Admiral Horatio Nelson defeated a combined fleet of French and Spanish ships in the Battle of Trafalgar, putting an end to Napoleon's ambition of invading England.

1805–1808 Napoleon added Venetia, Dalmatia, Liguria, Tuscany and some Austrian territories to his Italian kingdom.

1806 Joseph Bonaparte, Napoleon's brother, was made the king of Naples. In 1808 French General Joachim Murat replaced Joseph, who was installed as the king of Spain.

1807 France ended its war against the Third Coalition, comprising Britain, Russia, Austria and Prussia, with the Treaties of Tilsit. Signed at Tilsit in northern Prussia, France and Russia became allies under the terms of the treaty. Additionally, the two countries agreed to help each other in disputes.

1807 American engineer and inventor Robert Fulton designed the first commercially successful steamship *Clermont*. The boat sailed between New York and Albany, completing the 240-km journey in 32 hours. Fulton later designed several other steamboats, including the world's first steam warship.

1808 Russia invaded and occupied Finland. Alexander I of Russia made Finland a Grand Duchy and by the Treaty of Hamina, Finland was brought under Russian rule.

1808–1814 Britain joined Spain and Portugal's war for independence from the French. Napoleon was defeated in the Peninsular War and Ferdinand VII ascended the Spanish throne. The war was fought in the Iberian Peninsula.

1809–1813

1809 James Madison was elected the fourth president of the United States.

1809 France defeated Austria in the Battle of Wagram. In this battle, 154,000 French troops led by Napoleon fought against 158,000 Austrian troops led by Archduke Charles. The Austrian troops were deployed around the village of Wagram near Vienna. The attack of the French forces forced the Austrians to retreat. About 40,000 Austrians and 34,000 French died.

1809–1882 British naturalist Charles Darwin lived during this time. His research and writings contributed greatly to the understanding of the evolution of life forms. He wrote *On the Origin of Species by Means of Natural Selection* based on his theory.

1811 Paraguay overthrew its Spanish colonial rulers and declared independence.

▶ *The French army returning from Moscow were taken by surprise by an early and severe winter. Half the army perished.*

1811–1812 British craftsmen formed groups called Ludds and revolted against the industrialization of the textile industry. The Luddites, who attacked factories and damaged machinery, were arrested, brought to trial and hanged.

1812 Emperor Napoleon invaded Russia and defeated the Russians in the Battle of Borodino. In this battle, 130,000 French troops fought against 120,000 Russians led by Mikhail Kutuzov. The French lost about 30,000 men, while 45,000 Russians were killed or wounded. Napoleon captured Moscow but was soon forced to retreat.

1812 Helsinki was made the capital of Finland.

1812 United States went to war against Britain due to the latter's unfair maritime practices. The war ended two years later with the Treaty of Ghent.

1812–1870 British author Charles Dickens lived during this time. *David Copperfield*, *A Tale of Two Cities* and *Great Expectations* are some of his most famous works and are considered to be English classics.

1813 Combined Austrian, Russian, Prussian and Swedish forces ended French control over Germany and Poland by defeating France in the Battle of Leipzig (or the Battle of Nations).

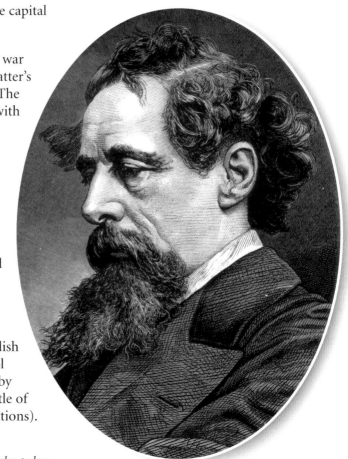

▶ *Charles Dickens remains popular today. His books have never gone out of print.*

1813–1817

1813 United States forces defeated British and Indian troops in the Battle of Thames at Ontario and gained control over northwest America.

1814 Paris was invaded by European allies and Napoleon was defeated and exiled to the island of Elba.

1814 The Bourbon dynasty came back to power in France with the coronation of Louis XVIII.

1814 Denmark and Sweden ended their war by signing the Treaty of Kiel.

▲ *The Battle of Waterloo was the last battle of Napoleon Bonaparte.*

1814–1815 Following the end of the Napoleonic Wars, the balance of power and partitioning of all disputed European countries and provinces were undertaken in the historic Congress of Vienna, which was attended by all major European powers.

1814–1838 Christian missionaries arrived in New Zealand. They were soon followed by European traders.

1815 Napoleon returned to France and raised a new army, but was defeated in the Battle of Waterloo by a British army under the Duke of Wellington, aided by the Prussians. Napoleon was exiled to the island of St Helena.

▶ *The Duke of Wellington.*

1816 Argentina declared its independence from Spain, and named itself the United Provinces of the Río de la Plata.

1816 The exiled Bourbon king Ferdinand IV returned to Sicily and ascended the throne of the kingdom of the Two Sicilies, formed by the unification of Sicily and Naples.

1817 James Monroe was sworn in as the fifth president of the United States.

. . . **FASCINATING FACT** . . .

Haiti won independence from its French colonial rulers in the late 18th century through its slave revolt, led by Toussaint-Louverture. Toussaint was a black slave who was inspired by the works of French philosophers and their views on freedom and human rights. His determination and victory are even greater considering that his opponent was Napoleon Bonaparte, one of the most gifted military leaders in the world. In recognition of his feat, Touissant is also called 'black Napoleon'.

1817–1820

1817 Chilean revolutionaries led by Bernardo O'Higgins defeated the Spanish forces ruling Chile. O'Higgins became the supreme director of Chile.

1817–1818 The First Seminole War was fought between United States troops and the Seminole tribe of Florida. The war was a consequence of United States campaigns to recapture runaway slaves living among the Seminole, which were opposed by the tribesmen. In 1818,

3000 United States soldiers led by Major General Andrew Jackson attacked. The Seminole were defeated and agreed to allow free use of Seminole lands by American settlers.

1818 The capture of Pensacola Bay by the United States forces led to Spain transferring Florida to the US.

1818 The British East India Company established control over much of India.

▼ *Simón Bolívar led the revolution against Spanish rule in New Granada.*

1818–1823 German historian and economist Karl Marx lived during this time. He wrote *Communist Manifesto* and *Das Kapital*, which were the basis of a school of thought called Marxism (the foundation of Socialism and Communism).

1819 Eleven people were killed in the Peterloo Massacre at Manchester, England, when the cavalry attacked a peaceful meeting of people gathered to protest against unemployment and high food prices.

1819 Latin American revolutionary forces led by Simón Bolívar defeated Spanish forces in the Battle of Boyacá and liberated New Granada.

1819 An expedition of the East India Company, headed by Sir Stamford Raffles, established itself in Singapore.

1820 In Italy, the Neapolitan Revolution led by the rebel group of Carbonari was suppressed by Austrian forces that came to the rescue of Ferdinand I, King of Naples. General Gugliemo Pepe was the leader of the

▲ *Karl Marx spent much of his life in poverty, supported by his friends. He established the philosophical basis of later Communist movements.*

revolt. The revolt drew support from the middle class and the poor people.

1820 George IV was crowned king of the United Kingdom following the death of his father George III. During his reign, George IV sponsored the restoration of Windsor Castle.

1821-1824

1821 The Treaty of Córdoba was signed, giving Mexico independence from Spain.

1821 Latin American forces led by Simón Bolívar defeated the Spanish in the Battle of Carabobo, liberating Venezuela.

1821 The Gold Coast in Africa became a British colony.

▲ *Claude Monet's* Garden in Giverny. *The Impressionism style of painting developed in the 19th century, chiefly in France.*

1821 Argentinian General José de San Martín drove out the Spanish rulers of Peru and liberated the country.

1821 The Ottoman Turks defeated the Greek revolutionary forces in the Battle of Dragasani. The Greeks continued their campaign for independence.

1821 Dom Pedro (Pedro I), son of King John VI of Portugal, declared Brazilian independence from Portugal and became the first emperor of Brazil.

1823 The Mexican monarchy of General Augustin de Iturbide was overthrown and the Mexican Republic was established.

1824 British-led Indian forces captured Rangoon and defeated the Burmese in the First Anglo-Burmese War. It ended with the signing of the Treaty of Yandabo in 1826.

1824 Charles X ascended the French throne following the death of his brother Louis XVIII. His July Ordinances imposed strict restrictions on the press. Although popular with the aristocracy and the Catholic Church, Charles X proved to be extremely unpopular among industrial workers.

1824 Malacca, occupied by the British during the Napoleonic Wars, was transferred to the British East India Company.

...FASCINATING FACT...

Impressionism, a major artistic style of the 19th century, got its name from the unique and revolutionary paintings of this period. Capturing the effect of light was the main objective of this artistic style. The majority of impressionistic paintings were landscapes in which the play of light on water, the leaves of a tree or a patch of grass was shown by means of dabs and flecks of colours. The form and shape of objects were usually blurred and appeared to shimmer as the painting was meant to represent the artist's impression of a fleeting moment in time.

1824-1826

1824 Frenchman Louis Braille invented Braille, a writing system using raised dots to enable blind people to read. His system was based on a method developed by Charles Barbier. In Braille system, characters embossed on paper are read by passing the fingers over the page. The system is based on a matrix of six dots arranged in two columns of three dots each. 63 combinations can be created using this system, which stand for numbers, letters, punctuation marks and common words. The Braille code for English was adopted in 1932.

1824 South American revolutionary Antonio José de Sucre defeated the Spanish forces at Ayacucho in Peru.

1825 Danish chemist Hans Christian Orsted became the first person to successfully produce aluminium. He had earlier shown that electric current flowing in a wire can deflect a magnetized compass needle. He also discovered piperine, one of the components responsible for the smell of pepper. The unit oersted, used to measure the strength of magnetic fields, was named after him.

1825 In Australia, Van Diemen's Land (now known as Tasmania) became a separate colony.

1825 In South America, Bolivia gained independence and Antonio José de Sucre became its first president in the following year.

1825 John Quincy Adams became the sixth president of the United States.

1825 British engineer and inventor George Stephenson made a steam-powered locomotive for the first passenger railway, between Stockton and Darlington in England. The train could carry 450 passengers.

1825 Alexander I, Emperor of Russia, died. His younger brother Nicholas I ascended the Russian throne. During his reign he suppressed a revolt in Poland and supported the rule of the Austrian Hapsburg dynasty over Hungary.

1825 Russian revolutionaries staged the Decembrist Uprising against Nicholas I, but the revolt was swiftly put down.

1826–1827 Frenchman Nicéphore Niepce produced the first permanent photograph using a technique he called heliography.

▶ Puffing Billy, *the oldest surviving steam locomotive. It had a considerable influence on the work of George Stephenson, one of the chief pioneers of the railway locomotive.*

1827–1830

1827 A combined fleet of British, French and Russian ships destroyed a Turko-Egyptian fleet in the Battle of Navarino. The superior guns of the European fleet destroyed three-quarters of the Turko-Egyptian fleet. This was the last significant battle between wooden ships and led to the expulsion of Greece from Turkey.

1828 Uruguay was recognized as an independent country following its revolt against Brazil.

1828 Russia invaded Persia and defeated the Persian forces, forcing them to sign the Treaty of Turkmanchai, whereby Russia got all Persian lands north of the Caspian Sea.

▼ *The use of steam power in ships became a practical idea after James Watt's success with his steam engine.*

1828–1829 Russia invaded Anatolia, defeated the Turks and forced them to sign the Treaty of Edirne, whereby Russia got the eastern shore of the Black Sea, Georgia and parts of Armenia.

1828–1910 Russian novelist Leo Tolstoy lived during this period. *War and Peace* and *Anna Karenina* are two of his best known works.

1829 Andrew Jackson was elected the seventh president of the United States. He strengthened the powers of the presidency over the individual states.

1829 The British colony of Western Australia was established. The first group of settlers who arrived there were led by Captain James Stirling. This was Australia's first non-convict colony. In 1886, gold was discovered in Western Australia and constitutional autonomy was granted by the British in 1890.

1830 France invaded Algeria, swiftly suppressing Algerian forces and occupying the African kingdom. By 1847, the French had established military control in Algeria and were successful in establishing civil rule in the late 19th century.

1830 Charles X of France was forced to give up his crown and Louis Philippe, Duke of Orléans, was crowned king of the French. During his reign, Louis Philippe introduced moderate democratic reforms. He strengthened France's position in Europe and supported Britain in forcing the Dutch to recognize Belgian independence. He faced several rebellions and attempts on his life during his rule.

1830 Belgium won its independence from the Netherlands, and Brussels was made its capital. Leopold I was chosen as king by the Belgian National Congress.

1830-1835

1830 William IV ascended the throne of the United Kingdom and Hanover, following the death of his brother George IV.

1830 The Mormon sect was founded by Joseph Smith in New York.

1831 British scientist and inventor Michael Faraday published his findings regarding the generation of electricity through electromagnetic induction.

1832 The Egyptian ruler Muhammad Ali defeated the Ottoman army in the Battle of Konya, in central Anatolia. Earlier that year, Ali had captured Damascus in Syria from Sultan Mahmud II.

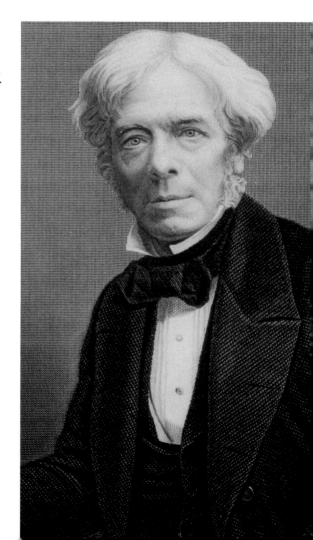

▶ *Michael Faraday, known for designing ingenious experiments, was largely self-educated.*

1833 The Slavery Abolition Act was passed by the British parliament, granting all slaves in the British Empire their freedom.

1833 William Lloyd Garrison, American journalist, founded the American Anti-Slavery Society, the main organization behind the Abolitionist movement in the US.

1833 Isabella II ascended the Spanish throne after the death of her father Ferdinand VII. Her ascension was opposed by Don Carlos, brother of Ferdinand VII, and led to the first Carlist War. Don Carlos and his followers were defeated in the war.

1834 Sir Robert Peel, founder of the Conservative Party, became prime minister of the United Kingdom. He was responsible for repealing the Corn Laws that had restricted the import of food grains to the United Kingdom.

1835 Ferdinand I became the emperor of Austria. He was simple-minded and left government to his nobles.

1835–1836 American inventor Samuel Colt invented the revolver. His revolvers were widely used during the American Civil War.

...FASCINATING FACT...

In the 1830s, British mathematician and inventor Charles Babbage began developing the Analytical Engine, a digital computer. His work drew a lot of attention and one of the people interested in it was the Countess of Lovelace, Ada Augusta King. Lady Lovelace, who was a mathematician, created a programme for the Analytical Engine. Unfortunately, the first computer program ever written was never used because Babbage never completed his computing device!

1835-1838

1835–1840 The Boers of South Africa began a mass migration from the British-controlled Cape Colony. They eventually settled in Transvaal and the Drakensburg Mountains, and in the area near the Orange River.

1835–1842 Native Americans of Florida were defeated by United States troops in the Second Seminole War and forced to move to a site close to the Mississippi. Seminole villages were burned and their crops destroyed. Faced with starvation, the tribesmen surrendered.

1835–1852 Chile was ruled by the harsh and cruel dictator Juan Manuel de Rosas.

1836 The Peruvian-Bolivian Confederation was formed when Bolivia defeated Peru. The Confederation was broken following its defeat by Chilean forces in 1839.

1836 Texas declared its independence from Mexico.

1836 Alamo, in San Antonio, Texas, was besieged by Mexican forces. Under 200 men defended the fort against 3000 Mexican troops for 13 days before the fort was captured. After the Texas revolution, Sam Houston was elected the first president of the republic of Texas.

1837 William IV died and his niece Victoria was crowned queen of the United Kingdom.

1837 Martin van Buren was elected the eighth president of the United States, but he struggled to cope with a financial crisis.

1837–1839 Members of the British working class launched the Chartist Movement, named after the People's Charter of 1838. They demanded equal rights and participation in parliamentary elections. The movement was led by Feargus O'Connor. The parliament accepted some of their demands and the movement declined.

1838 American inventor Samuel J Morse invented Morse Code. In this system, letters, numbers and punctuation marks are represented by a sequence of dots, dashes and spaces. Its modified version, the International Morse Code, is more precise and simpler, and was adapted in 1851. In Morse Code, signals are transmitted as electrical impulses. Related mechanical and visual signals are also employed.

▶ *Victoria was the first British monarch to use the title 'Empress of India', given to her in 1876.*

1838–1840

1838–1839 The first German and Scottish immigrants arrived in Australia.

1838–1842 British forces based in India invaded Afghanistan. They defeated the ruling monarch and established the exiled monarch Shah Shoja.

1839 French painter and inventor Louis-Jacques-Mandé Daguerre presented the daguerreotype process by which clear permanent photographs could be taken. This technique was based on the finding that if a copper plate coated with silver iodide was exposed to light, fumed with mercury vapour and fixed by a solution of common salt, a permanent image could be obtained.

1839 British blacksmith Kirkpatrick Macmillan invented the first practical bicycle. His machine was propelled by pedals, cranks and drive rods.

1839 Slaves aboard the Spanish ship *Amistad* revolted. The 53 slaves who had been abducted from Sierra Leone killed the captain and took control of the ship. Later, the ship was intercepted and the slaves underwent trial. Defending council John Quincy Adams successfully argued that the slaves should be freed. Donations helped them return to Sierra Leone in 1842.

1839 American inventor Charles Goodyear discovered vulcanization. In this process sulphur is added to heated rubber, making the rubber more elastic and waterproof.

1839–1842 Britain defeated China in the Opium War and made China sign the Treaty of Nanking. Britain was given Hong Kong and the British traders were given greater privileges.

1839–1906 French painter Cezanne lived during this period.

1840 New Zealand's North Island became a British colony.

1840 Queen Victoria married the German Prince Albert.

▶ *Queen Victoria and Prince Albert. Queen Victoria was the last monarch of the House of Hanover. She was succeeded by the House of Saxe-Coburg-Gotha, the royal family of her husband Prince Albert.*

1840-1845

1840 Frederick William III died. His son Frederick William IV was crowned king of Prussia.

1840 British educator Rowland Hill organized the modern postal system in Britain, devising the first pre-paid postage stamp.

1840–1917 French sculptor Auguste Rodin lived during this period. His sculptures *The Thinker* and *The Kiss* are among the world's most celebrated works of art.

1840–1926 French painter Claude Monet lived during this period. He was one of the most important artists of the Impressionist style.

▶ *British officials were sent to govern India during what is now called the Raj – the period of British imperial rule in India.*

1841 William Henry Harrison became the ninth president of the United States, but he achieved little before his sudden death.

1842 American physician John Gorrie invented a system of refrigeration and air-cooling through experiments conducted to provide air-conditioned rooms for patients suffering from fever.

1843 In the Battle of Miani, Sindh was conquered by the British in India and brought under the Bombay Presidency.

. . . **FASCINATING FACT** . . .
The world's first postage stamp, the Penny Black, a one-penny stamp with Queen Victoria's profile against a black background was produced in 1840. It was used for letters weighing less than half an ounce. For heavier letters the Twopenny Blue was used, which was similar, except that its background was blue.

1843 George Williams founded the Young Men's Christian Association in London, England. It initially had just 10 members. The first YMCA club in the United States was formed in the 1850s. Today YMCA programmes include sports and formal and informal education. The YMCA now operates in dozens of countries and also runs hotels, residential halls and cafeterias.

1845 In India, the Sikh kingdom of Punjab was defeated by British forces at Sobraon and forced to sign the Treaty of Lahore – Kashmir and Jalandhar went to the British. Kashmir was later sold to Gulab Singh, ruler of Jammu.

1845 James Knox Polk was elected the eleventh president of the United States, beginning an active foreign policy.

1845-1848

1845 Texas became part of the United States.

1845–1846 In India, British colonial forces defeated the Sikhs of Punjab and took control of the land between the Sutlej and Beas Rivers. A British government representative was posted in Lahore.

1845–1849 Ireland suffered the Great Potato Famine when entire crops of potato, the staple Irish food, were ruined. The famine was a consequence of the appearance of blight, the potato fungus. About 800,000 people died as a result of the famine. A large number of people migrated to Britain, the United States, Canada and Australia.

1846 American Elias Howe invented the first practical sewing machine. It revolutionized the garment industry.

1846–1848 In the Mexican War, United States forces defeated the Mexicans and occupied Mexico City. Under the Treaty of Guadalupe Hidalgo, the United States bought New Mexico, Utah, Nevada, Arizona, California, Texas and Colorado for 15 million dollars.

1847 The American Medical Association was founded in Philadelphia by 250 delegates representing 40 medical societies and 28 colleges. It is now the largest association of doctors in the United States with about 300,000 members.

1848 A series of revolutions started in various parts of Europe, beginning with Sicily, and spreading to France, Germany and Austria. They were mostly unsuccessful in bringing about any political change, and were all eventually suppressed.

1848 The February revolution in France forced King Louis-Philippe to give up his throne and France became a republic.

1848 Gold was first discovered in California in the American River. Nearly 80,000 people immigrated to California within a year, hoping to strike it rich.

1848 Britain took control of the area between the Orange and the Vaal Rivers in South Africa, and named it the Orange River Sovereignty. The Boers forced them to leave the area in 1854 and formed an independent Orange Free State.

▼ *In 1841 the population of Ireland was about 8 million. Around 800,000 to one million people died during the years of famine.*

1851–1853

1851 Victoria in Australia became a separate colony, with Melbourne as its capital. It is Australia's second smallest state, but was the first state in the country to develop its industrial sector.

1851 The English physicist Frederick Blakewell demonstrated the first practical facsimile machine at the World Fair in London. His system consisted of rotating drums that worked to transmit and receive recorded pictures.

1851 The discovery of large gold deposits to the northwest of Melbourne led to the Victorian Gold Rush. This period, which lasted until the early 1860s, led to an unprecedented population growth – soaring from about 75,000 to over 500,000 by 1860.

1851–1929 The German inventor Emile Berner lived during this period. He is most remembered for inventing the disc record gramophone.

1852 Napoleon III, the grandson of Napoleon I, was elected to be the emperor of France. He is believed to be the first to lay the foundations for a family welfare system. During his reign, craftsmen and artists formed associations to get finance for insurance.

1852 In the Second Anglo-Burmese War, British forces captured Lower Burma. While the war ended in British victory, it proved expensive for the East India Company, costing them £1 million and making them unpopular with those in India who had to pay the bill.

1853 Japan and the United States signed the Kanagawa Treaty, allowing the United States to establish a base in Japan and conduct trade. It was the first treaty that Japan signed with a Western country and was forced on Japan by American warships.

▶ *The Second Anglo-Burmese War (1852) was provoked by the British, who wanted access to the teak forests in and around Pegu, and also wanted to secure the gap in their coastline stretching from Calcutta to Singapore.*

1853 Maria II of Portugal was succeeded by her son Pedro V. He reigned as the king of Portugal until 1861, during which time he developed the railway and uplifted the public health system. Ironically, he died of cholera at a young age.

1853 The Crimean War was fought between Russia and an alliance comprising the Ottoman Empire, the kingdom of Sardinia, Britain and France. The war is best known for the futile and almost suicidal charge of the Light Brigade of British cavalry. The war ended in defeat for Russia.

1853–1890 The Dutch artist Vincent Van Gogh lived during this period. He pioneered the Expressionist style of painting.

1854–1857

1854 The Suez Canal in Egypt was opened, connecting the Mediterranean Sea with the Red Sea.

1855 Alexander II was crowned the Tsar of Russia. He is most remembered for the efforts he made to liberate serfs.

1855–1868 Thailand signed diplomatic treaties such as the Bowring Treaty with Britain, USA and other powerful European countries. These treaties were, however, considered to be unfair, subordinating Thailand to an inferior position.

1856 The Crimean War ended with the Treaty of Paris. This treaty was signed between Russia and the Ottoman Empire with its allies, England and France.

◀ *The 1857 Sepoy Mutiny in India began in Meerut and then spread to Delhi, Agra, Kanpur and Lucknow.*

1856 British inventor Henry Bessemer invented a process by which steel could be mass-produced in a cost-effective manner. In 1879, Bessemer was knighted and also awarded a Royal Society fellowship.

1856–1939 Austrian neurologist Sigmund Freud lived during this period. His path-breaking work was responsible for the development of psychoanalysis.

1856–1860 France and Britain defeated China in the Second Opium War, forcing it to grant more rights and privileges to foreign traders.

1856–1950 Irish playwright George Bernard Shaw lived during this period. He is the author of popular plays such as *Pygmalion*, *Apple Cart* and *Man and Superman*, and was awarded the Nobel Prize for Literature in 1925.

1857–1858 The Sepoy Mutiny among Indian troops in British service spread rapidly to military stations all over northern and western India. It was eventually suppressed by British troops. The 1857 Revolt later came to be thought of as the first collective Indian movement against British colonial rule.

1857 American inventor Elisha Otis designed and installed the first ever elevator, in New York.

....FASCINATING FACT....
Florence Nightingale's heroic services during the Crimean War are legendary. She worked tirelessly and cared for the sick and wounded, even during the night, thus earning the nickname 'Lady with the Lamp'. In 1907, she became the first woman to be awarded the Order of Merit.

1858–1861

1858 The British Parliament passed the Government of India Act, ending the rule of the East India Company and bringing India under British rule.

1858 Hyman Lipman from Philadelphia, USA, received the first patent for a pencil with an attached eraser. However, the patent was later cancelled, because there was nothing new about the invention.

1859 The Maoris of New Zealand clashed violently with European settlers, heralding the beginning of the second Maori Wars.

1859 In the United States, rich deposits of silver were discovered in Comstock Lode, Nevada. This marked the start of the mining boom in Nevada and a turning point for the state's economy.

1859 Under Napoleon III, France declared war on Austria to free all Italian and Sardinian territories from Austrian rule. This war lasted for only three months, but it proved to be very bloody.

1859 Russian forces invaded Dagestan, forcing its leader, Imam Shamil, to surrender. Dagestan became a part of Russia as the Dagestanskaya region.

1860 The Confederate States of America was formed when 11 southern states broke away from the United States. Jefferson Davis was elected as the Confederacy president. The 11 states of the Confederacy were North Carolina, South Carolina, Florida, Alabama, Georgia, Arkansas, Mississippi, Louisiana, Tennessee, Virginia and Texas.

1860 Vladivostok was founded in eastern Russia as a military outpost of the Russian Empire.

1861 Victor Emmanuel II became the first king of Italy. The capital city changed from Turin to Florence, and in 1870, Emmanuel II made Rome the official capital of Italy.

1861 William I ascended the Prussian throne after the death of his brother Frederick William IV.

▲ *The USS* Monitor, *the first American Union ironclad battleship, is best known for its battle with the Confederate ironclad* Virginia.

1861–1863

1861 Republican Abraham Lincoln was sworn in as the 16th president of the United States. Before he entered politics, Lincoln worked as a rail-splitter, a lawyer and a store clerk!

1861 Kansas was officially declared the 34th state of the United States. The name Kansas was derived from the Sioux word Kansa, and means 'people of the south wind'.

1861 The American Civil War began, with the Confederates making their first attack on Fort Sumter in South Carolina.

1862 In the American Civil War, the Federal Army gained victories at Fort Henry, Fort Donelson and New Madrid. They occupied Corinth and Memphis in Tennessee, while the Federal Navy took control of New Orleans.

1862 Confederate forces led by Robert E Lee defeated the Union Army in the Seven Days' Battle. Also known as the Seven Days Campaign, the week-long battle ended after Lee forced General McClellan and his Army of the Potomac to retreat.

▲ *Lincoln's Gettysburg Address is one of the most famous speeches ever delivered in the United States.*

1862 In the American Civil War, Confederate forces dealt Union forces a crushing defeat at Fredericksburg in Virginia.

1862 General Bartolomé Mitre became the president of Argentina, and Buenos Aires was established as the capital city. Apart from being a statesman and a general, Mitre was also a historian, poet and journalist.

▼ *The Vicksburg Campaign allowed the Union forces to cut off the Confederate states located west of the Mississippi River, from those that lay to the east.*

1863 President Lincoln made his Emancipation Proclamation, promising to free all slaves in the Confederate states. The document officially banned slavery in the country, and also allowed slaves to join the military forces.

1863 The Battle of Gettysburg was fought between the Confederates and Union forces. After intense fighting, and the loss of nearly 20,000 lives on both sides, the Confederates withdrew from the fight.

1863 In the American Civil War, Vicksburg was captured by Union forces, dividing the Confederate states in two.

1864–1867

1864 In the US Civil War, Union forces led by General William Tecumseh Sherman captured Atlanta, raided Georgia, and went on to capture Savannah.

1864 Denmark was defeated by the combined forces of Prussia and Austria, and was forced to give up the provinces of Schleswig and Holstein to joint Prussian-Austrian control.

1865 Ulysses S Grant, commander of the Union forces, captured Richmond and forced Confederate general Robert E Lee to surrender.

1865 In North Carolina, Confederate general J E Johnston surrendered to Union general William T Sherman. The American Civil War ended with the Confederate states being forced to rejoin the United States.

▶ *Ulysses Grant was born Hiram Ulysses Grant. While registering at West Point, a Congressman erroneously recorded him as Ulysses Simpson Grant, a name the future president liked so much that he kept it.*

1865 On Good Friday, President Abraham Lincoln was shot dead at Ford's Theatre in Washington. The assassin was John Wilkes Booth, a supporter of slavery and an actor by profession. Andrew Johnson succeeded Lincoln as the president of the United States.

1866 In the Seven Weeks War, Prussia defeated the combined forces of Austria, Hanover, Saxony, Bavaria and some minor German states, and established itself as the leader of German states. The German Confederation was formed with Berlin as its capital.

1866 American businessman Cyrus Field laid the first-ever telegraph cable across the Atlantic Ocean between Newfoundland and Ireland, allowing for the first transatlantic telegraph communication.

1867–1959 The American architect Frank Lloyd Wright lived during this period. The Prairie style of architecture, designed by Wright, greatly influenced modern residential architecture in the United States.

1867 Russia sold Alaska to the United States for over seven million dollars.

1867 The Swedish scientist Alfred Nobel patented his famous invention, the explosive dynamite.

. . . FASCINATING FACT . . .

The half dime, a silver coin worth five cents, was first minted in the United States in 1793. In 1866, the United States Congress declared the half dime coin as defunct, replacing it with the nickel. By 1873, the half dime coins were redundant.

1868–1870

1868 William Ewart Gladstone, the leader of the Liberal Party (Whigs), was elected Prime Minister of Britain. Gladstone holds the British records for the longest-ever Budget speech and the longest-serving chancellor.

1868 The Tokugawa shogunate in Japan came to an end after a political revolution called the Meiji Restoration. Subsequently, Emperor Meiji ascended the throne as the first modern emperor of Japan, ruling the country himself instead of through a military shogun.

▲ *The ownership of the Suez Canal remained in French and British hands until 1956.*

1868 Isabella II, Queen of Spain, was forced to flee the country due to a revolution led by democrats and powerful and wealthy rebels who wanted to establish themselves in the Spanish government.

1868 Since the late 18th century, British convicts were transported to European settlements in Australia to aid nation-building. The need for these convicts, however, gradually diminished, and in 1868, the last shipment of British convicts arrived in Australia.

1869 The Suez Canal, which connected the Red Sea with the eastern Mediterranean Sea, was opened. The canal is the world's longest artificial canal without locks, and took about ten years to build. It was also the first canal to serve as a direct link between the Mediterranean Sea and the Red Sea.

1869 Victoria became the first Australian colony to pass an Aboriginal Protection Act. The act attempted to provide for the housing, employment and general well-being of the native population.

1869–1954 The French painter Henri Matisse lived during this period. His famous figure compositions in bright colours led to the development of the Fauvist style.

1870 German states led by Prussia defeated France in the Franco-Prussian War. Victory signified the end of the domination of France in Europe, and marked the beginning of a unified Germany under the leadership of Prussia. The new state was dubbed the Second Reich.

1870 Napoleon III of France was forced to step down from the throne after losing the Franco-Prussian War, and the Third French Republic was established.

1870 Amadeus, a son of the king of Italy, became Spain's constitutional monarch, but was forced to give up the throne within three years.

1870–1878

1870 French occupation of Rome ended, and Rome became part of Italy. French troops had been protecting the power of the pope to rule Rome. After Italy captured Rome, the pope went into voluntary exile inside the Vatican.

1872 The Yellowstone National Park in the United States was established, giving the world its first national park.

1874 Alfonso XII, the son of Isabella II, became the king of Spain. He reigned as king until 1885, when he died of tuberculosis.

1876 Queen Victoria of Britain was crowned the Empress of India. The first ruler to take up residence at the Buckingham Palace, Queen Victoria ruled for a longer period of time than any other British monarch.

1876 Scottish-born American inventor Alexander Graham Bell invented the telephone. Bell later went on to establish the Bell Telephone Company.

1877 American inventor Thomas Alva Edison developed the phonograph.

▲ *The first complete sentence spoken on the telephone was by Alexander Graham Bell telling his assistant Watson, "Watson, come here; I want you."*

He also created the world's first research laboratory and named it the Invention Factory. Known as one of the most successful inventors in history, Edison patented over 1000 inventions in his lifetime.

1877 The American-based British photographer Eadweard Muybridge invented the zoopraxiscope, a forerunner of the contemporary movie projector. The device showed a series of still photographs in rapid succession.

1877–1878 Russia and Turkey fought their last war, with Serbia, Bosnia and Herzegovina and Bulgaria also siding against the Turks. The war ended with Russia's victory. Turkey signed the Treaty of San Stefano, which liberated Montenegro, Bosnia and Herzegovina, Serbia and Romania, and gave a large part of Bulgaria to the Russians.

1878 At the Congress of Berlin, the trio of Britain, Austria-Hungary and Germany forced Russia to cancel the Treaty of San Stefano and sign the Treaty of Berlin. The agreement meant that the Ottoman Turks got back all territories given to Russia in the Treaty of San Stefano, and Bosnia-Herzegovina went to Austria-Hungary.

1878 Victor Emmanuel II died and Umberto I was crowned king of Italy. Umberto I was respected for his generous and kind-hearted nature, earning him the title Umberto the Good.

▼ *Buckingham Palace is still the official London residence of the British sovereign.*

1879–1885

1879 Thomas Alva Edison invented the electric light bulb. Of Edison's many achievements, one of his greatest was the development of the world's first practical lighting system. He also established the first-ever company for the distribution of electrical power.

1879 In eastern South Africa, British forces defeated the Zulus in the Zulu War and annexed Natal (now KwaZulu/Natal), a territory in South Africa.

1880 The world's first electric street light was installed, in Indiana, USA. The light was situated above a court house, and cost approximately $100.

1881 Alexander III became the tsar of Russia after his father, Alexander II, was assassinated. The reign of Alexander III was marked by economic reforms, but savage political repression.

1881–1973 The Spanish-born French artist Pablo Picasso lived during this period. He developed a style of painting known as Cubism. A painter, sculptor, printmaker, ceramic artist and a stage designer extraordinaire, Picasso fashioned more than 20,000 different works of art.

1882 British forces occupied Cairo in Egypt, marking the beginning of the British Protectorate that ruled the country until 1922.

...FASCINATING FACT...

The USS *Monitor*, engineered by the Swedish-American John Ericsson, was the first American Union ironclad battleship. It took part in the first-ever battle between two ironclads. The vessel was described as a 'cheesebox on a raft', as it consisted of a huge iron turret and two cannons on an extremely flat deck.

◄ During the first 20 years of his life, Alexander III had no prospect of succeeding to the Russian throne because he had an elder brother, Nicholas.

1884 German engineers Gottlieb Daimler and Wilhelm Maybach invented the first engine that could run on petrol. In 1897, Daimler also developed the Daimler Victoria, the first-ever taxi, complete with a fare meter.

1885 In India, the Indian National Congress was formed to work towards the cause of India's independence from Britain. Founded by Englishman A O Hume, the Indian National Congress became the first-ever Indian political party.

1885 German engineer Karl Benz developed and commercialized the world's first car, the three-wheeled Benz car. He later joined forces with Daimler to form the automobile company Daimler-Benz, which later came to be known as Mercedes-Benz.

1884 Germany colonized the African province of Togoland. Gustav Nachtigal, an African strategist, signed a treaty with the chief of Togovillage for exclusive possession of the Togoland coast.

1886–1891

1886 Upper Burma was brought under British control, bringing the Anglo-Burmese Wars to an end.

1886 The Statue of Liberty, a gift from France to the United States, was dedicated to the nation by American President Grover Cleveland. Designed by the French sculptor Auguste Bartholdi, the statue took nine years to complete. It was shipped to the United States in 350 separate pieces, and was put together only once it reached its destination.

▶ *The Eiffel Tower is made of over 18,000 pieces of iron held together by two and a half million rivets. It took about 300 workers to erect the tower.*

1887 The British East Africa Company was established in Zanzibar, having been granted coastal areas by the sultan of the kingdom. Zanzibar became a British protectorate in 1890.

1888 The American inventor George Eastman invented and marketed the first Kodak camera, which was small, lightweight and looked like a wooden box. Eastman's invention of the film roll and camera meant that photography became popular across the world. He named his camera Kodak because he liked the letter 'k'.

1889 The British South Africa Company was granted a royal charter and given a vast stretch of land in south-central Africa. The company, established by the British imperialist Cecil Rhodes, was originally a London-based mercantile organization.

1889 The Brazilian monarchy was overthrown in a military takeover and the first Republic of Brazil was founded.

1889 Carlos I ascended the Portuguese throne and proved to be economically inept.

1889 The Eiffel Tower was built in Paris for the World Exhibition, which was held to celebrate the 100th anniversary of the French Revolution. Built by Gustave Eiffel, the wrought-iron structure remained the tallest in the world until the Chrysler building was completed in 1930.

1890 The famous Dutch artist Vincent Van Gogh committed suicide when he was just 37. He went to a wheat field in Auvers-sur-Oise near the city of Paris and shot himself in the chest.

1891 A liberal government came to power in New Zealand, marking the beginning of a period of economic growth in the country. John Ballance assumed the post of prime minister. He introduced various reforms to improve the country's economy.

1893–1898

1893 The Independent Labour Party was founded in England as a representative body of the British working classes. The party was established under the leadership of Scotsman James Keir Hardie.

1894–1895 Japan established itself as a major power when it defeated China in the Sino-Japanese War. The Treaty of Shimonoseki liberated Korea from China, while Japan was given Taiwan and the Liaotung Peninsula in Manchuria.

1895 Nicholas II, the last Tsar of Russia, ascended the Russian throne after the death of his father Alexander

▶ *Tsar Nicholas II and his family lived a privileged life, far removed from the realities of life in Russia. Nicholas abdicated the throne when the October Revolution broke out in 1917. He and his family were killed by the Bolsheviks after the revolution.*

III. Nicholas proved to be a gentleman and a benevolent, if weak, ruler. He presided over an economic boom, but cracked down heavily on any political unrest.

1895 South Australia passed a Female Suffrage Act, whereby all South Australian women were given the right to vote and to stand for elections.

> **. . .FASCINATING FACT. . .**
> In 1899, an Italian baker called Raffaele Esposito invented the classic pizza. When King Umberto and Queen Margherita visited Raffaele's restaurant, the baker decided to decorate his flattened bread with the colours of Italy. He added tomato, mozzarella cheese and basil as the topping to represent the red, white and green colours of the Italian flag. That is how the classic pizza came to be known as the Margherita pizza!

1895 France captured Antananarivo in Madagascar and declared the island kingdom a French Protectorate. The monarchy was allowed to continue, but its power was greatly reduced.

1895 The German physicist Wilhelm Conrad Röntgen took an x-ray of his wife's hand, the world's first x-ray of the human body. He was awarded the first Nobel Prize for Physics in 1901.

1896 The Italian physicist Guglielmo Marconi invented radio telegraphy. In 1909 he received the Nobel Prize for his pioneering work.

1897 German engineer Rudolf Diesel invented the world's first diesel engine and displayed it at the Paris World Fair. He designed his engine to operate on a wide range of fuels, including peanut oil and coal dust.

1898 British and Egyptian forces led by General Kitchener conquered Sudan in Africa and established a British-Egyptian administration. While the administration was meant to be a joint affair, it was the British Empire that made all the important decisions and policies.

1898–1899

1898 Robert Allison from Pennsylvania, USA, purchased a Winton car after seeing an advertisement in the *Scientific American* journal. He was the first person to buy an American automobile.

1898 The United States declared war against Spain in support of the Cuban struggle for independence, and defeated them in naval battles off the Philippines and Cuba. Spain agreed to give up its claim to Cuba.

1899–1902 British imperial forces defeated the Boer settlers of South Africa after a long, close-fought war. The war ended with the Treaty of Vereeniging, by which the Transvaal province and the Orange Free State became Britsh colonies.

1899–1945 German dictator Adolf Hitler lived during this period. Hitler originally wanted to be an artist and had applied to the Vienna Academy of Fine Arts in Austria. However, he was rejected by the institute.

▼ *Ladysmith Camp. British troops on active service in Transvaal.*

1899–1961 American novelist Ernest Hemingway lived during this period. *A Farewell to Arms* is his most famous work. He was awarded the 1954 Nobel Prize for Literature.

1900 The British South Africa Company took control of the administration of northern and southern Rhodesia, now Zambia and Zimbabwe respectively.

1900 In China, the government-sponsored Boxer Rebellion against foreigners and Christians was put down when international forces captured Peking and forced the Ch'ing empress to flee.

1900 Russia invaded and occupied Manchuria until 1904.

1900 Vittorio Emanuele III ascended the Italian throne when his father Umberto I was assassinated. He accepted democratic reforms and ruled through Parliament.

1900 The independent Republic of Hawaii became a part of the United States.

▼ *As well as receiving the Nobel Prize for Literature in 1954, Hemingway won the Pulitzer Prize in 1952 for his novel* The Old Man and the Sea.

1901 The Commonwealth of Australia Constitution Act was passed by the British Parliament, establishing the Commonwealth of Australia. The Act unified the colonies of New South Wales, Queensland, Tasmania, Victoria, South Australia and Western Australia.

1901 Queen Victoria, the British monarch and Empress of India, died at the age of 81. She left special instructions for her funeral, requesting that her sons personally place her inside the coffin. In addition, since the queen did not like black funerals, the whole of London was decorated in purple and white! The queen was succeeded by her son Edward VII.

1901 The Platt Amendment, passed by the United States Congress, laid down conditions that reduced Cuba's independence in return for the withdrawal of American troops stationed at Cuba since 1899.

◀ *William McKinley was the third of the four American presidents to have been assassinated.*

1901 The first ever Australian parliament was inaugurated at Melbourne.

1901–1971 The American musician and singer Louis Armstrong lived during this period. Armstrong, one of the earliest and most important jazz musicians, played the trumpet. His style and compositions have greatly influenced generations of musicians.

1901 William McKinley, the president of the United States, was shot by an anarchist called Leon Czolgosz. Theodore Roosevelt became the 26th president of the United States.

1901 The Boxer Rebellion in China ended with the Peace of Beijing.

1901 The first Nobel Prizes were awarded to Wilhelm C Röntgen for Physics, Jacobus H vant Hoff for Chemistry, Sully Prudhomme for Literature and Emil A von Behring for Physiology or Medicine. Frédéric Passy and Jean-Henri Dunant shared the Nobel Prize for Peace.

▲ *Until the 19th century, ordinary people knew little about new fashions of the rich, or foreign styles. Fashion plates (hand-coloured engravings) spread the news of latest trends.*

1901 The Italian physicist Guglielmo Marconi received the first trans-Atlantic radio signal, sent from England to Newfoundland. The message was the Morse code for 'S'.

1902-1903

1902 French illusionist and filmmaker Georges Méliès produced *Le Voyage dans la lune* (A Trip to the Moon), a science-fiction story in 30 scenes. It was the first film of its kind and was also the first to be shown internationally.

1902 Japan and Britain signed the Anglo-Japanese Treaty in order to protect their respective interests in Korea and China.

1902–1984 American photographer Ansel Adams lived during this period. He played an important role in the development and recognition of photography as a fine art form.

1902–1968 American novelist John Steinbeck lived during this period. His most famous book was *Grapes of Wrath*. He was awarded the Nobel Prize for Literature in 1962.

1902 The Republic of Cuba was established under the leadership of Tomás Estrada Palma.

1902 The Australian Parliament passed the Commonwealth Franchise Act, whereby all women were given the right to vote. However, Aborigines, Asians and Africans were still not given the right to vote.

1903 American engineer, projectionist and cameraman Edwin S Porter made *The Great Train Robbery*, the first motion picture edited to show continuous motion from more than one angle. It was also the first box office hit and a predecessor of the Western genre.

1903 French physicists Marie Curie, Pierre Curie and Henri Becquerel were awarded the Nobel Prize for Physics for their research on radioactivity.

1903 Edwin Binny and C Harold Smith produced the first ever crayons with charcoal and oil. To make their invention practical for children to use, Binny and Smith mixed paraffin wax and industrial colours to make 'child-friendly' crayons. Alice, Binny's wife,

named the crayons Crayola by putting together the French words *craie* (meaning 'chalk') and *ola* (meaning 'oily').

1903–1950 British novelist George Orwell lived during this period. His greatest works are *Animal Farm* and *Nineteen Eighty-Four*. The author's pen

▲ *Marie Curie (left) and her daughter (right). Marie Curie was initially not allowed to attend universities in Russia and Poland because she was a woman.*

name was George Orwell, while his real name was Eric Arthur Blair. Born in the Bengal region of India, Orwell worked as a policeman before he embarked on a career in writing.

1903

January 10, 1903–May 20, 1975 The British sculptor Barbara Hepworth lived during this period. Her new and original style influenced many 20th-century artists.

April 1903 In the Russian province of Kishinev mobs attacked Jews, killing 45 and wounding more than 600. Nearly 1500 Jewish homes were looted.

May 29, 1903–July 27, 2003 The British-born US actor Bob Hope lived during this period. One of America's greatest entertainers, he performed for more than 80 years in a variety of roles as a comedian, singer, dancer and actor in vaudeville, on Broadway, in Hollywood, on radio and on television.

July 1–19, 1903 French cyclist and journalist Henri Desgrange organized the first Tour de France bicycle race. The event was so popular that it has been held every year since its inception.

July 11, 1903 King of Serbia Alexander I Obrenovich and his wife Queen Draga Mashin were killed by rebel army officers. The nobleman Peter Karageorgevich became king and followed a pro-Russian policy.

July 16, 1903 The American industrialist Henry Ford founded the Ford Motor Company. Henry Ford introduced the concept of assembly-line production of cars, which heralded a revolution in the automobile industry.

August 1903 The Russian Social-Democratic Workers' Party split into two groups – Bolsheviks and Mensheviks. At the Second Congress meeting of the party, its two leaders, Vladimir Lenin and Julius Martov, had an argument that led to the party being divided into two.

August 2, 1903 The Macedonians rose in protest for freedom from Ottoman rule with the Macedonian Ilinden Uprising, but the Ottoman Turks suppressed the uprising, killing hundreds of people and destroying nearly 20 villages.

▼ *Many Russian Jews moved to other countries, such as the United States, following violence against them in Russia.*

September 25, 1903–February 25, 1970 The American painter Mark Rothko lived during this period. Among the most significant artists of the 20th century, he pioneered the abstract expressionism style of painting. This style was marked by free and spontaneous expression of emotions.

October 28, 1903–April 10, 1966 The British novelist Evelyn Waugh lived during this period. Regarded as one of the most gifted satirical novelists of his time, *Brideshead Revisited* is considered to be his greatest novel.

1903-1904

November 3, 1903 With the help of the United States, Panama separated from Colombia and became known as the Republic of Panama. The United States paid Colombia $25 million in compensation so Panama could be recognized as independent.

November 18, 1903 The United States and Panama signed the Hay–Bunau-Varilla Treaty. It gave the United States exclusive rights to the Panama Canal and committed the United States to protect Panama in return.

December 17, 1903 The American inventors Wilbur Wright and Orville Wright invented the first powered flying machine. The Wright Brothers named their aeroplane the *Flyer*. The maiden flight of the Wright *Flyer*, at Kitty Hawk in North Carolina, lasted about 30 seconds.

1903 The first ever transcontinental trip by car was completed successfully, lasting 52 days between San Francisco and New York.

▶ *Kitty Hawk, a town located in Dare County, North Carolina, became famous when the Wright Brothers made the first powered flight from a sand dune in the Kill Devil Hills.*

January 11, 1904 The Herero people of southwest Africa revolted against their German colonizers. The revolt was unsuccessful and over the next few years nearly 60,000 Hereros were killed in clashes with German forces.

February 8, 1904 The Russo-Japanese War broke out with a Japanese fleet making a surprise attack on the Russian navy at Port Arthur.

April 8, 1904 England and France began a period of friendly cooperation by signing the Entente Cordiale.

May 4, 1904 Sir Frederick Henry Royce of England manufactured the very first Royce car. The car, which was designed at Royce's Manchester factory, had two cylinders, a three-speed gearbox and an open, four-seat body.

May 11, 1904–January 23, 1989 The Spanish artist Salvador Dalí lived during this period. He was one of the most significant artists of surrealism and soon became one of the greatest painters of the 20th century. Dalí's paintings were mainly a reflection of his dreams. Surrealism essentially drew on the subconscious mind and fantasies, uniting these with conscious reality.

1904 The brothers Auguste and Louis Lumière of France patented the first commercially successful process of colour photography. The brothers named their process the Autochrome Lumière, which went on the market in 1907 and remained the only one of its kind until 1935.

. . .FASCINATING FACT. . .

Surrealism was born out of the need to break out of the regular and predictable forms of imagery used in art and literature. In surrealism, the artist or writer presents a very realistic image in a very unrealistic or dreamlike situation, which results in the final image being startling and unexpected. Some of the most famous images used in surrealistic paintings were Salvador Dalí's melting clocks and Rene Margritte's mirror.

1905

January 22, 1905 The Russian police opened fire on workers participating in a peaceful march at St Petersburg, Russia. More than 100 people died in the massacre and several hundred were wounded. The 'Bloody Sunday' marked the beginning of the 1905 Russian Revolution. The massacre was followed by strikes in other cities, peasant uprisings and mutinies in the army. The uprising led to the establishment of an elected parliament, but the tsar kept real power for himself.

May 27–29, 1905 In the Russo-Japanese War, the Japanese fleet destroyed the Russian Baltic fleet completely in the Battle of Tsushima.

June 7, 1905 Norway separated from Sweden and Hakon VII was crowned king of Norway.

June 30, 1905 German physicist Albert Einstein published the 'Theory of Relativity'.

August 9, 1905 The Russo-Japanese Treaty of Portsmouth recognized

▶ *As British viceroy of India, Lord Curzon reduced taxes and reformed the legal system, but upset many in the civil service.*

Japan's control over Korea and also gave Japan the Liaotung Peninsula, South Manchurian railroad and half of Sakhalin Island. China got back southern Manchuria.

1905 The Cullinan diamond was found at the Premier mine in Transvaal, South Africa. It was named after Sir Thomas Cullinan, who discovered the mine. Weighing 3106 carats in uncut form, it is the largest diamond ever found. It was presented to Britain's King Edward VII. Cut into nine large and 100 smaller pieces, it became part of the British Crown Jewels.

1905 Chinese revolutionary leader Sun Yat-sen founded the Alliance Society.

September 18, 1905–April 15, 1990 Swedish-American actress Greta Garbo lived during this period. *The Torrent, Anna Karenina* and *Camille* are some of her most famous films.

October 13, 1905 During the Russian Revolution, workers on strike formed the first worker's council, or 'soviet', at Ivanovo-Vosnesensk. Similar councils were formed in other parts of the country.

October 16, 1905 In India, British Viceroy Lord Curzon divided the province of Bengal into east Bengal and west Bengal. This caused widespread unhappiness among the Bengalis and accelerated the Indian nationalist movement.

375

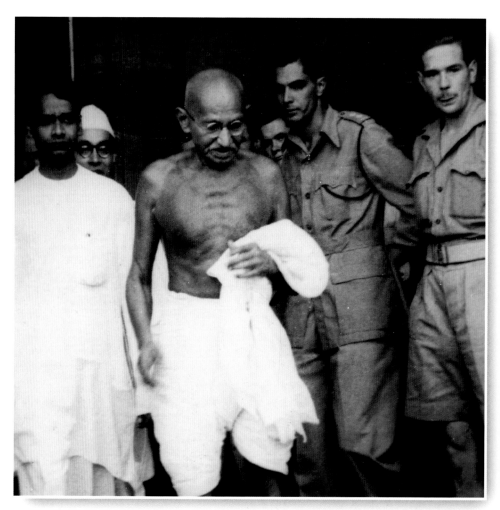

1905 The first German submarine, the U-1, was built. The letter U stood for *Unterseeboot* (meaning 'undersea boat'). Germany was the first country to employ submarines in war during World War I.

October 30, 1905 Tsar Nicholas II issued the October Manifesto, ending the absolute power of the crown and promising to establish the Duma, which would create a Russian Constitution.

November 28, 1905 The Irish nationalist party Sinn Féin was founded. In the Irish language, Sinn Féin means 'ourselves'. The goal of the party is the independence of Ireland.

February, 1906 HMS *Dreadnought* was launched by the British Navy. It was the first truly modern battleship, powered by steam turbines and fitted with big guns. The ship was 160 m long and could carry a crew of about 800 men.

◀ *Mohandas Karamchand Gandhi was called 'Mahatma', which means 'great-souled'.*

March 7, 1906 Finnish women were the first in Europe to be given the right to vote. By the following year, women were elected to the Finnish Parliament.

April 18, 1906 San Francisco was hit by a devastating earthquake.

April 23, 1906 The Russian Duma drafted the Fundamental Laws, which served as the Russian Constitution.

May 19, 1906 The Simplon railroad tunnel between Italy and Switzerland was opened. The Simplon is the longest railroad tunnel in the world.

June 6, 1906 The Zulus of Natal revolted against the poll tax imposed by the South African government. The revolt was suppressed and its leader was killed.

September 1906 In South Africa, Mohandas Karamchand Gandhi led a peaceful and non-violent protest against the Government of Transvaal's order that all Asians had to be registered with the government and be fingerprinted.

1906-1907

September 1906 American film producer and director J Stuart Blackton made the first animated film, *Funny Phases of Funny Faces*.

September 29, 1906 The Cuban election led to a disputed result and riots. United States troops occupied Cuba to control the situation.

December 24, 1906 Canadian-American Reginald A Fessenden broadcast the first radio programme, from his transmitting station at Brant Rock, Massachusetts, USA. It featured poetry reading, music and a speech.

1907 Italian educator Maria Montessori founded the first Montessori school, which applied a system of teaching researched and developed by her. The system was so successful that it is still in use today.

1907 American inventor Lee de Forest invented the Audion tube, which was used for broadcasting sound through radio waves. The Audion tube led to the development of radio, telephone and television.

1907 British-Indian author and poet Rudyard Kipling was awarded the Nobel Prize for Literature. His most famous works are *Kim* and *Jungle Book*.

...FASCINATING FACT...

Before Wilbur and Orville Wright became famous for their experiments with aircraft, the brothers sold and repaired bicycles. In 1896 they manufactured their first Van Cleve bicycle and a few years later they designed yet another bicycle called St Claire. Their designs were successful and they made as much as $3000 a year. By the early 1900s they became increasingly involved in aircraft design and stopped making bicycles.

▶ *The two* Jungle Books *written by Rudyard Kipling have become children's classics.*

June 15–October 18, 1907 United States President Theodore Roosevelt called the Hague Convention, which was attended by 44 countries. Several rules of war and the rights and duties of neutral and warring countries were written into law, though not all countries agreed to them.

July 6, 1907–July 13, 1954 Mexican painter Frida Kahlo lived during this period. She is famous for her self-portraits.

August 2, 1907 Following the killing of French workers in Casablanca, Morocco, French warships bombed the city and French troops were stationed in Casablanca.

November 13, 1907 French bicycle maker and inventor Paul Cornu flew the first helicopter.

1908

1908 British army officer Robert Baden-Powell founded the Boy Scout movement. He wrote *Scouting for Boys* in the same year. In 1910, he founded the Girl Guides (later named Girl Scouts) with his sister Agnes and his wife Olave.

February 1, 1908 King Carlos of Portugal and his elder son were killed by rebels from the Portuguese army. Carlos' younger son Manuel ascended the throne.

March 25, 1908–April 16, 1991 British film director David Lean lived during this period. *Lawrence of Arabia, Dr Zhivago* and *The Bridge on the River Kwai* are some of his masterpieces.

July 8, 1908–February 4, 1975 African-American musician Louis Jordan lived during this period. Jordan, who sang and played the saxophone, greatly influenced the development of rhythm and blues, and rock and roll.

August 1908 The Chinese monarchy presented its proposal for gradually adopting constitutional rule in China.

August 27, 1908–February 25, 2001 Australian cricketer Sir Donald Bradman lived during this period. One of the most outstanding players in cricketing history, he scored 6996 runs and his average of 99.94 runs per match remains a world record. He retired from first-class cricket in 1949 and was knighted in the same year.

October 6, 1908 Austria announced its decision to make Bosnia-Herzegovina a part of the Austria-Hungary Empire. This decision angered the natives of Bosnia-Herzegovina as well as Serbia and the Ottoman Turks, who both wanted to control the disputed area.

October 10, 1908 The province of Bulgaria declared its independence from the Ottoman Empire. Bulgarian prince Ferdinand was made the first king of independent Bulgaria.

October 10, 1908 The Belgian Parliament declared the Congo Free State in Africa a Belgian colony.

December 28, 1908 A powerful earthquake in Italy destroyed the town of Messina and killed 75,000 people.

▶ *Robert Baden-Powell's role in the siege of Mafeking during the South African War made him a national hero in Britain.*

1909–1910

1909 United States marines took over Nicaragua, following an American-backed revolt against President José Santos Zelaya. Zelaya was forced to resign and Adolfo Díaz was made president in 1911.

January 28, 1909 Cuban Liberal leader José Miguel Gómez was elected the president of Cuba.

February 12, 1909 The National Association for the Advancement of Colored People (NAACP) was founded in New York. It played a vital role in the fight against racism in the US.

April 6, 1909 American explorer Robert Peary claimed to have reached the North Pole along with Afro-American Matthew Henson. The point Peary actually reached is now thought to have been 50–100 km short of the North Pole.

July 25, 1909 French inventor Louis Blériot flew across the English Channel in his monoplane. This was the first flight across open sea.

March 23, 1910–September 6, 1998 Japanese film director Akira Kurosawa lived during this period. *Seven Samurai*, *Throne of Blood* and *Ran* are some of his best-known movies.

May 31, 1910 Transvaal, Cape Colony, Orange Free State and Natal joined together to form the Union of South Africa. The first elected prime minister of the new republic was Louis Botha.

August 22, 1910 Japan annexed Korea, remaining there till the end of World War II.

August 27, 1910–September 5, 1997 Mother Teresa lived during this period. She founded the Missionaries of Charity in Calcutta (now Kolkata), India. She dedicated her life to serving lepers and the poor. Mother Teresa recieved the Nobel Peace Prize in 1979 and was beatified (declared 'blessed' by the Pope) in 2003.

1910–1911 Portuguese revolt against the monarchy forced King Manuel II to flee. The Portuguese Republic was formed and Manuel José de Arriaga was elected its first president.

▲ *The plane in which Louis Blériot flew across the English Channel was called* Blériot XI.

▲ *The sinking of the liner* Titanic *revealed that safety measures then in force did not include enough lifeboats.*

1911 American aviation pioneer Glen H Curtiss developed the first successful seaplane. Aircraft designed by Curtiss were used by the United States Air Force during World War I.

1911 Polish-French scientist Marie Curie won her second Nobel Prize, this time in Chemistry.

June 22, 1911 George V was crowned king of the United Kingdom.

September 28, 1911 Italy declared war against Turkey in order to take control of Cyrenaica, Fezzan and Tripolitania in North Africa.

October 10, 1911 Chinese troops rose in revolt and occupied the capital city Wu-ch'ang. Sun Yat-sen, leader of the Chinese Nationalist Party, was appointed as the head of the new Chinese republic.

December 12, 1911 The reunification of east and west Bengal was announced by King George V.

December 14, 1911 Norwegian explorer Roald Amundsen became the first person to reach the South Pole.

January 28, 1912–August 11, 1956 American painter Jackson Pollock lived during this period. He was one of America's most important Abstract Expressionist painters.

February 1912 The Qing monarchy of China gave up their claim to the throne. Sun Yat-Sen resigned from the leadership of the Chinese republic, making way for Yuan Shikai.

April 14–15, 1912 The British luxury liner *Titanic* sank in the Atlantic on its maiden voyage to New York from Southampton, England. Over 1500 passengers and crew were killed in the tragic accident.

... FASCINATING FACT ...

The White Star Line built the *Titanic*, the largest and most luxurious ship of its time. It was built to beat rival Cunard Line's *Lusitania*. When the *Titanic* was built two other sister ships, *Olympic* and *Britannic*, were also made. The *Olympic* served as a transport ship during World War I and was retired and auctioned off bit by bit in 1935. The *Britannic* was used as a British hospital ship during World War I.

1912-1914

July 30, 1912 Japanese Meiji emperor Mutsuhito died. His son Yoshihito ascended the throne.

October 8, 1912 The Balkan League, comprising Greece, Serbia, Bulgaria and Montenegro, declared war on the Ottoman Empire to free Macedonia from Turkish rule.

October 14, 1912 United States President Theodore Roosevelt was shot while campaigning at Milwaukee, Wisconsin. Roosevelt survived the assassination attempt.

March 18, 1913 George I, King of Greece, was assassinated. His son Constantine I ascended the Greek throne.

April 1913 Woodrow Wilson was elected the 28th president of the United States.

May 30, 1913 The Ottoman Turks lost to the Balkan League in the First Balkan War. This defeat cost them Albania and Macedonia.

September 12, 1913–March 31, 1980 American athlete Jesse Owens lived during this period. He won four gold medals in the 1936 Berlin Olympics and held the world record in long jump, which was unbeaten for 25 years.

September 12, 1913–January 4, 1960 Algerian-French novelist, essayist and playwright Albert Camus lived during this period. *The Stranger*, *The Myth of Sisyphus* and *Exile and the Kingdom* are some of his works. He was awarded the Nobel Prize for Literature in 1957.

1914 British comedian and director Charlie Chaplin began his career in Hollywood movies with *Making a Living* and *Kid Auto Races at Venice*. It was in the latter that he first appeared wearing his familiar baggy trousers, tight coat, battered hat, floppy shoes and little moustache.

January 1, 1914 The Northern and Southern Nigeria British Protectorates were joined together to form the British Colony and Protectorate of Nigeria, with Lagos as its capital.

▲ *American athlete Jesse Owens. After his superb performance in the 1936 Berlin Olympics foiled Hitler's intention to show Aryan racial superiority through the Games.*

1914

▲ *Archduke Francis Ferdinand and his wife Sophie, countess von Chotek, visited Sarajevo.*
Less than an hour after this photo was taken, they were both assassinated.

January 10, 1914 The Chinese parliament was dissolved and President Yuan Shikai became dictator of China. He was successful in quelling a revolt against his rule, but his efforts to establish his own dynasty failed.

1914 The American Society for Composers, Authors and Publishers (ASCAP) was established in New York City to protect the copyrighted musical compositions of its members. The society ensured that the composer was paid if his music was broadcast, commercially recorded or otherwise used for profit.

April 2, 1914–August 5, 2000 British actor Sir Alec Guinness lived during this period. After service in the Royal Navy, he appeared on stage in Britain, United States and Canada in *The Cocktail Party*, *Ross* and *Dylan*. He also starred in movies such as *Oliver Twist*, *Kind Hearts and Coronets*, *The Man in the White Suit* and *The Lavender Hill Mob*. He won an Oscar for his role in *Bridge on the River Kwai* and was knighted in 1959.

June 28, 1914 Archduke Francis Ferdinand, heir to the throne of Austria-Hungary, was killed at Sarajevo by a Serbian patriot.

July 28, 1914 The Austrian emperor Franz Joseph declared war against Serbia, starting World War I.

July 31, 1914 Russia joined the war to defend its ally, Serbia.

August 1, 1914 Germany declared war against Russia. Just two days after that it attacked France as well.

August 4, 1914 Germany invaded Belgium, a country that had not involved itself in the war.

August 4, 1914 US President Woodrow Wilson declared that the United States would not take sides or participate in World War I.

August 6, 1914 Austria-Hungary declared war against Russia. Later in the month, Japan declared war on Germany, after the latter refused to surrender the Chinese territory of Tsingtao to Japan.

389

1914

August 14, 1914 France and Germany fought the Battle of the Frontiers. This was a series of battles along the Franco-Belgian and Franco-German borders.

August 15, 1914 The Panama Canal was opened. Earlier, a French company had begun the construction of the canal, but the enterprise collapsed in 1889. In 1904, the United States was granted the Panama Canal Zone and the construction began in 1904. The canal enabled the ships travelling between the Atlantic and Pacific oceans to avoid the circumnavigation of South America.

◄ *William II was the German emperor (kaiser) during World War I. After the war, he went into exile in the Netherlands.*

August 26–30, 1914 German forces crushed the Russian army in the Battle of Tannenberg.

August 28, 1914 British naval forces defeated a German fleet in the Battle of Helgoland Bight.

September 6–12, 1914 In the First Battle of the Marne, French forces halted the invading Germans and pushed them back with the help of British Expeditionary Forces.

September 9–14, 1914 On the eastern front, German forces defeated the Russians in the First Battle of the Masurian Lakes.

October 19, 1914 British forces made a surprise attack on the Germans at Ypres (called 'Wipers' by the British). The Battle of Ypres continued for almost a month.

October 29–30, 1914 Turkey allied with Germany and the Turkish fleet, led by the German warship *Goeben*, attacked several Russian ports, including Odessa.

November 1, 1914 Russia, France and Britain declared war against Turkey.

December 25, 1914 A temporary and unofficial truce was declared during Christmas among troops on the Western Front.

...FASCINATING FACT...

Trench warfare was one of the most effective tactics used by the Germans in World War I. Three to four lines of long and deep trenches were dug at the battlefront, each with a protective barbed wire barrier. The trenches were cut in a zigzag fashion and were connected to one another through underground passages. They were large enough to accommodate first-aid stations, kitchens, toilets and ammunition stores.

1915

1915 French novelist Romain Rolland was awarded the Nobel Prize for Literature. His best-known novel is the ten-volume epic *Jean-Christophe*. His other famous books include *Mahatma Gandhi* and *Beethoven*.

January 24, 1915 In the Battle of the Dogger Bank, a British fleet defeated the Germans by sinking one of their cruisers and seriously damaging two others, forcing the Germans to flee.

April 22, 1915 German troops used poison gas to attack Allied forces in the Second Battle of Ypres, introducing the concept of chemical warfare.

April 25, 1915 Allied forces began their campaign against Turkey by attacking Gallipoli near the Turkish capital of Constantinople.

▶ *Orson Welles, along with John Houseman, formed the Mercury Theatre in 1937.*

May 6, 1915–October 10, 1985
American film maker Orson Welles
lived during this period. He wrote,
directed, produced and acted in
Citizen Kane, widely considered
to be one of the greatest movies
of the 20th century.

May 6, 1915 American economist
Paul Samuelson was born. His book
Economics is the bestselling US
textbook of all times. He was awarded
the Nobel Prize for Economics in 1970
for his contributions to nearly all
branches of economics.

May 17, 1915 British liner *Lusitania*,
returning from New York to Liverpool
carrying passengers and a mixed cargo,
was torpedoed by a German U-boat.
Nearly 1200 passengers were killed,
including 128 United States citizens.

November 1, 1915 In the Battle of
Coronel, the German navy defeated a
British fleet led by Sir Christopher
Cradock, sinking two of their big
cruisers and killing the British
commander.

December 8, 1915 British Admiral Sir
Doveton Sturdee led a fleet of eight
cruisers, including the HMS *Invincible*
and HMS *Inflexible*, to defeat the
Germans off the Falklands coast.

December 12, 1915–May 14, 1998
American singer and actor Francis
(Frank) Albert Sinatra lived during this
period. He sang in the blues, pop
and jazz styles, and also acted in over
20 movies.

1916

1916 The Professional Golfers' Association of America (PGA) was formed. Its purpose was to promote interest in professional golf and elevate the standards of the game. Based at Palm Beach Gardens, Florida, the association conducts 40 tournaments for its members each year, including four premier golf events.

February 21–December 18, 1916 France defeated Germany in the Battle of Verdun, one of the most important and longest military encounters in World War I.

April 5, 1916–June 12, 2003 American actor Gregory Peck lived during this period. *Days of Glory*, *Spellbound*, *Roman Holiday*, *To Kill a Mockingbird* and *Cape Fear* are some of his films.

April 22, 1916–March 12, 1999 American-born British violinist and conductor Yehudi Menuhin lived during this period. He was one of the most accomplished violinists of the 20th century.

April 24, 1916 Irish republicans began the Easter Rebellion in Dublin, taking control of the post office and other public buildings. British troops suppressed the revolt swiftly and its leaders were executed.

May 31–June 1, 1916 British and German fleets engaged in the Battle of Jutland, held to be the greatest naval encounter in World War I. There was no clear winner in this battle. Germany destroyed more ships and men, but the British retained control of the North Sea.

June 6, 1916 Li Yüan-hung became the president of China.

July 1–November 13, 1916 Britain introduced the battle tank for the first time in the Battle of the Somme, an Allied attack on German forces on the western front. The tanks could easily cross the muddy, uneven terrain, but suffered frequent mechanical failure. This long and expensive battle ended with no clear result.

August 1, 1916 The Chinese Parliament was established once again and General Tuan Ch'i-jui was elected as premier.

August 28, 1916 Italy joined the war against Germany and Austria-Hungary.

▼ *The game of golf started gaining popularity across the world in the 20th century, though it is believed to have been played in various earlier forms since sometime around the 15th century. However, the precise origin of the game is still a matter of debate.*

395

1916–1917

September 13, 1916–November 23, 1990 British writer Roald Dahl lived during this period. He was a popular and successful writer of both adult and children's fiction. *James and the Giant Peach* and *Charlie and the Chocolate Factory* are some of his books.

October 5, 1916 The Trans-Siberian Railroad, running from Moscow to Vladivostock, was completed. It was the longest single rail system in Russia.

November 7, 1916 Woodrow Wilson was elected president of the United States for the second time.

November 7, 1916 Jeannette Rankin from Montana became the first woman to be elected to the United States House of Representatives.

▼ *Russian soldiers joined the people of St Petersburg (called Petrograd at that time) in the revolution that broke out in March 1917. The tsar was forced to step down.*

... **FASCINATING FACT** ...

After the first modern Olympic Games were held in April 1896, the tradition continued every four years, except in 1916, 1940 and 1944, due to the world wars. The Olympic flag, designed by the founder of the modern Olympics, Pierre de Coubertin, was first seen in 1920 at Antwerp. Coubertin also created the Olympic motto, Citius–Altius–Fortius ('Faster–higher–stronger') and the Olympic oath.

December 1916 The Indian National Congress and the All-India Muslim League came together to sign the Lucknow Pact, a document that outlined the structure of an independent Indian government.

December 12, 1916 An avalanche in the Dolomite Mountains in the Italian Alps killed nearly 18,000 Italian and Austrian soldiers.

1917 The United States bought the Virgin Islands from Denmark for $25 million. The United States built a naval base there to protect the Panama Canal and prevent Germany from occupying the islands.

March 8, 1917 Riots broke out in St Petersburg. As soldiers joined hands with the common people, a revolution against the monarchy spread all over Russia.

March 11, 1917 Baghdad was captured from the Turks by British forces.

March 15, 1917 Tsar Nicholas II was finally forced to give up his throne and a provisional government came to power in Russia. The new government introduced many democratic reforms, but decided to continue the war and rapidly lost popularity to a rival group called the Petrograd Soviet of Workers' and Soldiers' Deputies.

1917

March 20, 1917 The United States War Cabinet voted in favour of participating in the World War.

April 9, 1917 The United States joined the war on the Allied side.

April 9, 1917 Canadian forces, fighting on behalf of the Allies, won the Battle of Vimy Ridge in France. Over 10,000 Canadians were wounded during the battle and over 3000 killed. The Germans lost 20,000 men.

May 5, 1917 A new provisional government was formed in Russia and Aleksandr Kerensky was appointed minister of war and navy. Two months later he was made prime minister of Russia.

June 27, 1917 Greece joined the Allied forces after pro-German king Constantine I abdicated in favour of his son Alexander I.

July 31–November 10, 1917 The Allied forces won the Battle of Passchendaele (the Third Battle of Ypres), but only at the cost of 700,000 lives.

August 28, 1917–February 6, 1994 American comic-book artist Jack Kirby lived during this period. He helped in the creation of about 400 characters, including superheroes such as Captain America, Spiderman, X-Men, Daredevil and the Fantastic Four.

September 1, 1917 German troops defeated Russian forces at Riga and occupied the northernmost part of Russia.

October 23, 1917 The American Expeditionary Forces in France joined the war.

November 7, 1917 The Bolsheviks, led by Vladimir Iilych Lenin, overthrew the provisional Russian government and established the Soviet Republic. In 1918, Lenin signed the Treaty of Brest-Litovsk with Germany. During the Russian Civil War that followed, he launched a campaign called 'Red Terror', aimed at eliminating political opponents. He also launched a series of economic reforms to meet Russia's pressing economic needs.

▲ *Canadian troops surrounded by trench mortar bombs during the World War I. The Canadian Corps won a decisive victory at the Battle of Vimy Ridge, although over 10,000 soldiers died.*

399

1917–1918

December 6, 1917 Finland declared its independence from Russia.

December 9, 1917 Britain defeated Turkish forces and their Arab allies and captured Jerusalem.

December 22, 1917 Russia began peace talks with Germany.

1918 Lithuania declared its independence from Russia and Germany.

January 28, 1918 Civil war broke out in Finland and the communist Social Democratic Party took control of several Finnish towns. The White Army, led by General Carl Gustaf Mannerheim, put down the revolt.

March 1918 An epidemic of Spanish influenza began in a military camp in Kansas. It spread swiftly to all parts of the world and claimed the lives of millions of people. The number of deaths due to influenza was greater than those caused by the war itself.

1918 Tsar Nicholas II and his family were captured by communist troops at Tsarskoye Selo and taken to Siberia. Later, they were moved to Yekaterinburg in the Ural Mountains. In July, Tsar Nicholas II and his family were executed by Bolshevik gunmen.

August 8, 1918 German forces launched the Second Battle of the Somme to capture Amiens before proceeding to Paris. German troops led by General Erich Ludendorff forced the British to retreat to Amiens. Over 200,000 British soldiers were captured in the battle. The Germans suffered 300,000 casualties. A counterattack by British and French troops forced the Germans to turn back, producing an unlikely victory for the Allies.

September 27, 1918 Allied forces broke through the Hindenburg Line, a fortification that the Germans had successfully defended until then.

October 3–4, 1918 Germany and Austria expressed their desire for peace in letters to the United States president, Woodrow Wilson.

▼ *Tsar Nicholas II and his family.*

1918–1919

October 28, 1918
Czechoslovakia declared its independence from Austria-Hungary. The Prague National Council elected Tomás Masaryk as the first president.

November 1, 1918 Belgrade, capital of Serbia, was recaptured by the Allies, following the surrender of Bulgarian forces.

November 9, 1918 Kaiser Wilhelm II, Emperor of Germany, fled to Holland.

November 11, 1918 Peace was declared and World War I ended.

December 1, 1918 The kingdom of Serbs, Croats and Slovenes was formed. It comprised Serbia, Montenegro, Croatia-Slavonia, Bosnia and Herzegovina, Slovenia and Dalmatia. The Serbian Karadjordjevic dynasty ruled the new kingdom.

◀ *Italian dictator Benito Mussolini was also known as 'Il Duce', Italian for 'the leader'.*

1919 American inventor Lee de Forest developed the Phonofilm, a process by which sound could be recorded on film. This was an important discovery in the development of motion picture history, as it led to the development of talkies.

1919 German architect Walter Gropius founded the Bauhaus school of design in Weimar, Germany. The institute played an important role in the development of architectural and interior design during the early 20th century.

February 23, 1919 Journalist and ex-soldier Benito Mussolini founded the Italian Fascist Party.

April 1919 In the Russo-Polish war, Poland successfully stood up against Russian attacks, with the help of France. The Treaty of Riga gave Poland parts of what are now known as Belarus and Poland.

April 13, 1919 British troops led by General Reginald E Dyer opened fire at a crowd of unarmed Indian protesters gathered at the Jallianwala Bagh in Amristar, India, killing several people.

. . . **FASCINATING FACT** . . .

Rasputin, the Siberian peasant-healer, is one of the most fascinating characters in Russian history. Rasputin's extraordinary healing powers made him a favourite of Tsar Nicholas II's Queen Alexandra. Jealous members of the court tried to get rid of him. A group of noblemen including the emperor's first cousin Grand Duke Dmitry and Prince Felix Yusupov assassinated him by poisoning him, shooting him and finally throwing him into the ice-filled Neva River.

1919

May 1919 The Amir of Afghanistan, Amanullah Khan, led Afghani forces in the Third Anglo-Afghan War. Afghanistan won its independence from Britain.

May 18, 1919–February 21, 1991 The British ballerina Dame Margot Fonteyn lived during this period. She travelled all over the world performing a variety of roles in classics such as *Swan Lake*, *Sleeping Beauty* and *Ondine*.

May 25, 1919 Volcano Kloet erupted in Java, killing 16,000 people.

June 28, 1919 Germany and the Allied countries signed the Treaty of Versailles. As a result, Germany lost about 10 percent of its European territory and promised to pay the Allies to make reparation for war damage.

July 20, 1919 Edmund Hillary, explorer and mountaineer from New Zealand, was born. Hillary, along with Tenzing Norgay, became the first to reach the summit of the Mount Everest.

August 11, 1919 The Weimar Constitution was passed by the German Assembly and the new German Weimar Republic was established with Friedrich Ebert as its first president.

September 10, 1919 Austria and the Allied countries signed the Treaty of Saint-Germain, whereby Czechoslovakia, Hungary, Poland and the kingdom of Serbs, Croats and Slovenes gained their independence.

October 28, 1919 The United States Congress passed the National Prohibition Act (also called the Volstead Act), banning the manufacture and sale of liquor. The prohibition was removed in 1933.

November 27, 1919 Bulgaria was forced to sign the Treaty of Neuilly, giving away large portions of its territories to Yugoslavia and Greece. Bulgaria also had to reduce its army to just 20,000 soldiers and pay compensation to countries it had fought against.

November 28, 1919 Nancy Astor became the first woman to be elected to the British House of Commons.

▼ *David Lloyd George, British prime minister (1916–1922) who guided his country through the latter part of World War I.*

1919–1921

December 24, 1919 Civil war broke out in Russia between the Red Army of the Communist government and the White Army of the anti-Communists. The Communists emerged victorious.

1919–1926 Spain fought the Rif War against the Rif and Jibala people of Morocco. The war ended with Spain's conquest of western Sahara.

January 2, 1920–April 6, 1992 Russian-born American author Isaac Asimov lived during this period. *Foundation, Foundation and Empire* and *Second Foundation* are some of his works.

August 10, 1920 Ottoman Turkey signed the Treaty of Sèvres. The treaty granted Armenia its independence and Greece won control over parts of Thrace (in the southeastern Balkans, Europe), Anatolia (in Turkey) and the Dardanelles (strait in northwestern Turkey). War soon broke out between Turkey and Greece over the extent of Greek territory.

◀ *Adolf Hitler began his autobiography* Mein Kampf *in prison following his arrest in 1923.*

December 1, 1920 General Álvaro Obregón was elected president of Mexico. Under his rule the civil war that had troubled Mexico since 1909 was put to an end.

December 16, 1920 A major earthquake in the Gansu province of China killed nearly 200,000 people.

1920 In Germany, the German Workers' Party was renamed the National Socialist German Workers' (or Nazi) Party when Adolf Hitler became its leader.

1921 French bacteriologists Albert Calmette and Camille Guérin developed the BCG (Bacillus Calmette-Guérin) vaccination against tuberculosis.

1921 Albert Einstein was awarded the Nobel Prize for Physics.

1921–1924 Mongolia drove the Chinese from its territory with the help of Russian forces. The Mongolian People's Republic was founded.

1921–1923

December 6, 1921 The Anglo-Irish Treaty was signed, which laid the foundation of the Irish Free State. The Northern Irish counties of Antrim, Armagh, Down, Fermanagh, Londonderry and Tyrone chose to remain under British rule.

January 1922 Micheal Collins, Irish Republican Army (IRA) leader, was made chairman of the provisional Irish government. Rebels opposed to the Anglo-Irish Treaty killed him on August 22.

February 2, 1922 *Ulysses*, an epic novel written by Irish author James Joyce, was published in Paris. It is considered one of the greatest literary classics of the 20th century.

June 10, 1922–June 22, 1969 American singer and actress Judy Garland lived during this period.

November 4, 1922 British archeologist Howard Carter discovered Pharaoh Tutankhamen's tomb in Thebes, Egypt.

December 6, 1922 The Irish Free State was established with William Thomas Cosgrave as its president and Timothy Michael Healy as its governor-general.

...FASCINATING FACT...

British archaeologist Howard Carter is well known as the person who unearthed Pharaoh Tutankhamen's tomb. Before he made this famous discovery, he had discovered six other royal tombs, including those of Hatshepsut and Thuthmose IV. In 1907 Lord Carnarvon began sponsoring Carter's quest for Tutankhamen's tomb. By 1922 Carnarvon had lost hope of finding anything and had ordered Carter to return home after one last season. Carter discovered the tomb on his last attempt!

December 30, 1922 The Union of Soviet Socialist Republics (USSR) was founded. It comprised Ukraine, Belorussia and the Transcaucasian Federation, as well as Russia itself.

1923 The International Criminal Police Organization (Interpol) was established in Vienna, Austria.

1923 Spanish inventor Juan de la Cierva invented the autogiro, a low-cost alternative to the helicopter that proved of use for only small aircraft.

▶ *The Golden Mask of Pharaoh Tutankhamen can be seen at the Egyptian Museum in Cairo.*

1923-1926

March 3, 1923 *Time* magazine's first issue was published.

September 1, 1923 A massive earthquake in Kwanto, Japan, destroyed the towns of Yokohama and Tokyo, killing about 143,000 people.

October 29, 1923 Turkey became a republic and Sultan Abdul Mejid II was sent into exile. The new government, headed by Kemal Ataturk, defeated Greece and regained much lost territory.

November 8–9, 1923 Adolf Hitler's Nazi Party led a rebellion called the Beer Hall Putsch against the Weimar Republic. They were unsuccessful and Hitler was arrested.

1924 Surrealism, an artistic and literary movement, was founded in France.

January 21, 1924 Russian Bolshevik leader Valdimir Iilych Lenin died.

April 3, 1924–July 1, 2004 American actor Marlon Brando lived during this period. He performed memorable roles in classic films such as *A Streetcar named Desire* and the *Godfather* series.

1925–1927 Benito Mussolini, prime minister of Italy, dissolved the Italian Parliament and became dictator of Italy.

June 17, 1925 The Geneva Protocol banned the use of chemical and biological weapons during war.

September 16, 1925 American guitarist B B King was born. He was responsible for the development of the 20th-century 'blues' style and greatly influenced his contemporaries and younger musicians.

1926 John Logie Baird of Scotland invented the first television transmitter, which was capable of showing crude, flickering images.

▶ *Ill-health forced Scottish engineer John Logie Baird to give up his job as an electric-power engineer in 1922. After his retirement, he devoted himself to television research.*

1926-1929

March 16, 1926 American scientist Robert Goddard tested the first liquid-fuelled rocket. It used liquid oxygen and gasoline.

August 6, 1926 *The Jazz Singer* became the first talking motion picture. It was produced by Warner Brothers and directed by Alan Crosland.

October 18, 1926 African-American songwriter, singer and guitarist Chuck Berry was born. He popularized the rhythm and blues and rock and roll styles of music.

April 22, 1927 The Great Mississippi Flood, considered the most destructive flood in the history of the United States, displaced about 700,000 people.

May 20–21, 1927 American pilot Charles A Lindbergh made the first non-stop solo flight across the Atlantic, from New York to Paris, in his monoplane *Spirit of St Louis*.

May 25, 1927–March 12, 2001 American author Robert Ludlum lived during this period. *The Bourne Identity*, *The Scarlatti Inheritance* and *The Osterman Weekend* are some of his books.

November 12, 1927 The Soviet Communist Party expelled Leon Trotsky. Joseph Stalin gained undisputed control of the Soviet Union.

1928 Russian-born American inventor Vladimir Zworykin patented his design for a colour television.

December 5, 1928 The Chaco War between Paraguay and Bolivia began.

1929 King Alexander I renamed the kingdom of Serbs, Croats and Slovenes as Yugoslavia, and assumed dictatorship of the country. The move ended three years of internal disorder and virtual civil war between the Serbians and the Croats.

▶ *Joseph Stalin (right), seen here with Lenin (left), was one of the most brutal dictators in history.*

1929-1932

May 16, 1929 The first Oscar awards were presented by the Academy of Motion Picture Arts and Sciences. The award for the best film went to *Wings*, directed by William Wellman. This was the only silent film to win the award. Emil Jannings and Janet Gaynor were awarded best actor and actress.

▲ *When it was opened in 1931, the Empire State Building was the tallest building in the world.*

October 25, 1929 The New York Stock Market crashed. This marked the beginning of the Great Depression, a period of global economic crisis.

1930 In Brazil rival factions of Fascists and communists fought each other in the streets. President Getúlio Vargas imposed military rule to enforce peace.

1930 British inventor Frank Whittle patented the jet engine. Practical construction problems meant it was not introduced for aircraft for years.

May 1, 1931 In New York, the 102-storey Empire State Building was opened.

March 9, 1932 The Japanese established the state of Manchukuo in Manchuria and appointed the last Qing emperor of China, P'u-yi, as head of the new state.

May 20–21, 1932 American pilot Amelia Earhart became the first woman to fly across the Atlantic.

June 24, 1932 The Promoters Revolution in Thailand overthrew the monarchy and established constitutional rule, with power held by the small group of 'promoters'.

August 17, 1932 V S Naipaul was born in Trinidad, in the West Indies. One of the foremost fiction writers of the 20th century, he was awarded the Nobel Prize for Literature in 2001.

November 8, 1932 Franklin D Roosevelt was elected the 32nd president of the United States.

...FASCINATING FACT...

'Blues' music, one of the most popular musical styles of the 20th century, traces its origins to African folk music. It developed in the southern plantations in America, sung by African slaves while working on the fields or at social gatherings in their quarters. When slavery was abolished, blues-influenced black American church music became popular. During the Great Depression the blues spread all over America.

1933-1936

1933 Nearly 11,000 out of the 25,000 banks in the United States had to close down due to losses suffered during the Great Depression.

January 30, 1933 Adolf Hitler became chancellor of Germany.

March 1933 The worst phase of the Great Depression ended and the American economy began to recover.

March 10, 1933 The first Nazi concentration camp was established at Dachau. Jews and other prisioners were tortured and kept under inhuman conditions in these camps.

August 2, 1934 Adolf Hitler assumed the title of *Führer* (leader) of Germany. He now had dictatorial power over Germany and began a rapid buildup of military power.

1935 Amelia Earhart became the first woman to fly solo from Hawaii to California.

January 8, 1935–August 16, 1977 American singer Elvis Presley lived during this period. He was one of America's greatest singing sensations between the mid-1950s and 1960s and was called the 'King of Rock and Roll'. *Heartbreak Hotel* and *Jailhouse Rock* are among his biggest hits.

October 3, 1935 Benito Mussolini sent the Italian army to invade Ethiopia.

October 12, 1935 Luciano Pavarotti was born in Modena, Italy. He is probably the most famous opera singer of the 20th century.

January 20, 1936 George V died and was succeeded by his son Edward VIII as king of the United Kingdom and emperor of India. Edward soon became embroiled in a scandal and constitutional crisis over his choice of Wallis Simpson, a divorced American, as his wife and queen.

▶ *Concentration camps were places where people were confined, mainly for political reasons, under inhumane conditions.*

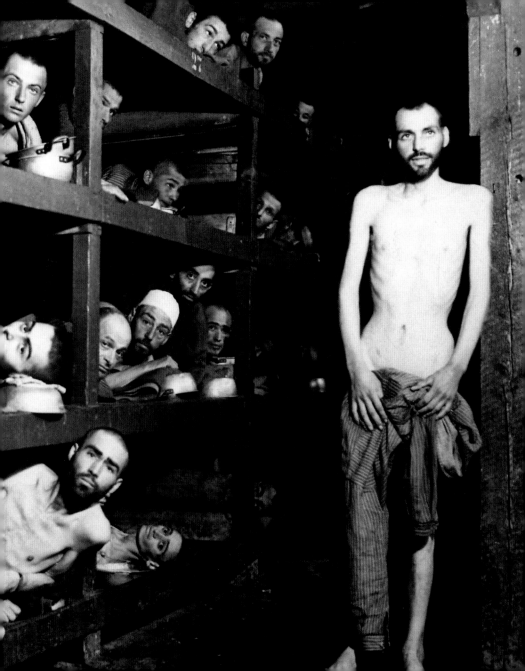

1936–1938

May 5, 1936 Italian forces captured Addis Ababa, the capital of Ethiopia, sending the Ethiopian monarch Haile Selassie into exile. Ethiopia was joined with Italian Somaliland and Eritrea to form Italian East Africa.

July 17, 1936 Civil war broke out in Spain when the Nationalist Party revolted against the ruling Republican government.

October 1, 1936 General Francisco Franco was declared the head of the nationalist Spanish government that was set up in the town of Burgos. After a bloody war, in which more than 500,000 people lost their lives, Franco and his troops established themselves in Madrid in March 1938.

November 3, 1936 Franklin D Roosevelt was re-elected to serve his second term as the president of the United States.

December 11, 1936 Edward VIII gave up his claim to the English throne and his brother George VI succeeded him.

January 1, 1937 General Anastasio Somoza García, commander of the Nicaraguan army, removed Juan Bautista Sacasa, the elected president of the country, from power. García took over the leadership of Nicaragua, and his family ruled the country until 1979.

May, 1937 Economic progress in the United States slowed down and the second phase of the Great Depression began.

June, 1938 The Great Depression finally ended.

July 21, 1938 The conflict between Paraguay and Bolivia ended with the signing of a treaty arranged by neighbouring countries and the United States.

September 29, 1938 Germany, Italy, France and Britain signed the Munich Agreement. Under its terms, part of Czechoslovakia (the Sudetenland) was ceded to Germany. Hitler later broke the agreement by conquering all of Czechoslovakia. France and Britain then began to prepare for war with Germany.

▲ *Edward VIII (second from left) became the only British monarch to resign voluntarily when he abdicated in order to marry Wallis Simpson.*

1939–1940

▲ *After World War II, Pablo Picasso joined the Communist Party and devoted his time to sculpture and ceramics as well as painting.*

April, 1939 Italian forces invaded and occupied Albania.

September 1, 1939 World War II began with the German invasion of Poland.

September 3, 1939 Britain and France declared war on Germany.

October 5, 1939 The Polish Army was completely routed and Germany took control of Poland. Germany and the Soviet Union shared Polish territories.

November 30, 1939 The Soviet Union invaded Finland as Finland refused to let the Russians establish a naval base in its territory. At first the Finns drove back the much larger Soviet armies and inflicted heavy casualties. Later, Stalin sent in vast numbers of Russian troops to defeat Finland.

1940 Russian forces occupied Lithuania, Estonia and Latvia.

March 6, 1940 The Russian Red Army defeated Finland and took over western Karelia, establishing a port on the Hanko Peninsula.

March 22–23, 1940 In India, the All-India Muslim League resolved to fight for the formation of a separate Muslim state.

1940 German forces invaded Denmark and Norway.

May 10, 1940 German forces made surprise attacks in the Low Countries (Belgium, The Netherlands and Luxembourg) and France. The Germans used a new form of warfare called blitzkrieg. They used tanks called panzers supported by aircraft to punch through enemy lines, and then advanced at high speed to disrupt enemy supply lines.

...FASCINATING FACT...

One of Pablo Picasso's most famous works of art is the massive mural *Guernica*, made for the Spanish pavilion at the 1937 Paris Exposition. This widely recognized symbol of war was inspired by the cruel destruction of the Spanish town of Guernica by German warplanes, on behalf of the Spanish dictator General Franco. One-third of Guernica's population was killed and the town was reduced to rubble to serve as an example to those rebelling against Franco's rule.

1940

May 10, 1940 Winston Churchill succeeded Neville Chamberlain as the prime minister of Britain.

May 26, 1940 Unsuccessful in defeating the German forces in France and the Low Countries, the British Expeditionary Forces were forced to leave for England.

May 27, 1940 Allied British forces were forced to pull out of Norway after holding out against the Germans for more than a month. Håkon VII, King of Norway, fled to Britain.

June 10, 1940 Italy declared war on France and Britain in support of Germany.

June 14, 1940 After taking Rouen and Asine, German forces entered Paris and spread out to the south, west and east of the country.

June 16, 1940 French premier Paul Reynaud resigned and World War I veteran Marshal Philippe Pétain succeeded him. France sent Hitler a peace note.

June 22, 1940 The Franco-German peace treaty was signed and two days later the Franco-Italian treaty was also made. German troops occupied more than half of France, including northern and northeastern France. The Italians took a small portion in the south. The rest of France that remained independent was ruled from the town of Vichy. The so-called Free French forces escaped to Britain and continued the war against Germany.

July–September, 1940 The Battle of Britain was fought between the Royal Air Force (RAF) and the German Luftwaffe. Germany made several air raids on England during this time, but the RAF won the battle. Hitler abandoned his plans to invade Britain.

1940 Japan signed treaties with Germany and Italy. These three countries and their allies were collectively called the Axis Powers.

▶ *Winston Churchill was awarded the Nobel Prize for Literature in 1953 and was knighted in the same year.*

1940–1941

November 1940 Romania and Hungary signed treaties of friendship with Axis Powers.

January 20, 1941 Exiled emperor Haile Selassie came back to power in Ethiopia after defeating Italian forces with the help of British troops.

March 1941 Bulgaria joined Germany in the war.

March 1941 Yugoslavia signed the Tripartite Pact (also known as the Three-Power Pact), joining the Axis Powers. The pact was originally signed by Germany, Italy and Japan on September 27, 1940.

◄ *The Japanese attack on the United States fleet at Pearl Harbor, Hawaii, hastened the entry of the United States into World War II. American casualties included over 180 aircraft and more than 5000 lives, from the military and the civilian.*

March 27, 1941 The Yugoslavian monarchy was overthrown and the army took control of the government. Yugoslavia's refusal to participate in the war caused the Axis Powers to invade the country a few days later.

March 28, 1941 The British Navy defeated the Italian fleet in the Battle of Cape Matapan. This World War II battle took place off the Greek coast.

April 6, 1941 German forces attacked and defeated Yugoslavia and Greece.

April, 1941 German Afrika Korps led by General Erwin Rommel expelled the British from Libya.

June 22, 1941 Germany invaded the Soviet Union. Other Axis Powers also declared war on the Soviet Union.

July 14, 1941 British forces, together with their Free French allies, invaded the Vichy French colony of Syria and established themselves in the country. They promised the Syrians they would become independent once the war was over.

▼ *A British soldier inspects a captured German panzer in North Africa.*

1941–1942

December 7, 1941 Japanese aircraft attacked Pearl Harbor in Hawaii. The United States reacted by declaring war on Japan.

December 11, 1941 Germany and Italy declared war against the United States.

January 8, 1942 English physicist Stephen Hawking was born. Despite being severely disabled, Hawking has contributed greatly to the study of astrophysics, and our understanding of black holes in particular.

January 17, 1942 American boxer Mohammed Ali was born. Known as Cassius Clay before converting to Islam, he was the first person to win the heavyweight championship thrice.

1942 Japanese forces attacked the Philippines, Hong Kong and Thailand.

February 14–15, 1942 Singapore was captured by Japanese forces and the British forces in Singapore surrendered.

May 1942 American forces in the Philippines were forced to surrender to the Japanese and the island country came under Japanese control.

June 1942 The United States defeated Japan in the Battle of Midway.

August 1942 The US defeated Japan in the Battle of Guadalcanal.

June–November 1942 British forces, led by Field Marshal Bernard L Montgomery, attacked the German Afrika Korps and defeated them in the Battles of El-Alamein.

...FASCINATING FACT...
During the World War II, six million Jews were killed by the Nazis in the Holocaust. Hitler believed that Aryans were superior to all other races, and that all inferior people should be used for slave labour or killed. The word Holocaust came from the Greek words *holo* (whole) and *caustos* (burned), meaning a burned offering or sacrifice that is totally consumed by fire.

▲ *Approximately 3000 United States naval and military personnel were killed or wounded during the attack on Pearl Harbor.*

1942-1944

September 13, 1942 After having successfully captured the Russian towns of Odessa, Kharkov, Sevastapol and Rostov, the Germans attacked Stalingrad. However, this time they were unsuccessful and lost 250,000 men.

November 27, 1942–September 18, 1970 American guitarist Jimi Hendrix lived during this period. He achieved great success and left a lasting impression in the world of rock, soul, blues and jazz music within his short solo career of just four years.

▼ *Around 5000 ships and 10,000 planes were employed in transporting troops during the invasion of Normandy by the Allies.*

1943 The Pentagon was built in Arlington, Virginia. It is the headquarters of the United States Department of Defense.

February 2, 1943 German forces suffered their first big defeat at Stalingrad, where they were forced to surrender. This was the beginning of the downfall of Nazi power.

May 13, 1943 German and Italian forces in North Africa surrendered to the Allies.

June 6, 1944 Allied Forces landed on the Normandy coast in France on D-Day.

July 1–22, 1944 The International Monetary Fund (IMF) and the International Bank for Reconstruction and Development (World Bank) were created at the Bretton Woods Conference held in New Hampshire.

July 20, 1944 Adolf Hitler survived an assassination attempt.

August 25, 1944 Allied forces liberated Paris from the Germans.

October 1944 United States forces regained control of the Philippines from the Japanese.

▼ *In the Normandy invasion, 156,000 American, British and Canadian troops landed at five beaches on the Normandy coast.*

1944-1945

October 2, 1944 The Polish uprising in Warsaw was put down by the Germans and the city of Warsaw was completely destroyed.

January 20, 1945 Hungary surrendered to the Allied forces.

February 6, 1945–May 11, 1981 Jamaican singer and songwriter Bob Marley lived during this period. He is considered one of the greatest reggae artists. His music is a combination of American, African and Jamaican styles.

April 12, 1945 Franklin D Roosevelt died and Harry S Truman became the 33rd president of the United States.

April 1945 Russian troops captured Berlin and the United States took Nürnberg.

April 28, 1945 Italian dictator Benito Mussolini was arrested during an attempt to escape across the frontier, and executed.

April 30, 1945 Nazi leader Adolf Hitler killed himself.

May 7, 1945 Germany surrendered unconditionally to the Allied powers.

August 6, 1945 The United States decided to use the atomic bomb against Japan. The first atomic bomb was dropped on Hiroshima using a special B-29 bomber of the American Air Forces. Almost the entire city was flattened and around 100,000 people were killed. A memorial park containing a museum and monuments has since been built in dedication to the victims.

August 9, 1945 The second atomic bomb was dropped on Nagasaki, a prominent shipbuilding centre in Japan. Again, the city was destroyed and between 60,000 and 80,000 people died.

▶ *United States aircraft bombed Nagasaki three days after the atomic bombing of Hiroshima, destroying almost one-third of the city.*

1945-1946

August 9, 1945 The Soviet Union invaded Manchuria. Within a few days they captured Emperor P'u-yi and conquered the country, taking over all stocks of food, gold and machinery.

August 14, 1945 Japan announced its surrender.

September 2, 1945 Communist leader Ho Chi Minh declared Vietnam's independence from France.

October 24, 1945 The United Nations was established.

1946 Supported by the Soviet Union, communists took control of most parts of Manchuria, northeastern China.

◀ *P'u-yi was the last emperor of the Qing dynasty in China. After World War II, he was tried as a war criminal by China but gained release in 1959.*

1946 John W Mauchly and John P Eckert invented the first electronic computer. It was called ENIAC (Electronic Numerical Integrator and Computer).

1946 The American Telephone and Telegraph Company (AT&T) introduced the first mobile telephones with radio receivers and transmitters that could be fitted in vehicles.

February 24, 1946 Colonel Juan Perón was elected the president of Argentina. During his leadership, his glamorous wife Eva Perón held considerable power and became very popular with the Argentinean public, especially the working classes.

June 2, 1946 King Umberto II of Italy was exiled and the people of Italy established a republic. Enrico de Nicola was named as the temporary president.

July 4, 1946 The Republic of the Philippines was established and Manuel Roxas became its first president.

... FASCINATING FACT ...
Eva Perón's rise to power from her humble and unhappy family background is almost a fairytale. It inspired British composer Andrew Lloyd Webber to create the hit stage musical *Evita* in 1978, which was performed 2900 times in its first run in London. In 1996 the screen version of *Evita* was made, with pop star Madonna playing the role of Eva Perón.

1946-1949

September 1946 King George II of Greece came back to power when the Greeks voted for the return of monarchy. This led to civil war against communist forces in northern Greece.

1947 American physicist and inventor Edwin Herbert Land developed the first camera that could take and develop pictures in a single process. The camera was available in markets the following year under the name of the Polaroid Land Camera.

1947 Russian weapons designer Mikhail Kalashnikov designed the AK-47 assault rifle for the Soviet Army. It is still one of the most widely used assault weapons today.

August 15, 1947 India gained independence from Britain and the separate Muslim state of Pakistan was formed. The part in the northwest was called West Pakistan, and the part to the northeast of India was called East Pakistan.

August 31, 1947 The United Nations recommended the creation of a separate Jewish state called Israel within the ancient Arab state of Palestine.

January 1, 1948 The General Agreement on Trade and Tariffs (GATT), signed by 23 countries, went into effect. International trade, tariffs, quotas and duties were governed by GATT.

February 2, 1948 The Republican government of Czechoslovakia was overthrown by the Czechoslovakian Communist Party backed by forces from Soviet Russia. Klement Gottwald was made head of the new Communist government.

May 1948 Daniel Malan led the Afrikaaner Party to victory in the South African elections. He was the first person to introduce the idea of apartheid (or racial differentiation) as part of government policy in South Africa.

April 4, 1949 Belgium, Italy, Canada, the Netherlands, Portugal, Denmark, Britain, France, Iceland, Norway, Luxembourg and the United States signed the North Atlantic Treaty, forming the North Atlantic Treaty Organization (NATO). It was a military alliance formed to counter the potential threat of Soviet invasion of Western Europe.

October 1, 1949 Mao Tse-tung, leader of the Communist party of China, proclaimed himself the chairman of the People's Republic of China. He is credited with implementing the programme of industrialization in the country, as well as for redistribution of land to the peasants.

▶ *Following the establishment of People's Republic of China, Mao ordered the redistribution of land and the elimination of rural landlords.*

1949-1954

October 16, 1949 The Greek civil war ended when the Greek army defeated rebel Greek communists with the help of United States forces.

February 10, 1950 American swimmer Mark Spitz was born. He is the only person to have won seven gold medals at a single Olympic Games (1972).

June 25, 1950 Communist North Korea invaded South Korea, beginning the Korean War.

February 6, 1952 Elizabeth II was crowned the queen of the United Kingdom following the death of her father King George VI.

April 1952 Military rule was ended in Bolivia when the National Revolutionary Movement (MNR) came to power. Víctor Paz Estenssoro became the president of Bolivia.

November 25, 1952 *The Mousetrap*, Agatha Christie's classic suspense play, was first staged at the Ambassadors Theatre in London. It set the record for the longest-running play at one theatre.

May 29, 1953 New Zealand mountaineer Edmund Hillary and Nepali Sherpa Tenzing Norgay became the first people to reach the top of Mount Everest, the highest mountain in the world.

July 26, 1953 Fidel Castro began his fight against the Cuban dictator Fulgencio Batista with an attack on the Moncada Military Barracks in Santiago de Cuba. The revolutionary movement is known as the 26th July Movement.

May 7, 1954 French forces were defeated by the Viet Minh in the Battle of Dien Bien Phu. The Geneva Accord temporarily divided the country into the northern Communist area and the southern non-Communist area.

October 31, 1954 The Algerian war for independence from French colonial rule began under the leadership of the National Liberation Front (FLN).

▶ *Agatha Christie first introduced her fictional Belgian detective Hercule Poirot in her 1920 novel* The Mysterious Affair at Styles.

1955–1956

April 12, 1955 The polio vaccine, developed by American physician Jonas Edward Salk, was introduced in the USA.

September 19, 1955 Argentinean President Juan Perón was overthrown by rebels belonging to the Argentinean military. He was forced to flee to Paraguay.

October 1955 Ngo Dinh Diem, the prime minister of South Vietnam, declared himself the president of the Republic of Vietnam.

January 1, 1956 The Republic of Sudan was established independent of Britain.

▶ *The Suez Canal is one of the world's most heavily used shipping lanes. Ships mainly travel in single-line traffic as the canal is narrow.*

March 2, 1956 Morocco declared independence from French rule and Sultan Muhammad V formed a constitutional government.

March 20, 1956 France granted complete independence to Tunisia. Habib Bourguiba became the president of Tunisia.

June 6, 1956 Swedish tennis player Björn Borg was born. He was the first person to win the Wimbledon five times in a row as well as four successive French Open titles.

...FASCINATING FACT...
Argentinean revolutionary Che Guevara was the chief architect of Fidel Castro's revolution against the Batista government in Cuba. Guevara was a practicing doctor, but his commitment to the Communist cause led him to abandon his practice and lead the Cuban guerrilla army to the liberation of Cuba. A widely read man and deeply interested in poetry, Guevara wrote books on socialism and guerrilla warfare. He was killed in the course of leading a failed revolution in South America in 1967.

July 26, 1956 Egyptian president Gamal Abdel Nasser declared complete ownership and control of the Egyptian government over the Suez Canal. Outraged by this, Britain and France invaded Egypt.

October 29, 1956 Israeli forces defeated Egyptian forces in Sinai, Egypt. British and French allied forces moved into Egypt and occupied the area along the Suez Canal.

October 1956 Hungarians revolted against Soviet rule, but the Russians suppressed the uprising.

1957–1959

March 25, 1957 West Germany, Italy, France, Belgium, Luxembourg and the Netherlands signed the Treaty of Rome, establishing the European Economic Community (EEC), also known as the Common Market. This organization later evolved into the European Union (EU).

▼ *The first artificial satellite to be launched into orbit,* Sputnik I *began the so-called space age. Weighing about 83 kg, it remained in orbit from October 1957 until January 1958.*

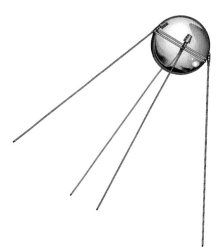

September 1957 François Duvalier became the president of Haiti. The country suffered his dictatorial and corrupt rule for 14 years.

October 4, 1957 The Soviet Union sent *Sputnik 1*, the first man-made satellite, into outer space.

1958 The first Flight Data Recorder box was produced, invented by Australian Dr David Warren. The box was able to record conversations and details about aircraft flights. Able to withstand crashes, it has proved to be an invaluable source of information.

1958 The first Grammy awards were given by the National Academy of Recording Arts and Sciences in the United States. Today Grammy awards are given in dozens of categories.

January 31, 1958 The United States launched *Explorer I*, their first space satellite.

February 1, 1958 Syria joined Egypt to form the United Arab Republic.

August 16, 1958 American singer and actress Madonna Louise Ciccone was born.

August 29, 1958 American singer, songwriter and dancer Michael Jackson was born. *Thriller*, *Bad* and *Dangerous* are some of his most successful albums.

January 1, 1959 In Cuba, rebel forces led by Fidel Castro overthrew Fulgencio Batista. The deposed leader was forced to flee the country. Castro took charge as commander-in-chief of the armed forces and shortly after, became head of the government. Castro improved health services in the country and worked towards improving literacy among the Cuban public. He later suppressed his opponents and banned all political parties except the Communist Party.

▲ *Fidel Castro was premier of Cuba from 1959 until 1976. He set up a one-party government to assume complete power.*

441

1960-1961

January 23, 1960 The USS *Trieste* bathyscaphe (deep-sea diving vessel) created history by reaching a record depth of 10,750 m in the Pacific Ocean. This part is called the Challenger Deep, the deepest known point in the oceans and located in the Mariana Trench. The vessel was manned by Jacques Piccard and Don Walsh.

1960 The French colony of the Republic of the Congo was granted complete political independence. In 1958, Congo had become an autonomous republic within the French Community, and Fulbert Youlou had formed the first parliamentary government.

October 1, 1960 Nigeria gained independence. In the same year, Madagascar, Mali, French Congo, Chad and Mauritania also became independent.

◀ Trieste *spent 20 minutes at the bottom of Mariana Trench, the deepest undersea trench known, located in the North Pacific Ocean.*

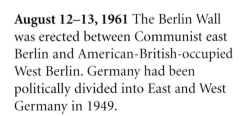

▶ *The first human traveller to outer space, Yuri Gagarin was conferred with the title of 'Hero of the Soviet Union' after his return.*

January 20, 1961 John F Kennedy became the 35th president of the United States.

April 12, 1961 Russian cosmonaut Yuri Gagarin became the first man to go into outer space. His spacecraft *Vostok 1* made an orbit of the Earth in 1 hour and 29 minutes.

April 17, 1961 The United States (supported by Cuban exiles) invaded the Bay of Pigs in Cuba. The invaders were defeated by Cuban communist leader Castro and his troops.

May 5, 1961 Alan B Shepard became the first American to go into outer space. His flight, on NASA's *Freedom 7* spacecraft, lasted for just 15 minutes.

June 19, 1961 Kuwait gained independence from Britain.

August 12–13, 1961 The Berlin Wall was erected between Communist east Berlin and American-British-occupied West Berlin. Germany had been politically divided into East and West Germany in 1949.

September 28, 1961 Syria declared its independence from the United Arab Republic.

443

1961-1963

December 1961 In Africa, Tanganyika became independent and Julius Nyerere became its first president.

December 19, 1961 Goa, Diu and Daman in western India were liberated from the Portuguese.

1962 British musical group the Rolling Stones was formed.

1962 The Central African countries of Burundi and Uganda gained independence from Belgium and Britain respectively. Burundi was ruled by the native Tutsi tribe and in Uganda a federal government was formed with Milton Obote as the head of state.

March 1962 General Ne Win overthrew the Burmese government led by U Nu and established military rule in Burma.

July 10, 1962 The first communications satellite *Telstar*, made by John Robinson Pierce of Bell Laboratories, USA, was launched into space. A giant antenna near Andover in Maine transmitted the first television signals and the images appeared on television screens all over the continent.

▲ *Marilyn Monroe, whose real name was Norma Jean Mortenson, was only 36 years old when she died.*

August 5, 1962 Marilyn Monroe, one of the greatest cinematic icons of all time, was found dead in her house in California, the United States. It is widely believed that she died from an overdose of sleeping pills, but her death remains shrouded in controversy.

October 1962 United States President John F Kennedy discovered that the Soviet Union placed missiles in Cuba aimed at United States cities. He demanded that the Russians withdraw the weapons. Following a period of tense weeks during which war seemed very likely, Russia finally backed down.

November 1962 Chinese troops entered India through Assam and began attacking Indian armed forces. The border region remains disputed to this day.

March 4, 1963 Six people charged with plotting to assassinate General Charles de Gaulle were sentenced to death.

May 25, 1963 The Organization of African Unity (OAU) was created with 30 independent African nations. Its aim was to promote unity and cooperation within Africa.

...FASCINATING FACT...

During the Great Depression, an unemployed salesman from Pennsylvania called Charles Darrow invented a game that involved buying, selling and renting real estate. It became very popular among his family and friends, and he was soon selling copies of the game to big stores. In 1935, Parker Brothers, an American toy manufacturer, bought the game from Darrow and Monopoly was born! Darrow became a millionaire and Monopoly is still one of the bestselling board games .

▼ *The Forth Bridge in Scotland was designed and built by English engineer Benjamin Baker in the 1880s. One of the first bridges with cantilevers (beams supported at one end and carrying a load at the other end or along the unsupported length), the Forth Bridge spans the Firth of Forth, the estuary of the River Forth.*

August 5, 1963 The United States, the Soviet Union and the United Kingdom signed the Nuclear Test-Ban Treaty in Moscow, banning all tests in land, water and outer space. Only underground testing was permitted.

August 28, 1963 In the United States, Martin Luther King, Jr, delivered his famous 'I have a dream' speech to 200,000 civil rights activists participating in the March on Washington.

November 1963 Ngo Dinh Diem, the dictatorial leader of South Vietnam, was killed by his army, and military rule was established.

November 22, 1963 John F Kennedy was shot dead by Lee Harvey Oswald in Dallas. He was succeeded by Lyndon B Johnson as United States president.

December 12, 1963 Kenya declared independence from British rule and Jomo Kenyatta became the first prime minister of the new nation.

July 2, 1964 The United States Congress passed the Civil Rights Act to end discrimination based on race, colour and religion.

August 2, 1964 The Viet Cong forces of North Vietnam attacked the American destroyer *Maddox* in the Gulf of Tonkin, causing the United States to escalate their efforts against communists in Vietnam.

August 18, 1964 British pop band the Beatles gave their first performance at Hamburg, Germany. They had been performing since 1956 as the Quarry Men and later as the Silver Beetles.

September 4, 1964 The Forth Bridge in Scotland was opened to the public. This suspension bridge was one of the longest single-span bridges in the world.

October 16, 1964 China became the fifth country (after the USA, USSR, Britain and France) to successfully test an atomic bomb.

1964-1966

October 24, 1964 Zambia (also called Northern Rhodesia) became independent, breaking away from the British-controlled Central African Federation. Kenneth Kaunda, president of the United National Independence Party (UNIP), became the president of the new republic.

December 1964 African-American civil rights leader Dr Martin Luther King, Jr, became the youngest person to receive the Nobel Peace Prize, at the age of 35.

February 1965 American warplanes began bombing North Vietnam.

April 1965 Pakistani tanks entered the Rann of Kutch in India and defeated the Indian forces posted in the area.

August 9, 1965 Singapore broke away from the Federation of Malaysia and became an independent state.

September 6, 1965 Indian forces began their attack on Lahore and Sialkot in Pakistan. However, fighting ended quickly due to pressure from the United States and the Soviet Union.

December 5, 1965 General Charles de Gaulle was elected as the president of France for the second time. De Gaulle was famous for forming the Fifth Republic, and also for propelling France to world-power status.

January 10, 1966 The Indo-Pakistan War of 1965 ended with the two countries signing the Tashkent Agreement.

June 30, 1966 The National Organization for Women (NOW) was founded in Washington, DC, by feminist Betty Freidan and Reverend Pauli Murray, the first African-American woman to become an Episcopalian priest. NOW has played an important role in the women's equal rights movements in America.

September 30, 1966 The Bechuanaland British Protectorate in southern Africa declared its independence. It renamed itself the Republic of Botswana.

▶ *Charles de Gaulle was responsible for ending the Algerian War.*

1967-1968

April 21, 1967 Greek military officer Colonel Georgios Papadopoulos overthrew the weak King Constantine. In 1973 the police chief Dimitrios Ioannidis took control of the country.

May 30, 1967 Civil war broke out in Nigeria when Lieutenant Colonel Odumegwu Ojukwu, the governor of the Eastern Region, declared the eastern part of the country independent. He named it the Republic of Biafra.

June 5–10, 1967 Israeli forces invaded Sinai, the West Bank, Jerusalem and the Golan Heights in Syria to prevent Egyptian and Iraqi forces from attacking Israel. The Six-Day War ended with Israel's triumph. Subsequently, the United Nations arranged for a cease-fire and passed a resolution demanding that Israel withdraw from 'occupied territories'.

September 1967 General Nguyen Van Thieu was elected the president of South Vietnam. The country was troubled by constant violence due to the increasing number of communist rebels who entered from the north.

December 3, 1967 South African surgeon Christiaan Barnard successfully conducted the first heart transplant operation.

...FASCINATING FACT...

The use of slang has existed for several years, especially among younger people. The youth of the 1960s too had their own slang. Many of them are words still in use today and many were so strange, one could never guess their meaning. For example, 'church key' was slang for a soda can opener; to 'ape' was to become extremely angry; to 'choose off' was to pick a fight; a 'drag' was a short car race; and a 'jelly roll' was a hairstyle!

1968 The British rock group Led Zeppelin was formed. They were among the most popular groups of the 1970s and played an important role in the development of heavy metal music.

January 30, 1968 The Viet Cong made a surprise attack on 36 South Vietnamese towns. The campaign became known as the Tet Offensive.

February 1968 In the Battle of Hue, South Vietnamese forces and United States troops defeated the North Vietnam Communists, driving them out of the religious centre of Hue.

April 4, 1968 American civil rights leader Dr Martin Luther King, Jr was shot dead by James Earl Ray at Memphis. The assassination resulted in riots in several cities across the United States.

May 10, 1968 Representatives of the United States and Vietnam met in Paris for peace talks.

▲ *Formed in 1968, the rock group Led Zeppelin remained popular through the 1970s. The group broke up in 1980.*

1968-1970

July 1, 1968 The United States, the Soviet Union, Britain and 59 other countries signed the Nuclear Non-Proliferation Treaty. The United States, the Soviet Union and Britain agreed not to provide nuclear weapons or information to other countries.

November 1968 Richard M Nixon was elected the 37th president of the United States.

1969 American President Nixon ordered the bombing of Cambodia to cut off supply routes from Cambodia to the Vietnamese Communists.

March 3, 1969–1971 Egypt and Israel fought the War of Attrition, supported by the Soviet Union and the United States respectively.

July 20, 1969 American astronaut Neil Armstrong became the first person to land on the Moon.

August 15–17, 1969 The Woodstock Music and Art Fair was held in Bethel, New York. Attended by more than 400,000 people, it was one of the most important cultural events of the 1960s.

1970 The Republic of Biafra's rebellion against the central government in Nigeria was ended when Biafra surrendered and joined Nigeria. About one million people died in the fighting and in the famine that followed.

January 1970 The Aswan High Dam, across the Nile in Egypt, was completed. Measuring over 110 m high and about 3828 m long, it was one of the largest dams in the world. The Aswan Dam was formally inaugurated in January 1971.

March 1970 Cambodian ruler Norodom Sihanouk was removed from power and General Lon Nol established himself as head of state. Civil war broke out in Cambodia due to conflicts between Vietnamese communists and Cambodian forces.

November 3, 1970 Salvadore Allende became Chile's first socialist president.

▶ *A licenced pilot since he was 16 years old, Neil Armstrong was the first human being to set foot on the Moon.*

1970–1973

December 1970 The Awami League led by Mujibur Rahman won the Assembly elections in East Pakistan. The party sought independence from West Pakistan, which retained a greater share of political and economic power.

January 25, 1971 In Uganda, Idi Amin overthrew Milton Obote, the head of state, and declared himself president of Uganda. During his reign he forced all Asians to leave Uganda, tortured and murdered several hundred Ugandans and supported the Palestinian war against Israel.

March 25, 1971 West Pakistani forces invaded East Pakistan and arrested Mujibur Rahman.

December 3, 1971 India attacked and defeated West Pakistan to liberate East Pakistan. East Pakistan gained independence and was renamed Bangladesh.

January 1972 Sheik Mujibur Rahman became the first prime minister of Bangladesh.

January 30, 1972 Thirteen Catholic activists were killed in Belfast by British troops who had come in to calm down the tension between the Protestant majority and Catholic minority in Northern Ireland. The event became known as 'Bloody Sunday'.

March 1972 Continuing violence between the Protestants and Catholics of Northern Ireland led to the British Parliament ending Home Rule and bringing Northern Ireland directly under British rule.

December 18–28, 1972 Hanoi, the capital of North Vietnam, was heavily bombed by United States forces even as peace talks were going on between the American representative Henry Kissinger and the Vietnamese representative Le Duc Tho at Paris.

December 23, 1972 Managua, the capital of Nicaragua, was hit by a devastating earthquake that destroyed the city and killed thousands of people.

1973 The 110-storey Sears Tower was opened in Chicago, Illinois. It was the world's tallest building until the Petronas Towers were built in 1996 in Kuala Lumpur, Malaysia.

▼ *The Sears Tower (left) in Chicago opened in 1973, though the construction was not completed till 1974. One of the world's tallest buildings, the Sears Tower reaches up to a height of 442 m.*

1973-1974

January 27, 1973 Fighting ended in Vietnam and in March, United States troops returned home. The war had claimed the lives of over two million people, including 58,000 Americans.

July 10, 1973 The West Indian island of Bahamas became an independent nation within the British Commonwealth.

July 17, 1973 Muhammad Zahir Shah, ruler of Afghanistan, was overthrown by Muhammad Daud, who established the Republic of Afghanistan.

September 11, 1973 The Chilean Socialist leader Salvadore Allende was killed and Augusto Pinochet established a military government in Chile.

October 6, 1973 Egyptian and Syrian forces made a surprise attack on Israel on the Jewish holiday of Yom Kippur. Although the attack was initially successful, Israeli forces soon entered Egypt and surrounded the Egyptian Third Army, forcing them to surrender.

▶ *The United States Supreme Court voted unanimously in the Watergate trial and ordered President Nixon to hand over taped recordings related to the scandal. Chief Justice Burger presided over the trial, ultimately forcing Nixon to resign.*

1974 The military government in Greece resigned and Constantine Karamanlis set up a democratic government, bringing back order and peace to the country.

January 1974 Israel agreed to return all territories it had captured the previous year and move out from the west bank of the Suez, as well as from an area on the east bank.

April 25, 1974 The dictatorship in Portugal was ended by rebel army officers who had founded the Armed Forces Movement. Military rule was established with General António de Spínola as the new president of Portugal.

456

July 15, 1974 Members of the Cypriot national guard overthrew Archbishop Makarios III, president of Cyprus. A few days later Turkish forces invaded Cyprus and occupied the northern part of the island.

July 24, 1974 The United States Supreme Court ordered President Richard Nixon to surrender White House tapes to special prosecutor Leon Jaworski, who was investigating the Watergate scandal. The controversy was related to the bungled attempt to bug the headquarters of the Democratic National Committee at the Watergate complex in Washington, DC. The operation was allegedly organized by Nixon.

457

1974-1975

July 27–30, 1974 After the Watergate Scandal was revealed, President Nixon was charged with obstruction of justice, failure to follow the law and refusal to cooperate with the investigating authority.

August 8, 1974 President Nixon resigned, owning up to his involvement in the Watergate scandal.

September 12, 1974 Ethiopian emperor Haile Selassie was deposed. Rebel army officers led by Major Mengistu Haile Mariam took charge of the country, establishing a socialist government.

March 25, 1975 Saudi Arabian king Faisal ibn Abd-al-Aziz was assassinated. He was succeeded by Prince Khalid ibn Abdul Aziz.

April 1975 General Lon Nol, ruler of Cambodia, was overthrown. Khmer Rouge, a Communist organization, took control of the Cambodian government. Pol Pot, the Khmer leader, became prime minister.

April 1975 Bill Gates and Paul G Allen co-founded Microsoft Corporation, the leading developer of computer software in the world today.

June 25, 1975 The Mozambique Liberation Front (also known as Frelimo) freed Mozambique from Portuguese rule.

June 26, 1975 Indira Gandhi, the prime minister of India, declared a state of national emergency. Freedom of press was restricted and many opposition politicians were imprisoned.

July 1975 The Soviet *Soyuz* spacecraft and the American *Apollo* met in outer space and conducted experiments for two days. It was the first joint venture space programme by the two countries.

August 1, 1975 Thirty-five European countries, the United States and Canada signed the Helsinki Accords. They recognized European borders established after World War II, agreed to uphold human rights and freedom, and promised to maintain friendly and cooperative relations with each other.

▲ *Indira Gandhi served four terms as prime minister of India, from 1966–1977 and then in 1980–1984. One of the highlights of her long stay in office was the declaration of a state of emergency throughout the country in 1975. The emergency period lasted 19 months.*

1975-1979

November 20, 1975 The Spanish dictator Francisco Franco died. Juan Carlos became king of Spain and introduced a democratic constitution.

January 21, 1976 The supersonic jet Concorde made its first flight from London to Bahrain. The aircraft was developed jointly by British Airways and Air France.

April 30, 1976 The South Vietnam government surrendered to the invading North Vietnam forces, who had taken over almost the entire country.

◀ *Ruhollah Khomeini, recognized in his own time as one of the supreme religious leaders ('grand ayatollah') in Iran, steered the revolution against the ruling shah. Khomeini remained in absolute power for over a decade.*

June 27, 1976 Palestinian terrorists hijacked an Air France flight from Israel to France and took the aircraft to Entebbe in Uganda. On July 4, an Israeli commando squad made a daring rescue operation to save the 103 Israelis who were being held hostage.

July 2, 1976 North and South Vietnam were unified and named the Socialist Republic of Vietnam. The capital of the new nation was Hanoi, and the southern city of Saigon was renamed Ho Chi Minh City.

July 5, 1977 The Pakistani president Zulfikar Ali Bhutto was imprisoned and later executed by General Mohammad Zia-ul-Haq, the army chief of staff. Zia-ul-Haq assumed dictatorship of Pakistan.

November 19–20, 1977 The Egyptian president, Anwar el-Sadat, made a historic visit to Israel. It marked the beginning of a peace process that ended the 30-year Egypt-Israel war.

April 27, 1978 Muhammad Daud, the president of the Afghanistan Republic, was killed by the Rebel People's Party. Following this, the Democratic Republic of Afghanistan was established. A communist government assumed power under the leadership of Nur Muhammad Taraki, who became president and prime minister.

July 25, 1978 Louise Brown, the first 'test tube baby', was born through the *in vitro* fertilization technique. The technique was developed by the British scientists Patrick Steptoe and Robert Edwards. Louis Brown's success story heralded a revolution in medical science, inspiring scientists to develop the IVF further. Today, test tube babies are commonplace for people who cannot produce children naturally.

February 5, 1979 The Grand Ayatollah, Seyyed Ruhollah Khomeini, led a revolution against the shah of Iran, overthrew the monarchy and established the Islamic Republic of Iran.

1979–1981

March 26, 1979 Anwar el-Sadat, president of Egypt, and Menachem Begin, prime minister of Israel, signed a peace treaty ending the war between the two nations.

March 28, 1979 The breakdown of the nuclear power plant at Three Mile Island in Pennsylvania, USA, caused a leakage of hydrogen and radioactive gases. Although the leak was contained within the plant, seven other nuclear plants in the United States were shut down for safety reasons.

April 1979 Rhodesia gained independence from the British and was renamed Zimbabwe.

July, 1979 Saddam Hussein became the president of Iraq.

August 27, 1979 Lord Mountbatten, former Viceroy of India, was killed when a bomb planted on his boat by the Irish Republican Army exploded.

December 25, 1979 Soviet forces invaded Afghanistan. They killed President Hafizullah Amin and made Babrak Karmal the president of Afghanistan. This led to the formation of large groups of rebels called *mujahideen* (soldiers who fight holy wars).

September 22, 1980 Saddam Hussein, president of Iraq, declared war against Iran.

1981 IBM introduced its first personal computer, the IBM PC.

...FASCINATING FACT...

Barbie Millicent Roberts (better known as 'Barbie') was designed in 1959 by Ruth Handler, the co-founder of Mattel, the American toy manufacturer. Barbie was named after Handler's daughter Barbara. Ken, who was introduced in 1961, was named after Handler's son.

1981 Pathologists in New York and California first discovered the presence of a new and deadly disease called AIDS (acquired immunodeficiency syndrome).

January 20, 1981 Ronald Reagan was sworn in as the 40th president of the United States.

◀ *Lord Mountbatten had directed the recapture of Burma during World War II.*

1981–1985

May 10, 1981 François Mitterrand of the Socialist Party was elected the president of France.

July 29, 1981 Charles, Prince of Wales, and Lady Diana Frances Spencer were married at St Paul's Cathedral in London.

April 2, 1982 Argentina invaded the British controlled Falkland Islands and took control of Port Stanley, South Georgia and the South Sandwich islands.

June 6, 1982 Israeli troops invaded Lebanon and defeated the Palestine Liberation Organization, which had established itself in Lebanon.

June 14, 1982 Argentina surrendered the Falkland Islands to Britain after being defeated in battles fought on both land and sea.

◀ *The interior of St Paul's Cathedral combines elements of Neoclassical, Gothic and Baroque architecture.*

1983 The first modern cellular telephone system, called the advanced mobile phone system (AMPS), developed by AT&T and Motorola, was introduced in Chicago.

June 1, 1984 The Indian army stormed the Golden Temple in Amritsar to flush out the Sikh militants hiding there. This operation, called Operation Bluestar, was ordered by Prime Minister Indira Gandhi.

October 31, 1984 Indira Gandhi, the prime minister of India, was assasinated. Her son Rajiv Gandhi became the next prime minister.

December 3, 1984 A poisonous gas leak from a pesticide plant in Bhopal in Madhya Pradesh, India, killed 3800 people and injured many more.

March 10, 1985 Mikahil Gorbachev was elected the general secretary of the Communist Party of the Soviet Union. His programmes of modernizing the Soviet economy and giving more independence to communist states that were part of the Soviet Union led to the breakup of the USSR.

1985–1989

November 1985 Microsoft Corporation introduced the Windows Operating System to its computer software.

February 20, 1986 The Russian space station and laboratory *Mir* was launched into outer space.

February 25, 1986 Leader of the opposition Corazon Aquino became president of the Philippines when the corrupt ruling president Ferdinand Marcos fled the country.

April 25–26, 1986 An accident at the nuclear power plant at Chernobyl, Ukraine, killed 32 people. Several thousand people and animals were affected by the radiation.

▼ *A glacier in Prince William Sound, Alaska. Glacier ice covers about 10 percent of land area.*

February 22, 1987 A new constitution for Ethiopia officially took effect. In September, Major Mengistu Haile Mariam was elected the president of the People's Democratic Republic of Ethiopia.

1987 Palestinians began the *intifada*, or 'shaking off', against the Israelis. The revolts included riots, strikes and demonstrations in various places controlled by the Israelis.

▲ *Oil spills constitute a major environmental problem. Besides the economic loss, the effect on the ecological system can be considerable.*

1987 The United Nations Environment Programme (UNEP) published the Montreal Protocol. It confirmed that the ozone layer above the Antarctic had thinned considerably.

December 1988 A new parliament called the Congress of People's Deputies was created in the USSR.

1989 British scientist Tim Berners-Lee invented the World Wide Web while working with the European Particle Physics Laboratory (CERN) at Geneva, Switzerland.

1989 *Exxon Valdez*, one of the largest oil carriers ever built, crashed into a reef in Prince William sound, Alaska, and spilt 11 million gallons of oil. This oil spill was one of the worst in history.

1989-1990

January 7, 1989 Emperor of Japan Hirohito died. He had ascended the throne in 1926 and had been Japan's longest reigning monarch. Prince Akihito succeeded him.

January 20, 1989 George H W Bush was sworn in as the 43rd president of the United States.

November 9, 1989 The Berlin Wall was brought down. Communist governments across Eastern Europe gave way to democracy in the following months.

December 16–22, 1989 Communism ended in Romania when the dictator Nicolae Ceauçescu was forced to flee Bucharest due to a popular uprising. He was later arrested and executed.

▼ *The Channel Tunnel was destined to be a link between the UK and France. Trains would travel at speed through two rail tunnels bored beneath the seabed of the English Channel.*

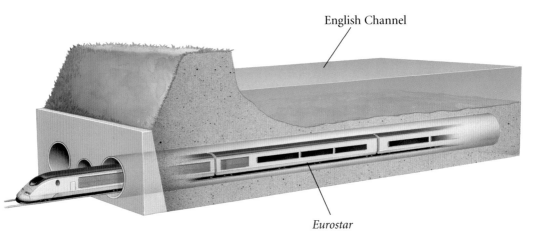

English Channel

Eurostar

January 1990–January 1992 The Communist Federation of Yugoslavia broke up into the separate countries of Serbia, Bosnia and Herzegovina, Macedonia, Croatia and Slovenia.

January 3, 1990 Manuel Noriega, dictatorial military leader of Panama, surrendered to US forces who invaded Panama. Guillermo Endara Galimany, (elected in 1989) was made the new president of Panama.

February 11, 1990 Nelson Mandela, the leader of the African National Congress, was released from prison after 26 years. His long struggle against discrimination ended apartheid in South Africa.

March 1990 The Congress of People's Deputies elected Mikhail Gorbachev the president of the USSR.

March 11, 1990 Auguste Pinochet, leader of Chile's military government, was forced to make way for Patricio Aylwin, elected by the Chilean public.

December 1, 1990 Channel Tunnel workers from the UK and France meet 40 m beneath the English Channel seabed, establishing the first ground connection between the UK and mainland Europe since the last Ice Age.

...FASCINATING FACT...

The world has seen some of the most amazing inventions in small things. One such is the safety pin. It was invented accidentally when American inventor Walter Hunt was absent-mindedly twisting a piece of wire while wondering how to pay off a $15 debt. Although Hunt patented his invention in 1849, he probably did not think much of it, because he sold the patent for just $400!

1990-1991

1990 The Leaning Tower of Pisa in Italy was closed to the public after it was declared unsafe.

March 11, 1990 Lithuania declared its independence from the Soviet Union. However, the Soviet Union recognized the declaration formally only in September 1990, after abortive attempts at applying military and economic force.

March 21, 1990 Namibia gained independence from South Africa. In 1989, elections were held in Namibia under the supervision of the United Nations (UN). Sam Nujoma, leader of the victorious South West Africa People's Organization (SWAPO), became president.

April 25, 1990 NASA launched the Hubble Space Telescope. It is capable of taking highly accurate and clear pictures of distant objects in space.

May 29, 1990 The Russian parliament elected Boris Yeltsin the president of the Russian republic.

August–September 1990 The Iran-Iraq War finally ended and both countries began working towards establishing friendly relations.

August 2, 1990 Iraqi forces made a surprise attack on Kuwait, starting the Persian Gulf War. The United States, NATO and Arab forces from several countries came together to free Kuwait from Saddam Hussein and his army.

October 3, 1990 East and West Germany were reunified. Helmut Kohl became the first chancellor of the unified nation.

January 16–17, 1991 The Persian Gulf War began with Operation Desert Storm, an intense air raid on Iraq by the United States and its allies.

February 24, 1991 Allied forces entered Kuwait and southern Iraq, and recaptured the city of Kuwait within three days.

▶ *The Hubble Space Telescope orbits around the Earth at 600 km above the ground. It was launched in 1990 by NASA.*

1991-1993

February 28, 1991 American President George Bush declared the end of the Persian Gulf War. Kuwait was once again independent.

May 21, 1991 Indian Prime Minister Rajiv Gandhi was assassinated.

November 1991 Chechnya declared its independence from the USSR and established itself as a republic under the leadership of Dzhozkhar Dudayev.

December 25, 1991 Mikhail Gorbachev resigned from the post of president of the Soviet Union. By this time all the 15 communist countries that were once part of the USSR had declared their independence and 11 of these had formed the Commonwealth of Independent States (CIS). The chief goal of the CIS is to promote common interests of the member nations.

April 7, 1992 Serbian forces began to attack the Bosnian capital Sarajevo and took control of the eastern part of Bosnia. In the next two years, hundreds of Bosnians were killed and thousands were forced to flee.

April 27, 1992 The Federal Republic of Yugoslavia was formed by Serbia and Montenegro. Belgrade was made its capital. Yugoslavia was renamed Serbia and Montenegro in 2003.

August 7, 1992 Buckingham Palace, the official residence of the British royal family, was opened for public viewing for the first time.

January 1, 1993 Czechoslovakia was split into the Czech Republic and Slovakia.

January 20, 1993 William (Bill) Jefferson Clinton succeeded George H W Bush as the president of the United States.

September 1993 Marc Andreessen developed the Mosaic web browser with technical support from the National Center for Supercomputing Applications at the University of Illinois. Mosaic popularized the use of the World Wide Web.

▶ *Buckingham Palace contains 600 rooms and is surrounded by 50 acres of gardens.*

1993-1996

1993 The French submersible *Nautile* dived down to the wreck of the *Titanic* to recover artefacts.

May 10, 1994 Nelson Mandela became the president of the Republic of South Africa.

December 1994 Netscape Communications Corporation, co-founded by Marc Andreessen, introduced the Netscape Navigator web browser.

January 1, 1995 The World Trade Organization (WTO) was established to control international trade. It replaced the earlier GATT.

▲ *The titanium-hulled, deep-sea submersible* Nautile *is capable of working at depths of up to 6000 m.*

March 22, 1995 Russian cosmonaut Valery Polyakov returned to Earth after spending 438 days on the *Mir* space station.

May 17, 1995 Mayor of Paris Jacques Chirac was elected president of France.

...FASCINATING FACT...

The 50-km-long Channel Tunnel between England and France opened on May 6, 1994, allowing people to travel between the two countries in just 35 minutes. Built over a period of seven years, it took about 15,000 workers to construct this rail tunnel. The first passengers travelled on November 13, 1994.

November 4, 1995 Israeli Prime Minister Yithazk Rabin was fatally shot by a Jewish rebel opposed to a deal with the Palestinians. Rabin was attending a rally in Tel Aviv.

1996 British scientist Ian Wilmut and his colleagues at the Roslin Institute at Edinburgh, Scotland, created Dolly the sheep. She was the first mammal to be cloned from an adult cell, and the subject of much controversy. Dolly later gave birth to a female lamb named Bonnie, the first of four lambs.

January 20, 1996 Yasir Arafat was elected president of the Palestinian Authority, ruling Palestinian areas of the Gaza Strip and West Bank.

December 29, 1996 The civil war in Guatemala was ended after 36 years. The state and the leaders of the Guatemalan National Revolutionary Union finally signed a peace treaty.

▶ *South African statesman Nelson Mandela.*

475

1997-2000

July 1, 1997 Hong Kong was handed over to China by Britain. It was made a special administrative region under the direct control of the Chinese government.

August 31, 1997 Diana, Princess of Wales (and former wife of Charles, Prince of Wales), was killed in an automobile accident in Paris. Her funeral was held at London's Westminster Abbey on September 6.

May 1999 Pakistani forces crossed over the Line of Control in Kashmir and took control of some border areas, leading to the Kargil War between India and Pakistan.

June 16, 1999 The African National Congress won the South African elections again. Nelson Mandela stepped down and Thabo Mbeki became the new president.

September 1999 Mireya Moscoso Rodríguez, leader of the Arnulfista Party, was elected the president of Panama. She was the first woman to occupy this position in Panama.

October 11, 1999 General Pervez Musharraf, chief of the Pakistan army, overthrew Nawaz Sharif, prime minister of Pakistan, and seized power.

December 31, 1999 The United States gave up its exclusive rights to the Panama Canal.

December 31, 1999 Russian President Boris Yeltsin resigned and Vladimir Putin replaced him. In March the following year, Putin was formally elected to the post after he won the general elections. His term was marked by an upturn in the country's economy and reforms in administration.

May 12, 2000 President Kim Jong II of North Korea and President Kim Dae-jung of South Korea met in Pyongyang, North Korea. They agreed to call off the state of war that had existed between the two nations since 1950.

May 24, 2000 After occupying southern Lebanon for 20 years, Israeli troops in the area were finally withdrawn.

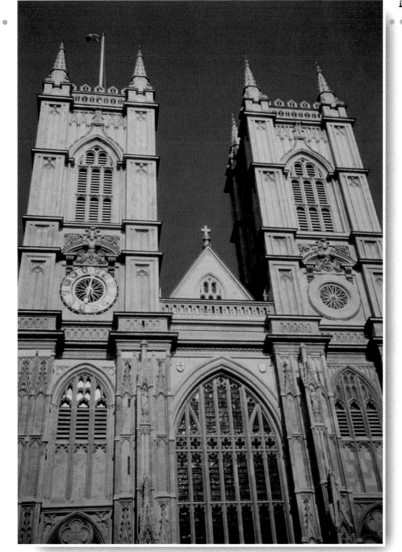

◀ *The funeral service for Diana, Princess of Wales, was held at Westminster Abbey in London. At the ceremony, singer and composer Elton John paid tribute to the late princess with his song, 'Candle in the Wind'.*

477

2000-2001

June 10, 2000 Syrian president Hafez al-Assad died, and his son Bashar Assad succeeded him.

2001 The Islamic organization the Taliban controlled most parts of Afghanistan. It began by taking control of Kandahar in 1994 and then other parts of the country.

January 16, 2001 Laurent Kabila, president of the Democratic Republic of Congo, was shot dead by rebels. His son Joseph Kabila became the new head of state.

January 19, 2001 Philippine Vice President Gloria Macapagal Arroyo took over as president of the country, replacing Joseph Estrada.

January 20, 2001 George W Bush was sworn in as the 43rd president of the United States.

February 6, 2001 The Likud Party won the elections held in Israel. Party leader Ariel Sharon became the prime minister of Israel.

February 16, 2001 American and British warplanes made a surprise attack on Iraq, destroying several anti-aircraft radars and other important military bases.

March 23, 2001 The abandoned Russian space station *Mir* came down to Earth. Its pieces fell into the Pacific Ocean.

June 1, 2001 In Nepal, King Birendra and other members of the royal family were massacred, apparently by the Crown Prince Dipendra, who later shot himself. Birendra was king of Nepal for 29 years.

June 7, 2001 Tony Blair, leader of the British Labour Party and prime minister of the United Kingdom since 1997, was re-elected to his second term.

▶ *Launched into an Earth orbit in 1986, the Russian space station* Mir *was inhabited by human beings for about 14 years, allowing them to conduct scientific research in various areas including astrophysics and biotechnology.*

2001–2003

July 23, 2001 Megawati Sukarnoputri was sworn in as the fifth president of Indonesia. She was the president for over three years.

▲ *The completion of 50 years of Queen Elizabeth II's reign in 2002 was marked by celebrations that included concerts, fireworks and a ritual march to St Paul's Cathedral.*

480

September 11, 2001
The twin towers of the World Trade Center in New York were hit by passenger aircraft hijacked by Al Qaeda militants. A short while later, the Pentagon in Washington was also similarly attacked. More than 3000 people were killed in these horrific incidents.

October 7, 2001
Kabul, Kandahar, Jalalabad and Mazar-e Sharif in Afghanistan were bombed by American and British warplanes.

December 22, 2001
The Taliban was defeated and driven out of Kandahar, the Afghani capital. A temporary government was established with Hamid Karzai as the new leader of Afghanistan.

January, 2002 Euro coins and notes were introduced in 12 countries of the European Union.

May 19, 2002 The Pacific island of East Timor became an independent nation. East Timor's President Xanana Gusmao took over as the leader of the first native government after 450 years of foreign rule.

May 24, 2002 Russia and the United States formally ended the Cold War by signing an agreement to cut down their respective nuclear arms programmes.

May 26, 2002 Alvaro Uribe was elected the president of Colombia.

June 3, 2002 A 'Party in the Palace' was organized at Buckingham Palace as part of British queen, Elizabeth II's, Golden Jubilee celebrations.

January 18, 2003 Protests against the proposed war by the United States against Iraq were held in New Zealand, Japan, Russia and several European countries.

2003

January 27, 2003 United Nations Chief Weapons Inspector Hans Blix presented his report on Iraq. It stated that there was no evidence of nuclear weapons in Iraq. The report also added that the Iraqi government has yet to accept the need to destroy weapons of mass destruction.

January 28, 2003 The Likud Party won the Israeli elections and its leader Ariel Sharon remained prime minister of Israel.

February 1, 2003 NASA's *Columbia* space shuttle exploded just 16 minutes before its scheduled landing at Cape Canaveral in Florida, USA. All seven astronauts on board were killed and the debris was scattered over a wide area covering Texas, Louisiana, Arkansas, Arizona and New Mexico.

February 6, 2003 American Secretary of State Colin Powell presented evidence of Iraq hiding weapons of mass destruction and providing shelter to Al Qaeda terrorists at a United Nations Security Council meeting.

February 15, 2003 Nearly 750,000 people gathered in London to protest against the proposed war against Iraq. Thousands joined similar peace marches in Germany, France, Italy, Spain and Greece.

March 12, 2003 The Serbian Prime Minister Zoran Djindjic was assassinated in Belgrade.

March 13, 2003 The first case of the deadly SARS virus was reported in Hanoi, Vietnam. The influenza-like epidemic had begun to claim several human lives in China, Hong Kong and Vietnam.

March 19, 2003 American and British air forces began their first attacks on Baghdad, Mosul and Basra in Iraq.

April 4, 2003 American troops and tanks entered Baghdad, the capital of Iraq, and captured the airport. Hundreds of Iraqis fled the city. The next day, American and Kurdish forces jointly captured the Iraqi town of Mosul.

May 1, 2003 American President George W Bush announced the end of all major military operations against Iraq.

▼ *The United Nations flag carries the official emblem of the organization in white against a blue backdrop. The emblem is a circular world map, as projected from the North Pole, enclosed within olive branches – a symbol for peace.*

2003–2004

May 27, 2003 Celebrations were inaugurated to mark the 300th anniversary of St Petersburg in Russia. The city was called Leningrad during the communist regime.

May 21, 2003 A powerful earthquake in Algeria, North Africa, killed more than 2000, injured nearly 9000 and left almost 51,000 people homeless.

October 24, 2003 The supersonic jet Concorde made its last flight.

December 12, 2003 Paul Martin was elected the 21st prime minister of Canada.

▼ *St Petersburg, Russia. Tsar Peter the Great of Russia laid the foundation for the city in 1703.*

December 14, 2003 American troops captured Iraqi dictator Saddam Hussein at Tikrit, Iraq.

December 27, 2003 A severe earthquake hit the ancient city of Bam, in Iran, killing about 28,000 people and injuring almost the same number.

January 4, 2004 *Spirit*, the six-wheeled robot made by the United States space agency NASA, landed on Mars.

March 2, 2004 A group of terrorist suicide bombers killed 100 people and wounded 300 in the holy Muslim city of Karbala, and killed 58 people and wounded 200 others at Baghdad in simultaneous attacks at both places.

March 11, 2004 Three trains were blasted simultaneously in Madrid during the morning rush hour, killing nearly 200 and wounding more than 1400 people. Islamic militants were believed to have been responsible. As a result, the Spanish public elected a new government and withdrew its support for the war in Iraq.

March 14, 2004 Vladimir Putin was elected the Russian president for the second time.

... **FASCINATING FACT** ...

The world's first passenger train, which ran from Stockton to Darlington in England, travelled at 24 km/h. It was the fastest means of transporting passengers and coal during the Industrial Revolution. Today the Maglev train that runs between the Shanghai airport and the city centre is the world's fastest commercial train. It can travel at 430 km/h and while in motion its carriages float 10 cm above the track!

2004

April 6, 2004 American marines, tanks and helicopters attacked the Sunni Muslim centre of Fallujah in Iraq. Many rebels were captured and several were killed.

April 23, 2004 Two trains carrying explosive substances collided at Ryongchon in North Korea, near the China border. Nearly 3000 people were killed in this accident.

April 30, 2004 Jean-Bertrand Aristide, Haiti's first president, was forced to resign by rebel forces. Chief Justice Boniface Alexandre was appointed as the new president of the island.

May 9, 2004 Chechen President Akhmad Kadyrov was killed in a bomb blast along with five others while attending Victory Day celebrations at Chechnya's capital Grozny.

May 19, 2004 Dr Manmohan Singh of the Congress Party became the prime minister of India. His party had won the general elections, defeating the ruling Bharatiya Janata Party (BJP).

June 24, 2004 Simultaneous terrorist attacks in five Iraqi cities killed nearly 300 people.

June 27, 2004 The American administration of Iraq ended and the governance of the country was given back to the Iraqis.

July 2004 Large parts of South Asia were affected by severe floods. Nearly three million people in Bangladesh were left homeless, and hundreds lost their lives in Nepal and the eastern Indian states of Assam and Bihar.

August 11, 2004 American marines, helicopters and tanks launched a heavy attack on the Iraqi holy town of Najaf.

September 1, 2004 Chechen rebels held nearly 1000 school children hostage at a government-run school in Beslan, southern Russia. The crisis ended two days later when some mines were set off, allegedly by the rebels. More than 320 people were killed and several more wounded.

▲ *The Kuwait Towers were built in 1978. After the Iraqi occupation of Kuwait in 1990–1991, the United Nations instituted a committee to investigate the possession of dangerous weapons by Iraq and accordingly have them destroyed.*

487

Index

A

489

494

English Parliament 116, 137, 150, 218, 222, 234, 236, 239, 240, 242, 244, 248, 251, 272
Council of St Albans 116
Currency Act 289
English Catholics 207
Gunpowder Plot 207
Iron Act 289
Slavery Abolition Act 335
Entente Cordiale 372
Epicurus 60
Eric XIV 190, 193
Escalante, Silvestre Vélez de 300
Espinosa, Juan Salazar de 180
Esposito, Raffaele 362
Ethiopia 416, 418, 424, 467
Italian East Africa 418
new constitution 467
People's Democratic Republic of Ethiopia 467
socialist government 458
Euphrates 16, 30
Euripides 54
European Union 440, 481
Explorer I 440

F

Faisal ibn Abd-al-Aziz 458
Fallen Timbers, Battle of the 314

Fallujah in Iraq 486
Faraday, Michael 334
Fatimid Caliphate 91
Fehrbellin, Battle of 258
Fessenden, Reginald A 378
Finland 213, 321, 323, 400, 421
Civil war 400
Hanko Peninsula 421
Helsinki 323
independence 400
Russian Red Army 421
Russian rule 321
Social Democratic Party 400
western Karelia 421
White Army 400
Finnish Parliament 377
Flanders 166, 172, 199, 249
Fleurus, Battle of 269
Flight Data Recorder 440
Florida 179, 189, 192, 198, 272, 294, 306, 326, 336, 348, 394, 482
Pensacola 272, 326
Spanish colonists 189
St Augustine 192, 198
Fonteyn, Dame Margot 404
Forbidden City 139
Ford, Henry 370
Formigny, Battle of 146
Fort St James 243
Fort Ticonderoga 291, 300, 302

Fox, George 240
Francis I 164, 170, 172, 173, 175, 177, 180, 184, 287, 295, 304
Battle of Pavia 170
Field of the Cloth of Gold 164
Italian Wars 164
Treaty of Cambrai 175
Treaty of Madrid 172
Treaty of Toledo 180
Treaty of Westminster 173
Francis Ferdinand, Archduke 388, 389
Francis of Assisi 116
Franco, Francisco 418, 460
Franklin, Benjamin 289, 300, 304
American Post Office 300
Frederick II 119, 120, 190
Innocent IV 120
Pope Honorius III 119
throne of Austria and Styria 120
treaty of San Germano 119
Frederick the Great 285, 286, 308
French and Indian War 290, 294
Louisborg 290
Treaty of Paris 294
French Congo 442
French East India Company 256
frescoes 162
Freud, Sigmund 347
Frobisher, Sir Martin 196

Baffin Island 196
Frobisher Bay 197
Fulton, Robert 321
Fyodor II 208
Fyodor III 258, 262

G

Gabriel, Daniel Fahrenheit 281
Gagarin, Yuri 443
Gainsborough, Thomas 284
Galileo Galilei 227
Gama, Vasco da 156, 157, 170
Cape of Good Hope 157
Portuguese viceroy 170
Gandhi, Indira 458, 459, 465
Golden Temple in Amritsar 465
Operation Bluestar 465
Sikh militants 465
Gandhi, Mohandas Karamchand 377
Gandhi, Rajiv 465, 472
Garbo, Greta 374
Garland, Judy 408
Gascony 146
Gaul 71, 80
Geneva Protocol 410
George IV 327, 334
George V 384, 416
Georgia 70, 137, 202, 217, 333, 348, 352, 465
Georgian style of architecture 283
German submarine 377
German U-boat 393
Germanic tribes 84
Germany 71, 86, 100,

503

505

508

Z

Acknowledgements

All artworks are from Miles Kelly Artwork Bank

The Publishers would like to thank the following picture sources whose photographs appear in this book:

p226 Macduff Everton/CORBIS, p231 Farrell Grehan/CORBIS
p259 Jeremy Horner/CORBIS, p293 Bettmann/CORBIS
p365 Pictorial Press.com, p451 Pictorial Press.com

All other photographs from:

Castrol, CMCD, Corbis, Corel, digitalSTOCK, digitalvision
Flat Earth, Hemera, ILN, John Foxx, PhotoAlto, PhotoDisc
PhotoEssentials, PhotoPro, Stockbyte